Property   Dawn ♡ **W9-BFY-418**
                    DANNY

H - 250 - 474-7192

C   250 ~ 882-6299

A Widow's Awakening

Dawn,

It was <u>so</u> nice
to meet you + your
silver sparkle :)
I hope you find
my book of
interest + all
the very best
to now!
take care,
Maryann Page

A Widow's Awakening

Maryanne Pope

pink
GAZELLE
PRODUCTIONS INC.
www.pinkgazelle.com

Pink Gazelle Productions Inc.
www.pinkgazelle.com
Calgary, Alberta, Canada

Library and Archives Canada Cataloguing in Publication
Pope, Maryanne, 1968-
A widow's awakening / by Maryanne Pope.

Includes bibliographical references.
ISBN 978-0-9810643-0-7

I. Title.
PS8631.O644W53 2008   C813'.6   C2008-904736-2

Cover design by Neil Gilbert at Elbowroom Design
Typesetting and page layout by One Below

Printed in Canada at Friesens

The text pages have been produced on 100%
post-consumer recycled paper.

FSC
Mixed Sources
Cert no. SW-COC-001271
www.fsc.org
© 1996 Forest Stewardship Council

First edition, second printing September 2010

For John

And don't you know that God is Pooh Bear?
—Jack Kerouac, *On the Road*

Where there is great love
there are always miracles
—Willa Cather

Preface

Writing is not life, but sometimes it can be a way back to life.
—Stephen King

On September 29, 2000, my husband – a Calgary police officer – died in the line of duty. We were both thirty-two at the time and had been together as a couple for eleven and a half years and married for four.

A Widow's Awakening is a work of creative non-fiction. The people, events and my psychological reaction to them are real, however many of the conversations have been modified. The names, dogs included, are fictional – or U/C (undercover) names as they say in the police world.

Virginia Woolf once wrote that the trick to life is to be able to 'put together the pieces.' A *Widow's Awakening* is how I made sense of the unacceptable. Right or wrong, enlightenment or insanity, awareness or post traumatic stress disorder, or some combination thereof, this is my journey through the first year of grief.

Contents

Prologue

1994
Abbotsford, British Columbia, Canada

"Know what would be cool to do someday?"

"What's that?"

"Walk on a really long, straight road through the middle of a cornfield."

I'd laughed. "What . . . like in Iowa or somethin'?"

"It doesn't matter where, dill. It's the experience I'm after."

"Oh. And what would that be?"

"Freedom."

"How so?"

"Well, in my mind I see this huge field – it doesn't have to be full of corn, but that would work. So I'm walking along on this road but since the corn stalks are taller than me, I can't see what's on the other side."

"Probably more corn."

"Smartass. What I mean is that I couldn't see what was beyond the cornfields."

"Oh."

"But I could more or less see the road ahead and if I stopped and turned around, I could see where I've been."

"But why would that make you feel free?"

"I dunno." He'd shrugged his shoulders with that little smirk on his face. "It's just something I always wanted to do."

PART I
Relationship

August 9, 2000
Calgary, Alberta, Canada

"What the heck are ya doin' in there?" I ask through the bathroom door.

"Whaddya think I'm doing?

"Well, I know THAT. But why are you taking so long?"

"I always take this long," he says. "You should know that by now."

I sit on the edge of our bed. "But what else do you do in there?"

"If I tell ya, will you leave me alone?"

"Deal."

"I calculate things."

I laugh. "Like what?"

"Financial stuff."

"Hence the calculator."

"Mmmm . . . hmmm. But at the moment, I'm actually working on my U/C name."

"That stands for undercover, right?"

"Yup."

"In case you get on with the Priority Crimes Unit?" I ask.

"Uh huh."

"When do you hear back from them?"

"Any day." Then, with a giggle that sounds so funny coming from such a big guy, he says, "You can go now."

One

Sunday September 17, 2000
7:00 a.m.

"And I'm gonna drape my leopard print scarf over my head, like this . . ." I say, motioning with my hands within the confines of the cramped cubicle. "And, of course, I've got my Jackie O sunglasses!"

"Of course," Mark says, crossing one long leg over the other.

"I will be SO damn cool in that convertible!"

"That you will, my friend."

Mark is a police officer and close friend of my husband, Sam. They graduated from the same police recruit class four years ago. I'm a report processor with the same police service, and Mark and I are just finishing up an incident report. On a Saturday night/Sunday morning shift such as this, the reports are mainly alcohol-related occurrences like impaired driving, assault with a weapon, sexual assault and robbery, or early morning crimes of opportunity, also usually alcohol-related, such as property damage, theft and break and enters. All the good stuff.

Sam's job is to catch the bad guys; mine is to write about them.

"Got what you needed, Adri?"

"Yup."

"Say hi to Sam for me," Mark says, gathering up his papers. "And tell him we'll have to do lunch again soon."

"It's been awhile, hasn't it?" He, Sam and another two of their buddies from recruit class often meet for lunch or beers downtown.

Mark nods. "Too long."

"I'll tell him."

He stands up. "And I hope you guys have an awesome vacation."

"We will!"

His is the last report of my shift so I sign off the phone,

place my logbook, headset and photo of Sam into my locker and drive home.

"Woohoo . . ." I whisper in Sam's ear as I crawl into bed. "We're on holidays my furry friend!"

Rolling over to face me, he grins and mumbles, "Spoon."

I flip over, so my back is touching his chest, and he wraps an arm around me. Our dog, a Shepherd-cross, jumps up on the end of the bed and all three of us fall asleep.

When I wake up, Sam has both our bags packed and has taken the dog and her little blue suitcase filled with cookies, chew toys and a blanket to the kennel.

My mom drives us to the airport and the three of us have dinner together before catching our flight to Los Angeles. Sam seems OK with this arrangement, which surprises me because his relationship with my mother has been pretty much derailed since our wedding four years ago. Sam is Greek Orthodox; I'm not. Sam is strong-willed and stubborn; so is my mother. We ended up getting married in an Anglican Church ceremony, which Sam had agreed to for me. I had insisted upon this partly to appease my mother and partly because I strongly disagreed with a condition the Greek Orthodox Church would have placed upon us. Had we been married there, we would've had to promise to baptize and raise any future children Greek Orthodox. I refused to make a promise I did not agree with and therefore could not keep. My mother hadn't acknowledged Sam's religious sacrifice – for not being married in his church means not being buried by it – and relations between Sam and my mother had never improved.

Anyway, the airport restaurant uses a big piece of brown paper as a tablecloth and guests are given a bunch of crayons to draw with.

"Hi," our waitress says, writing her name upside down on the tablecloth so we can read it.

When she leaves, Sam and I try writing *our* names upside down – but he gets the first letter backwards and we laugh.

After dinner, we ditch my mom at security and head to our

departure gate, where we're waiting for our flight to LAX when I tell Sam that the last report of my shift had been with Mark. He asks me how Mark is doing.

"He seemed fine. I mean, he looked OK."

"Looked?" Sam shifts in his chair to face me. "Wasn't he on the phone?"

"No. He came right into records to give his report."

"But don't most of us *phone* the reports in?"

"Usually, yeah. Anyway, he said to say hi and to . . ."

I'm interrupted by the announcement of our names over the loudspeaker. Sam and I look at each other then walk over to the departure counter.

"Are we at the right gate?" I ask the woman, handing her my ticket.

She looks at it. "No. This flight is going to Toronto."

Sam and I sprint through the airport to the correct gate, just in time to catch our flight to L.A..

"That was odd," I say, once we're on the plane. "I could've sworn we were at the right gate."

"Me too."

We arrive into LAX around 10:00 p.m., pick up our red rental convertible, put the top down and head east towards Vegas.

Once we're past the city limits, Sam leans back in his chair and looks to the sky. "Check out those stars, eh?"

We drive in silence for awhile. Then I thank him for having dinner with my mom.

"She's a control freak," he says, "but I do admire her strength."

I turn to him. "That almost sounded like a compliment."

"Seriously, Adri. She did a great job raising you and your brothers on her own. That couldn't have been easy."

"Are you feeling all right?"

He smiles. "But now she has to let you go."

"It's hard for mothers to do that – no matter what age their kids are."

"I'm sure it is. But if they've done their job well, what's the problem?"

"She's alone, Sam. *That's* the problem."

He looks at me. "Not yours, it isn't."

Tonight, we make it as far as Barstow.

After a mammoth American breakfast in the morning, we continue towards Vegas. But as cool as I *look* in my leopard scarf and Jackie O sunglasses, somewhere around Baker I start feeling uncomfortably warm.

"Uh Sam, it's getting pretty hot. I think you're gonna have to put the top up."

"No problem." He pulls over and puts the top up.

Twenty minutes later, I ask him to put it down again. He pulls over and does so. Ten minutes after that, I tell him I'm too hot again.

"Oh for God's sake," he snaps, "this is ridiculous!"

"I can't help it! I'm melting over here."

"We're almost there."

"Fine." I yank off my scarf, as the wind's whipping it into my eyes, and replace it with a ballcap.

"You're such a baby sometimes, Adri."

"I am not. *You* just happen to enjoy an inhuman level of heat."

"You were the one who insisted on renting a convertible."

"I didn't hear you complaining."

"Well it's costing us a bloody fortune."

"It's a little fucking late to tell me that now."

"Nice language," he says. "You sound like a sailor."

We drive in silence until the Vegas hotels come into view.

"Wow!" I say.

Sam nods. "Very cool."

But when we're checking into our swanky hotel, our credit card gets denied. Mortified, Sam phones the bank to sort it out and is told the rental car agency has put a hold on funds. The bank agrees to temporarily raise our credit limit. Again.

After taking our suitcases up to the room, we test the bed just to make sure it's working properly, and then head out onto the Strip in search of the ultimate buffet. We make it a block when Sam spies a store advertising helicopter rides.

"That'd be awesome," he says.

"Let's see what it would cost."

"It'll be too expensive."

"It doesn't hurt to ask."

So we go in and Sam asks the girl at the counter what a ride would cost.

"It depends on where you want to go, sir."

I smile at the 'sir.' Though only thirty-two, Sam's black hair is already two thirds gray, making him appear significantly older.

"How about the Grand Canyon?" he says.

"That would be about $500 for the two of you."

Food is more affordable. After a dinner of all the shrimp, crab legs, prime rib and bread pudding we can stuff in, we waddle over to the 'must see' buccaneer show. The pirates fighting over our heads is nothing spectacular but the way Sam stands behind me, with his arms tightly wrapped around my torso, is. Public shows of affection are rare.

Back in our hotel room, we make love again. Sam's on top so the pendants on his chain – his baptismal cross and St. Jude medal – keep hitting me in the mouth.

I shift them around so that they're resting on his back. "That's better," I say.

He smiles. "Protecting those perfect teeth of yours, are ya?"

Two

The next morning, we arrange our lounge chairs at the pool so that I'm in the shade while he's in direct sunshine.

"Can I least put some sunscreen on you?" I ask.

"I'm Greek – I don't need any."

"Oh for God's sake, you're gonna get skin cancer."

He tilts his chair back and closes his eyes. I watch a young couple with two children stationed a few feet in front of us.

"Look at that woman, Sam."

"Huh?"

"Over there." I poke him in the ribs.

He opens his eyes.

"How can she still be so skinny after having kids?" I ask.

"Maybe she doesn't eat."

"They look like a happy family, though."

"Those parents haven't sat still since we got here," he says, closing his eyes again.

I let a few minutes pass. "Sam?"

"Yeah?"

"Are you *sure* you don't want to ever have kids?"

"Oh God, Adri . . . let's not get into that again."

"You're right." I'm not going to take the chance of ruining a great day by pushing the matter – a sensitive one between us, to put it lightly.

"OK," I say, "one more question, then I'll leave you alone. How would you describe Vegas?"

Sam thinks a moment. "It's a stage where the seven deadly sins are not only prevalent, but encouraged."

"Ooohhhh . . . nicely done."

Silence.

"So," I continue, "what *are* the seven deadly sins?"

"Gluttony, lust, greed . . ." his voice trails off. "I can't remember them all now."

I look over at him, trying to snooze in the scorching mid-day heat.

"Sloth," I say, "that's another."

He gives me the thumbs-up.

Around four o'clock, we head out onto the strip again, starting at the hotel modeled after Venice. Hand in hand, we stroll across the bridge. Beneath us, a mock gondolier in a red scarf and striped shirt is singing in Italian as he paddles his replica gondola through replica canal waters. Sam stops on the bridge and puts his hand on my shoulder. We stand like this a moment, looking out over the canal. I close my eyes and listen to the music.

"As lovely as all this is," I say, turning to Sam, "it still seems a bit . . . fake."

He looks at me but says nothing.

"But *this* Venice is far cleaner and safer than the real place," I add.

"That's a good thing, then, is it not?"

I point to the artificial canal. "Yeah but look at the water. There's not one piece of garbage floating in there and it doesn't smell like shit."

"And the problem is . . ."

"This doesn't *feel* like Venice."

"This isn't Venice, Adri, it's Vegas."

"But what about people who haven't been to the real place? They'll totally get the wrong idea. This is beautiful but it isn't . . . authentic."

We continue walking towards the hotel foyer and as we get closer, we see a group of elderly tourists, staring – heads back, mouths open – at the ceiling. We follow their gaze and there, on the dome-shaped ceiling, is a magnificent painting.

"Ohhhh . . ." I say, "that *is* kinda cool."

"Real enough for ya, snotty-pants?"

I give Sam a mock punch on the shoulder.

"You saw the Sistine Chapel right?" he asks, as we walk out the hotel doors.

"Uh huh."

"That was amazing too, I bet."

"It really was. I mean, despite the fact that I was only twenty-one at the time and more interested in where my next beer was coming from."

He stops. "So you were in the real Rome, seeing *real* art and yet you didn't appreciate it?"

"I was young."

"I see. Left or right?"

"Ummmm left. Let's go check out New York."

We continue along the strip . . . past a two-block long artificial lake with dancing fountains, past a half-size Eiffel Tower, past a brightly-lit castle.

"There's so much of the world to see," Sam remarks.

"Uh huh."

"You're fortunate to have seen and experienced what you have."

"I realize that."

"Most people are lucky if they make it to Vegas in their lifetime," he adds, "never mind visiting the actual destinations these hotels were inspired by."

Half a block from the New York City skyline, I snap a photo of Sam with the replica Empire State Building in the background. A little further along, we stop beneath a smaller-scale Statue of Liberty.

"There she is," he says.

We stare up at her then look at each other.

"I still can't wait for us to go the real place," I say.

Sam gives me *the look* – the one that means 'that's enough.'

Inside, we stroll along the replicated streets of Manhattan, past steam rising from pretend manhole covers, to a bar where a crowd of people has gathered. Since Sam is over six feet, he can see over most of the heads.

"Oh, you'll love this," he says, pulling me to the side for a better view.

There's a guy singing and playing a piano as the patrons gather around, humming along and having a hoot.

Then I hear myself say, "I wonder if this is like a real bar in Greenwich Village."

"Regardless, *this* is pretty cool." Now there is an edge to Sam's voice.

"Yeah but . . ."

"We're in Vegas. Let's appreciate this."

"Don't you want to go to New York anymore?"

"Of course I do, but this is great in itself." Sam sweeps his arm across the scene as if waving a magic wand. "If you can't appreciate this, then what makes you think you'll enjoy the real New York?"

"C'mon, Sammy, lighten up! What would you *most* want to do in Manhattan?"

"Well . . . remember how in the *Catcher in the Rye*, Holden loved to sit on a park bench in Central Park and watch the ducks in the lagoon?"

I smile at Sam's use of a literary reference as he's not much of a reader. "Yeah."

"That's what I'd do."

Back on the strip again, he asks if I'm ready to go back to our own hotel. I shake my head. "Let's go check out the pyramid."

"Are you sure? It's already a really long walk back . . ."

He's right. And when we do finally begin the homeward trek, after a loop through the pyramid, our feet are aching and we're both irritable. On the way, we pass dozens of men slapping sleazy photographs of teenage prostitutes and strippers against their thighs.

"There's some authenticity for you," Sam remarks.

"What are they doing?"

"What do you think they're doing, Adri?"

"I know THAT. But why are they slapping the pamphlets against their legs?"

"Because it's obviously against the law to *verbally* solicit customers."

"And pimping out teenagers isn't?"

We walk in silence until the erupting volcano outside our hotel comes into view.

Sam laughs. "Go big or go home."

"What?"

"I was just thinking how Vegas is such a 'go big or go home' kinda place."

Tonight we have the lustful, in-front-of-the-hotel-room-mirror kind of sex couples tend to have on vacation, away from the pressures of daily life.

In the morning, I awake to find Sam has gone downstairs and brought us back coffee and muffins for breakfast in our room. We sit at the table in the corner, looking out the window at the dormant volcano.

I turn to Sam. "Thank you."

"For?"

"Everything. This is awesome."

As we leave Vegas in our convertible – top down – I remark: "That was quite somethin', huh?"

Sam nods.

"All that *stuff* in the middle of the desert . . ."

He nods again.

I look over at him. "But now it's quiet time?"

"Bingo," he says with a wink. So I put a sock in it for awhile.

"How are you doing over there?" he asks, half an hour later.

"I'm getting kinda hot."

Laughing, he pulls over and puts the top up.

When we check into our hotel in Tusayan, the clerk tells us the sunset at the Grand Canyon is at 6:28 p.m. so if we want to catch it, we better get our tails in gear. Back into the convertible we hop and speed towards the canyon, arguing over whether or not we should take a helicopter ride.

"I'll call them on the cell phone, Sam."

"We already know it's gonna cost too much."

"But you want to go."

"Adri, chill . . . it's no big deal."

"At least let me phone and find out."

"We already know it's gonna be five hundred bucks."

"That was from Vegas," I say, punching in the number. Then it hits me: isn't *being* at the Grand Canyon enough? I push end and place the phone on the floor. "I just thought seeing the Grand Canyon from a helicopter would be amazing."

"Have you ever been up in one?"

I shake my head.

"It's great. It's like you get to see . . . a bigger piece of the picture."

Three

Around the next corner, patiently waiting millions of years, is the Grand Canyon. Sam pulls into a turnoff and switches off the engine. We walk around to the front of the car and stand side by side, staring out over the landscape.

"This isn't the place they told us to see the sunset," I say.

He sighs. "I know. We'll keep going."

We get back in the car and follow the instructions to the best place to observe the sunset, which is right beside the gift shop. I ask Sam what time it is.

He glances at his watch. "Six-twenty."

"I'll be right back."

Inside, the salesgirl is ringing in two coffee mugs with the Grand Canyon plastered on the side when Sam appears beside me.

"They're for our moms," I explain.

"Just because we're on vacation doesn't mean we have to buy everyone presents."

"Relax. It's only a few bucks."

"But we have to be really careful with our money. You know that. And couldn't you have at least waited 'til after the sunset?"

The girl wraps up the mugs, sticks them in a bag and hands it to me. I want to throw the damn things *into* the canyon.

Back outside, we aren't alone. We choose a vacant rock a couple of feet from some moron loudly reciting poetry to his much younger – and clearly embarrassed – female companion. Sam and I exchange looks.

"It's Sven!" I whisper. Sven is the name of my imaginary and supposedly ideal lover. Mythical Sven loves to hike, ski and read by the fire. He spends his day scaling mountains, listening to me talk and, apparently, reciting poetry as the sun sets over the Grand Canyon. Thank God I didn't get the husband I asked for when I was a teenager.

"Then that must be Sasha," Sam replies, nodding to the woman. Sam's imaginary and supposedly ideal lover goes by the name of Sasha. Mythical Sasha is a porn star with big hooters and no voicebox. All she wants to do is have sex all day, sometimes with other women. I'm about the furthest thing from a Sasha, except for the sex – but with just the two of us, thanks.

The poet finally shuts up so all two hundred of us can enjoy the sunset in peace.

After a dinner of fajitas and beer back in Tusayan, we stumble back to our hotel room and Sam immediately races into the bathroom.

"Ummm," he says, when he finally comes out again, "would you mind if I slept in my own bed tonight?"

"No."

"It's just that I'm really full and my stomach hurts . . ."

For as long as I've known Sam, he's always had problems with his digestive system. "Sam, it's OK. I understand."

Still, it is strange waking up in the morning and seeing him in the other bed.

"I was hoping you'd sleep in," he says.

"No way! We gotta see the sunrise."

By 5:30 a.m., we're back in the convertible and make it to the Canyon just in time to see the first light appear on the horizon. Once the sun is fully in the sky, I suggest we take a walk. Sam nods but I can tell he isn't into it. He'll want to be hitting the road since we have an eight-hour drive ahead of us, whereas I want to cram as much as possible into the time we have left. Seeing the Grand Canyon isn't enough; it would be better from a helicopter. The sunset isn't good enough; I have to see the sunrise too. If I had my way, I'd drag Sam halfway down *into* the canyon, just to experience that as well.

We're five minutes along the path when we come to a large open rock face. I walk quickly towards the drop-off.

"Adri!" Sam yells. "Don't go so close to the edge."

I stop and turn to him. "I'm nowhere *near* it."

"Yes you are. Don't be stupid!"

"Fine." I sit down, still a good three feet from the edge. "Can you take my picture here then?"

He takes my photo, then turns and starts back towards the car. Our walk is over.

The drive back to L.A. is long and hot and neither of us says much. I try to keep the number of top up versus top down requests to a minimum. It's me who finally breaks the silence. It usually is. "Do you believe in evolution?" I ask.

He continues staring straight ahead. "No."

"That's ridiculous!" I snap. "Evolution isn't something you 'believe' or 'don't believe' – it's a scientific *fact*."

"Then why did you ask the question?" He reaches over and turns on the radio.

We don't speak again until the first sign for San Bernadino appears. "That's where that pilot I told you about lives," Sam says. "The one who flies a police helicopter. He said to call him when I was down here and he'd take me up for a ride."

"No way! Are you gonna call him?"

"Nope."

"Why not?"

"Because this is our vacation and I don't want to do anything work-related."

I shift to get a better look at Sam. Passing on the chance to meet up with a cop from another country is strange enough behavior for him. Not seizing the opportunity to go up in a police helicopter is unexplainable. Sam eats, sleeps and breathes police work.

"But *why?*"

"I know you want to get to Knots Berry Farm for dinner."

Granted, I'd heard that the dinner specials at Knots Berry Farm were not to be missed – and had insisted we wait until then to eat dinner. But by the time we sit down in the restaurant booth, Sam's ready to throttle me. "My wife has dragged me here all the way from the Grand Canyon," he tells our waiter.

"Ah," replies the waiter. "I promise you it will be worth the wait."

He didn't have to sit in a convertible, driving through the sweltering desert heat with a bitchy wife wearing a leopard print scarf, baseball cap and Jackie O sunglasses.

I watch Sam devour the basketful of warm biscuits, three pieces of fried chicken, mashed potatoes with thick gravy and kernel corn. Also down the hatch goes a gallon of boysenberry punch and a huge piece of boysenberry pie.

Back at our hotel, Sam runs to the bathroom so I put our leftovers into the mini-fridge, climb into the kingsize bed and fall fast asleep.

Four

Friday September 22ⁿᵈ, 2000

Today is Sam's friend's wedding at Disneyland, the original reason for our trip. I put on a black dress.

"You look beautiful," he says, as we're leaving our hotel room.

"Thank you." I stand on my toes to kiss him. "You're rather dashing yourself."

In the foyer, the desk clerk waves us over to the reception desk. "You're going to Disneyland today, right?"

"Yup!" I say. "Any tips?"

"Use the fast passes," he advises, "and find a good spot to watch the fireworks."

"Oh yeah?" says Sam, clearly not as enthused as I.

The clerk nods. "You don't want to miss Tinkerbell flying through the sky . . . it's actually pretty neat how they do it."

Sam smiles politely and I laugh.

At the luncheon reception after the ceremony, Sam and I sit with the photographer and his family. I listen as Sam asks the teenagers questions about their lives and career plans. After the reception, we head into the hotel bathrooms to change into more comfortable clothes. When I come out of the ladies room, Sam's waiting for me, wearing a white T-shirt with his fuzzy blue vest over top, khaki shorts and white runners. He crams my shoes and clothes into the knapsack and puts it on his shoulders. "Let's roll."

I almost have to jog to keep up with him. "We've only got one day," he explains, "so we have to coordinate our moves."

"Couldn't we come back tomorrow?"

Sam smiles but I can see right through him. He knows that if he can make *today* fabulous for me, he won't have to spend a second day – and a Saturday yet – at Disneyland.

"Where are we headed?" I ask, a little out of breath as I trot along beside him.

"You said you wanted to go to Splash Mountain so let's get that reserved first."

"Geez. It's like you've come up with a . . . whaddya call it? An operating plan?"

"An *Ops* plan," he corrects me. "And yes, I have."

After we reserve Splash Mountain, he relaxes so I ask him about his questions to the teens at lunch. "You seemed genuinely interested in them," I say.

"I was."

"It's just that you're so negative about kids now."

"I'm not an asshole, Adri."

"I know."

"I liked them. They were polite and seemed like they actually gave a damn."

I sigh. "There are a lot of decent people out there."

"Yeah well, I just don't happen to deal with the good ones on a regular basis."

When we arrive at Splash Mountain at our scheduled time, we walk through the express lane to the front of the line, proud as peacocks at our fast pass planning finesse. At the very top of the ride, there's a section where the little log cars float along in the water as large stuffed chipmunks sing to each other: "*Zippity do dah, zippity yay, my oh my what a wonderful day.*"

We're bobbing along in our log car when Sam puts his arm around my shoulders and watches me watching the chipmunks. I feel so happy and safe, like I'm a kid again – I mean before I knew my parent's marriage wasn't going to make it.

"*Zippidy do dah, Zippity yay,*" sing the ever-cheerful chipmunks, "*I got a feeling something's coming my way.*" Then the tranquility ends as our log car drops into the waiting pool of water.

"Did you *feel* that?" I ask Sam, as we're climbing out of the log car.

"What? The drop?"

"No – at the top before we dropped down . . . it was like magic or somethin'."

One eyebrow goes up. "You wanna go again then?"

"Nah." I give him a little wave of my hand. "It's never the same the second time."

So instead, we race around Disneyland like two over-sized kids; stuffing our faces with popcorn and hotdogs, jumping on and off rides, and smugly passing exhausted parents wiping ice-cream off their screaming children's faces.

In the late afternoon, we find a place to watch the parade and hoot and holler as our favourite characters walk by. I snap a picture of Sam with Grumpy Dwarf and tease him about the likeness. As the last float goes by, we somehow end up *in* the parade, laughing and waving at the crowd as we walk along.

After dinner, Sam secures us a prime spot behind a garbage can to watch the fireworks. "This way," he says, "nobody can stand directly in front of us."

We're waiting for the show to begin when Sam squeezes my hand and nods towards our left. "Check it out. It's the Pooh family."

Sure enough, there's mom, dad and two little kids, all sporting yellow fuzzy jackets with Winnie the Pooh crests. We watch their stroller and sippy-cup antics until a woman's voice comes over the loudspeaker: "*Believe* . . . there's magic in the air . . ."

I smile at Sam and then kapow! The show begins in an explosion of light.

But just before Tinkerbell descends from the sky, Pooh *Grandma* suddenly appears to my right. I hadn't noticed her earlier but the matching yellow fuzzy reveals her heritage. She looks at me and says, "Excuse me. I have to get by."

So I take a step back to let her pass and Sam does the same. But when she's in front of him, she falls and the back of her head hits the concrete. Sam immediately kneels down to help her as I run into the crowd, arms waving and yelling for an ambulance.

When I return, Sam's still kneeling on the pavement, speaking into her ear. The woman is breathing and her eyes are open but she's motionless, staring blankly into the night. As I watch Sam comfort her, it occurs to me that he can't just turn off being a police officer. The paramedics and security arrive and after Sam gives his witness statement, we walk away. I ask him if he thinks she'll be OK.

"I don't know," he says. "I mean, she really hit the back of her head *hard*."

"Did she trip?"

"Either that or fainted."

"Things like that aren't supposed to happen at the Happiest Place on Earth."

Sam doesn't say anything.

"So you probably want to go now, huh?" I ask.

To my surprise, he shakes his head. "No. You?"

I grin. "No."

He takes my hand. "Star Tours?"

"Yup."

We race back to the Star Tours Flight Simulator, walk through the empty lineup to the entrance then hop on the ride.

"Again?" I ask, once the ride's finished.

Sam winks. "I thought it was never the same the second time around?"

"It's not. It's *better*."

After our last tour through the stars, we head over to Sleeping Beauty's Castle and climb on a ride clearly intended for little kids. I turn to Sam, squished beside me in the tiny pink cart. "I can't believe you're doing this."

"Me neither."

Around midnight, we're making our way towards the exit and come across the old-fashioned merry-go-round. I look at Sam. "Whaddya reckon?"

"Last one?"

"Deal."

Sam chooses a white horse and climbs on. I hop on my horse, pull my camera out of the knapsack then lean back. "OK, Greekie . . . gimme a smile."

Gripping the brass pole, Sam smiles broadly and I snap the photo.

Five

Sam awakes the next morning to find me studying the map in bed.

"So what does the clipboard of fun say for today?" he asks.

I smile sheepishly. "I dunno."

"Yeah right."

"OK, what would *you* like to do today?"

He nods towards the mini-fridge. "Let's start with those leftovers."

I retrieve the Knots Berry Farm doggie-bag and return to bed where we watch TV while eating cold chicken and boysenberry pie. Sam expertly balances the containers on his chest, mindful of not wasting any unnecessary energy actually sitting up.

"That's quite a skill," I say, gently poking him in the ribs with my fork.

"What would you think about us visiting my mom's best friend today?" he asks. "She lives in San Diego and I know she'd love to meet you."

"Sure." But this surprises me. Visiting people is not high on Sam's list of preferred vacation activities.

Yet this evening, we find ourselves in San Diego, drinking peach juice and chatting with an older Greek couple at their kitchen table. Not twenty minutes into the conversation, we get onto the topic of death. The woman shows us a photo of an infant.

"Friends of ours lost a baby a year ago."

"That's too bad," says Sam.

"But she got pregnant again immediately."

"Oh my!" I say.

She looks at me. "I guess they felt that was best, Adri."

I nod my head and keep my mouth shut – but I wonder how someone could replace a dead child with a new one so quickly.

We're then taken on a tour of their home. At the top of the stairs, the woman stops outside a closed door and turns to face us. "My mother was widowed very young," she says. "She was a devout Greek Orthodox."

Sam and I nod our heads in somewhat baffled silence.

"I admired her absolute faith," she continues.

I smile. "Well that's good."

"And I guess I'm a pretty strong believer myself," she says, reaching over and opening the door. "This is my prayer room."

My eyes widen at the sight of the room filled with images and icons of Jesus, the disciples and saints. Pictures depicting Christian scenes as well as several gold crosses hang from the walls. Candles in red glass containers flicker gently, casting a reddish hue. The powerful scent of incense hangs in the air. Sam and I stay in the hall.

"Come on in," she says at our obvious hesitation, "it's safe in here!"

So we go inside and stand quietly a moment. Undoubtedly, it is peaceful.

As we're pulling out of their driveway half an hour later, I ask Sam what the heck that was all about.

"Ya got me."

"She's pretty religious, eh?"

"No kidding," he says. "But I couldn't *stand* the smell of that incense."

"I hear ya."

We drive in silence for a few minutes.

"Where were we recently where they were waving that stuff around?" I ask.

"My uncle's funeral."

I nod. "Right."

For the first time in our eleven and a half years together, I'd attended a Greek Orthodox funeral four months ago.

Sam glances over at me. "You were pretty upset that day, hey?"

When we'd got back into the car after the graveside service, I'd burst into tears. Sam's brother and sister had been with us.

"I just hated how we left your uncle all alone like that," I say.

"Adri, he was dead."

"I know! But it was so strange how one second, people were making such a fuss – wailing and throwing dirt on his coffin and then the next, the tears were gone and it was like, 'OK, what's for lunch?'"

Sam throws back his head and laughs. "Greeks are like that – very dramatic."

"I'll say."

"I guess we *could* have taken him to the reception . . ."

I look over at Sam.

"Wheeled his casket right on by the buffet table . . ."

"Sam!"

"Uncle, would you like a cookie?"

"Stop it!" Laughing, I reach over and swat him on the forearm.

The next morning, however, I wake to a growly husband.

"I'm very angry with you," he says.

"Why?"

"I had a dream that you cheated on me."

"Uh oh."

"With another cop."

"Who?"

"The one with the sexy voice."

I smile. I know who he's referring to because the guy is *really* good-looking, plus he practically purrs when he phones in a report to us girls at work. I went on a police ride-along with him years ago and we'd had a riot.

"I'm serious, Adri." Sam gets out of bed. "I can't believe how mad I am at you."

"It was a *dream*!"

He shakes his head. "It felt too real to be just a dream." With a snort, he heads into the shower. Today we're off to Universal Studios.

We're one of the first to arrive at the Waterworld show, so from our seats we watch other audience members walk in. And as people go past the massive water stage, representing a futuristic flooded earth, an actor pretending to be a maintenance man squirts them with a hose as they walk by. Most people can't figure out where the water is coming from and Sam howls watching their confused reactions.

"I'd love to be an actor," he says.

"Oh yeah?"

"Uh huh. Especially if I got to play the bad guy."

"Maybe that's why undercover work appeals to you so much?"

"Maybe."

After the show, I convince him to take the tram tour through the studio. When our guide isn't chirping half-truths about what's around the next corner, a director promotes his upcoming film on an overhead TV monitor. As our tram rolls along, I wave at Jaws, who is far more decrepit than dangerous since I last saw him twenty-two years ago; cringe at King Kong, who ought to be retired by now; and shrug at the old house that Psycho was filmed in forty years ago. I keep hoping we'll catch a glimpse of a new movie being filmed versus tired remnants of old sets. I tell Sam this.

"But they can't control what you might see on a live film set," is his reply. "They're only gonna show you what *they* want you to see. It's Hollywood – what do you expect?"

"To see movies being made . . . the behind-the-scenes stuff."

Our tram enters a burning building and the false floor collapses beneath us. The woman behind us screams. Sam rolls his eyes. "Better?"

By late afternoon, we've had more than enough. I suggest we go to Malibu for dinner and find a nice restaurant overlooking the sea . . .

Sam sighs. "Are you sure you want to go all that way?"

"Uh huh."

Of course, he's right. By the time we actually arrive in Malibu, the sun has set. Thus we sit in our ocean-view restaurant with no ocean view.

"*Chicken?*" I snip, after the waiter has left. "What the heck are ya ordering chicken for, when we're at the sea?"

"Because I feel like chicken."

"Don't you want fish?"

"No, I don't. I want chicken."

"I'm sorry, Sam . . . I guess I'm just tired."

He shakes his head and takes a drink of beer. "You're a weirdo."

Six

Monday is our last day of vacation and we spend it in Santa Monica, walking on the beach. We've walked for about twenty minutes when I suggest we go for a swim.

"You're on your own," Sam says. "I left my swim shorts in the trunk."

I open my mouth to ask a bitchy *Why?* But I catch myself. Instead, I say, "No worries. I think I'll still go in though."

"Absolutely! I'll hold your stuff."

So Sam stands on the sand while I run into the surf. I'm only in up to my calves when I stop, my childhood fear of sharks returning. I turn back to Sam and he nods, as if to say 'go on.' So I take a deep breath, run straight into the waves and dive under. When I come up, I check to make sure Sam's still keeping an eye on me and then I dive under again. When I come up this time and first open my eyes, Sam looks different – as if he's surrounded by some sort of haze. Or maybe it's the salt water in my eyes.

We walk back along the beach and on the way, come across a Spanish family splashing around in the water. Wordlessly, Sam and I both sit on the sand and watch.

"That's nice," he says a few minutes later, nodding towards the ocean. "I mean, the whole family playing together like that . . ."

I want to ask him if that will ever be us: mom, dad and a couple of kids? But deep down, I already know his answer. So I just nod. "It really is."

Then I reach over and scratch his scalp because he loves it when I do this.

He closes his eyes. "Mmmmm . . ."

"I've got one picture left, Sammy."

"Self-portrait?"

"Yup."

So I lean in and wrap both arms tightly around him. He leans back into me, holding the camera out at arms-length and snaps the last photo. As the film is rewinding, he glances at his watch. "We better get to the airport."

I laugh. "Our flight home isn't for hours."

"We might run into some heavy traffic. I mean, it is L.A.."

"True."

We walk back to the parking lot and are climbing the steps from the beach when we both see a disheveled-looking older woman sitting cross-legged in the sand. Her head is slumped over her chest and bottles and cans lie strewn around her.

"That's got to be a shitty way to live," Sam remarks, once we're in the car.

Frankly, his comment surprises me. Compassion for fainting Pooh Grandma is one matter; empathy towards a homeless alcoholic is something Sam has had very little of lately.

"Are you OK over there?" he asks, when he catches me staring at him.

I smile. "I'm thinking you better put that top down one last time."

"You betcha."

Once we're on the freeway, Sam says, "It's a big world out there. I'd forgotten how big it is."

I look over at him.

"But this trip has really made me realize there's so much more to life than our little city back home, Adri."

"Yeah . . ."

"It can be a cruel world – but it is a big one."

I giggle. "Have you been drinking coffee again?" Chatty Sam usually only comes out after a strong cup of coffee or a few beers.

He smiles. "I was just thinking how much it bothered me that I didn't get on with the Priority Crimes Unit."

"Oh?" We've scarcely talked about his work this trip.

"But now that I'm away from home, I realize there are so many other opportunities to work undercover."

"Such as?"

"CSIS, the FBI, CIA, Secret Service . . ."

"I think you'd need a green card for some of those, hon."

"My point," he says, "is that I've been thinking way too small."

"Oh."

We travel in silence for a few minutes. "Just out of curiosity," I say, "what would your undercover name have been if you *had* gotten on with Priority Crimes?"

"Some co-pilot you are," he replies, pointing to the airport exit sign as we drive past it. "Pay attention, will ya?"

"Oh shit. Sorry."

He taps his temple with his index finger. "That's why it's good to leave lots of extra time."

"You're a bit early for your flight," says the guy behind the check-in counter at the LAX airport.

"Yeah," I whisper under my breath, "like *five* hours."

As we walk away from the counter, I say to Sam, "You're the weirdo."

"I did get us here too early, huh?"

"Then again," I reason, "if we stayed at the beach much longer, we might have hit way worse traffic."

So, once we're through security, I find a comfy chair and devour the L.A. Times. Sam finds a spot at the bar and has a beer watching Monday Night Football. We wave at each other occasionally but for the most part, we do our own thing. The vacation is over.

Seven

Back home, I'm first out of bed first Tuesday morning. I put on coffee, write in my journal and do some catch-up reading from *Simple Abundance; A Daybook of Comfort and Joy* by Sarah Ban Breathnach, the closest thing to a bible for me.

The September 22nd passage mentions how once you're ready to start making connections, the revelations come quickly and from all places. "In the Old Testament," it reads, "God uses donkeys, rocks and burning bushes to deliver Divine messages, so don't question the validity of what you hear or how you hear it *if the truth resonates within*." The September 24th passage suggests that if you do what you love, the money will follow – but that it'll come from unexpected sources. For when you do start to follow your authentic path and use the gifts Spirit expects you to use, "you get a new employer: Spirit."

"Must be a pretty good sex scene."

I look up and see Sam walking into the living room.

I grin. "Not quite."

"Whatcha readin'?"

I hold up the familiar pink book. I've read it many times.

He nods and sits on the couch. "It's good to be home, huh?"

"Sam, I gotta get my shit together . . . with my writing, I mean."

He stands up again. "Let's go retrieve the hound."

Back home from the kennel, we're barely in the back door when the phone rings.

I answer it. "Oh, hi mom."

Sam rolls his eyes and walks out of the kitchen.

I tell her a bit about our vacation and then she asks if I have any ideas for Thanksgiving Dinner.

"Well," I reply, uttering words I do not mean, "we *could* have it here."

"That would be very nice, Adri."

"Except that I'm working most of that weekend. And I think Sam is actually working the whole weekend."

"I could cook the turkey," she says, "and we could all help out."

"I dunno mom, it really isn't that convenient . . ."

"Oh."

"But I'll see what Sam thinks," I finish.

I know damn well what he'll think.

"You're fucking kidding me, right?" is his actual response.

I cross my arms over my chest. "Nope."

"You wanna have fifteen people over for dinner – and we're both working?"

"That's right."

Sam glares at me then shakes his head slowly. My stomach tightens.

"You just don't get it do you?" he says then walks away.

Funny thing is I *do* get it. I just can't be bothered to say no to my mom because it's not worth the hassle. Sam, however, apparently thinks it is – and gives me the silent treatment to prove his point.

By Wednesday afternoon, he still hasn't said a word to me. Even Sasha, our dog, ignores me. She follows Sam around the house and lies beside him on the floor when he reclines on the couch, affectionately called – by him – The Perch.

Sam's scheduled to work his first shift back at 9:00 p.m. tonight but I overhear him on the phone telling his sergeant, Tom, he won't be in.

"You're taking another court day?" I ask.

"Yes."

Over the past four years, I can count the times on one hand that Sam has taken a day off work other than for vacation. Not going into work, especially since he's not speaking to me anyway, is odd. That it's a night shift he's missing, as opposed to a dayshift, is even stranger. Sam's a nightowl; I'm the earlybird.

We eat our dinner in silence. I know he's a stubborn Taurus but this is getting ridiculous. I fantasize about leaving him . . . moving to Vancouver, renting a little apartment and becoming a *real* writer by the sea. I'd take Sasha and the two of us would walk on the beach during breaks from my blossoming career as a novelist. This is what I'm thinking when I crawl into bed, alone, on Wednesday night.

Thursday morning, I'm working on my computer when I hear him upstairs in the kitchen, pouring his coffee. When he comes down stairs, I don't look up.

He walks by my desk. "Mornin'."

"Morning," I reply, in my iciest voice.

He walks over, lies down on the couch and flips on the TV. *Dink.* I resume typing.

Ten minutes later, he turns the TV off. "What do you do over there all the time in your little office?"

My silent treatment has been lifted.

"I'm building an empire," I say, referring to the fact that I was researching a stock price on the Internet. "And I also happen to be writing a novel, in case you've forgotten."

He sighs. "No, I haven't forgotten."

"Good."

"So what are you writing today?"

"I'm actually editing a poem I wrote about an old University Prof of mine – but it's supposed to be about *Liz's* former professor."

"Liz is the character based on you, right?"

"Uh huh," I say glumly. Fiction isn't turning out to be my strong point.

"Let's hear it."

"I dunno . . . it's in pretty rough shape."

"That's OK." Sam settles back into the couch and assumes his best thinking position: thumb beneath chin, index finger on cheek, middle finger above mouth.

The poem is a dreadful piece of writing. *Liz's* frustration about not living up to her potential, however, is crystal clear. When I finish, there isn't a peep from The Perch.

Hearing my own words out loud makes me realize I'm a spoiled brat wallowing in self-pity. And I'm blaming my lack of writing on having to work at a regular job.

"Very interesting," says Sam. "And what, exactly, did your Prof teach you that was so important?"

I jump up. "He taught me how to *think*! How we need to question the underlying assumptions that have led us to the mess we're in."

He takes his mug from the coffee table. "Let's go to the dog-park."

In the Jeep, he doesn't say much and the tension between us is palpable. Ten minutes into our walk the volcano erupts.

"I think you're trying to control me," I blurt.

He stops walking. "Why do you say that?"

"This Thanksgiving thing is a perfect example. It's as if whatever *you* say goes – but there are two of us in this relationship you know."

"I realize that. But having dinner at our place this year simply isn't convenient."

"Fine. But why do you have to be such a prick about it?"

"Don't swear, Adri."

"What's your fucking problem?"

"Don't raise your voice at me."

"You're not my goddamn father!" I scream. "Stop treating me like a child!"

"Then stop acting like one."

Steam is coming out of my ears by this point but Sam has more to say: "I just don't understand why you can't say no to anyone."

"Oh God, here we go," I groan, "back to my mother."

"I'm not mad at your mom anymore. It's you I'm disappointed in."

My stomach tightens. "Well, isn't that dandy."

"Do you even *want* to have the damn dinner?"

"No."

"Then maybe it's time you learn how to say that. And maybe you should spend less time pleasing everyone else and more time on *you* – and on us."

I blink back tears. "Sam, I feel like I'm not being my true

self around you anymore. I'm holding back on saying what I really think or feel because I know it'll lead to a fight."

"Seriously?"

"Yeah."

"Then don't do that anymore," he says. "Starting now."

"OK . . ." I take a deep breath. "I'm scared shitless I'm gonna wake up twenty years from now and *still* not have finished
writing a book."

He looks me in the eye. "You're probably right about that
– as long as you know that'll have been *your* choice."

I open my mouth – like a goldfish waiting to be fed – but
no words come out.

"I believe in you," he continues, "but until you make your
writing a priority and take it seriously, nobody else ever will."

"I don't have time to write!"

"Then find it."

"When? I have to work at a stupid clerical job."

"Not twenty-four seven, you don't. What happened to writing in the morning, before you leave for work?"

"I'm *trying*. But when the alarm goes off, I come up with a
bunch of excuses as to why the next day would be better. I keep
procrastinating."

"Then stop procrastinating."

"It's not that easy!"

"Nothing worthwhile ever is. There are no short-cuts."

"I get your goddamn point," I say through gritted teeth.

We stare at each other until Sam breaks into a goofy grin.
"Geez," he says, "I can be a real asshole, can't I?"

"I'll say."

"Adri look . . . you're the smartest person I know. It kills me
to see you wasting your potential racing around like a chicken
with its head cut off."

He looks so sad – but I know he's right. So I promise myself
to wake up at 5:00 a.m. tomorrow to start the next draft of my
novel before going in to work.

We walk back towards the parking lot, chatting about the

upcoming days. Sam's heading back to work tonight; I start again tomorrow morning.

At home, he has a quick bite to eat then takes a nap while I putter around the garage. But I catch myself fantasizing about how good it would be if I could work from home as a writer and not have to go to my regular job.

When Sam wakes up, he showers while I sit on the bathroom counter, chirping away at him. When he's finished, I hand him his towel.

Then, because my car needs to be fixed, I take it to the gas station and Sam picks me up there in his Jeep. He drives us to his work so I can drop him off because I'll need the Jeep to get to *my* work tomorrow.

"But how will you get home in the morning?" I ask as he pulls up behind his District's police station.

"Tom'll drop me off."

We get out of the Jeep and he hands me the keys.

I give him a quick kiss. "Have a good shift!"

He walks to the back door of the police station. I get in the driver's seat and am just about to drive away when I glance out the window and see that he's still standing outside, watching me. So I smile and wave but he just nods curtly then heads inside.

Eight

Friday September 29th, 2000

When my alarm goes off at 5:00 a.m., I push snooze.

I don't want to wake up. I don't feel like writing. Maybe tomorrow. I don't want to go back to work.

Ten minutes later, the alarm goes off again. I push snooze.

I don't wanna get up. Why do I have to type police reports for a living?

Ten minutes later, the alarm again goes off. Snooze is hit.

Holy shit, am I ever anxious. If I got up in the first place, I wouldn't be feeling this way. I hate my job.

I drag myself out of bed at 6:15, furious for not following through on my own promise to get up early and write. I quickly shower, scarf down a bowl of cereal, then throw an apple, chocolate pudding and granola bar into my blue vinyl lunch bag. I'm just about to put on my wool sweater with the three lamb faces on the front, when I notice Sasha's dog dishes are low. This concerns me, even though Sam will be home in less than an hour. "You never know," I say, topping up her food and water, "you just might be on your own today."

I drive downtown and, as usual, arrive one minute before 7:00. When my supervisor sees me in the hallway, she asks me to go into her office. I figure I must have made a mistake typing a report, back before I left on holidays.

She shuts the door and looks me in the eye. "Sam's fallen."

Perhaps a broken leg or arm. The thought flits into my mind and out again.

"You have to call his inspector right away," she says, handing me the phone number. "He's waiting to hear from you."

I'm puzzled as to why an officer with the rank of inspector wants to speak to me because inspectors don't phone in incident reports. So I sit down at my supervisor's desk and start punching in the first few numbers, when I make the connection between Sam's inspector and Sam's *fall*. This isn't about a report.

"Hi," I say when an older male voice answers the phone.

"Is this Adri?"

"Yeah."

"Sam's been in an accident."

"Oh."

"Where are you right now?"

"At work."

"Is your supervisor with you?"

I swallow. "Yeah."

"OK, listen to me. Sam's hit his head and we're on the way to pick you up."

"HIS HEAD?"

The room suddenly feels different — as if the air is being sucked out.

"Yes. He's at the hospital and we're going to take you to him."

Oh God no.

"Adri, are you there?"

"Uh huh."

"I need to talk to your supervisor now, OK?"

I hand the phone over. It feels as if my insides are caving in. I also have the oddest feeling that *something* has just begun.

My supervisor takes my arm and leads me from the office to the back alley behind the police station, where we wait for Sam's inspector to pick me up.

"We had an awesome holiday," I hear myself say.

Her eyes widen. "I'm really glad, Adri."

The police van pulls up and Sam's inspector and Tom get out. Tom gives me a big hug, which is normal since I know him. But then the inspector hugs me and this is worrisome because I've never met the man. The inspector gets back in the driver's seat and Tom opens the sliding back door for me. So I get in and he sits beside me.

Everything is wrong. I should be typing in my cramped cubicle, not sitting in the back seat of a police vehicle with Sam's sergeant, who is supposed to be driving Sam *home* right about now. I ask Tom what happened.

"Sam was investigating a break and enter when he fell through a false ceiling."

I look out the window. "I see."

"He hit his head, Adri."

"Where are we going?"

There is a pause, then: "The hospital."

I turn to look at him. "But which one?"

He tells me Sam is at the hospital in the northwest part of the city.

"Why didn't they take him to the one in the south?" I ask.

"Because he needed to be at the hospital with the best trauma unit."

Clunk. Like a coin landing on the bottom of an empty piggybank, the seriousness of Sam's injury hits me. You don't generally make it home to dinner when your day starts in a trauma unit.

"You know," I say, "we had a great vacation."

Nine

At Emergency, we're directed to a room where most of Sam's team is waiting – four or five officers, all of whom I know. When I walk in, they stand up and each person hugs me. I choose a seat beside Amanda, the only policewoman on Sam's team, and she puts her arm around me. I ask her what happened.

"We went to a break and enter. Sam went inside with the K-9 officer and his dog. Sam was searching an upper level in the building when he fell through the floor."

"He gonna be OK, though, right?"

"Adri, he *really* hit the back of his head hard."

"Did they catch the bad guy?"

She opens her mouth then closes it again. "Uh . . . I don't think so."

I stare at the floor. For the next ten minutes we all sit quietly. When I do glance up, I catch the bloodshot stares of Sam's team-mates. The observation of this anomaly – crying cops – tells me the truth; wordlessly, softly, gently.

A nurse enters the room and walks over to me. "Are you Sam's wife?"

I nod so she hands me a clear plastic bag full of clothing. I stand up to take the bag but when I look more closely, I realize the items are familiar. On top of Sam's black rain pants are his watch, chain, wallet and a twenty-dollar bill. I'm staring at these, astounded, when I hear a man's voice behind me: "It's OK, Adri, they're just giving you Sam's things . . . it doesn't mean anything."

Oh, but it does. It means *everything*. It means that wherever Sam is headed, he isn't gonna need to know the time or have twenty bucks for dinner.

But why would the nurse give me Sam's things before I've

even seen him or spoken to his doctor? This is like telling someone the end of a movie and then giving her a ticket to see it.

I sit down, reach into the bag and pull out Sam's watch and chain.

"His cross is missing," I say, panic rising, "and his St. Jude medal."

"We'll find them," Tom says.

"They're really important to Sam," I explain, as the air in this room is sucked out.

Tom tells one of his officers to ask the nurse about the pendants. I put Sam's watch on my wrist and am placing his chain around my neck when his inspector appears in front of me, perplexed.

Clearing his throat, he glances at the plastic bag in my lap. "I'm sorry, Adri, but I'm going to have to take Sam's personal effects."

"Oh?"

"For evidence. I'm not sure why they gave you that."

I hand him the bag but don't say anything about removing Sam's watch and chain. Nobody else does either.

The inspector leaves the room and Tom sits down next to me. "I think you better call Sam's parents."

Oh shit.

Sam's dad answers the phone. Despite my inability to speak Greek and his limited English, he understands perfectly well that Sam has been seriously hurt. Sam's sister, Angela, is staying with them so the phone is passed to her.

"How bad is it?" she asks.

"Pretty bad."

"Mom's at work. Should I go and pick her up?"

"I think they're going to talk to you about that right now."

I hand the phone to an officer and I hear him telling Angela that a police car is being sent to pick them up.

Then I phone my own mom and for the first time, I cry briefly. I feel very young and terrified in my wool sweater with the three lamb faces, clutching my vinyl blue lunchbag with the chocolate pudding inside.

An ER doctor comes in and gives us an update: critical but stable. That's one way to put it. The car is totaled but we're salvaging what parts we can, would be another.

"When can I see him?" I ask.

"Very soon."

Twenty minutes later, the social worker comes to get me and the two of us walk down the corridor together. I ask him how Sam is doing.

The social worker stops walking, so I do too. "He's in pretty rough shape, Adri."

I nod slowly and we resume walking. Then, for just a second, it's like I split in two. I'm physically beside the social worker yet I'm also *watching* the two of us walk.

When the social worker and I arrive at a set of doors, he takes my arm. Like arriving at a party too late and entering the banquet room to find the busboys clearing the tables, no one has to tell you it's over – you just figure it out. By the time I get to the strangely inactive emergency room, they've obviously given up on trying to save Sam and are instead merely stabilizing his body.

Since it was the back of his head that struck the concrete, Sam looks much the same as when I saw him last night. Except that now, he's unconscious, flat on his back, draped in a white sheet and has tubes sprouting out from his chest, neck and arms.

I race to his side and grab his unresponsive hand. I kiss his cheek and the real tears finally arrive, streaming down my face.

"I love you," I whisper in his ear.

No response.

"I love you."

Nothing.

"I love you, Sam."

My silent treatment has been reinstated.

And then it happens again: I'm holding Sam's hand and yet I'm also observing the two of us from a few feet away.

Then the social worker gently takes my arm and leads what's left of me out of the emergency room. He walks me to a waiting area in the intensive care unit where Sam's teammates, who've also been relocated, and several other officers are seated.

I again sit beside Amanda. "Why would Sam step through a false ceiling?" I ask.

"I don't know."

The number of cops in the room is growing by the minute. When I'm not being hugged by one of them, I stare at the floor. I don't understand why Sam's fall and the seriousness of his injury isn't a huge surprise to me. Instead, it feels as if I always knew this day would happen and now that it's actually unfolding, I know I have to keep it together for whatever lies ahead.

Someone tells me that Angela and Sam's parents have arrived so I go out into the hallway to see his parents stumbling towards me. Various family members are on either side of his mom, physically holding her up. She loudly cries out Sam's name, in Greek, over and over.

For privacy, we're moved into the attached quiet room for families. Sam's mom continues sobbing and his father holds her hand. Angela asks me what happened.

"Sam fell through a ceiling and hit his head."

"Is he going to be OK?"

"I'm not sure."

"He's going to be fine," Sam's mom says to me. "Right, Adri?"

"I don't know."

But I do know. I know Sam is going to die. I know his death is meant to be. And I know that someday, I'll be all right again. But I'm sure as hell not gonna tell his mother this.

Ten

After Sam's brother, Nick, and his expectant wife arrive, the emergency room doctor gives us an update: Sam has suffered a very serious head injury.

"Is he going to be OK?" Nick asks.

"It's a very serious brain injury," the doctor repeats. "He's in a deep coma."

Sam's mom breathes in sharply.

"When can we see him?" Angela asks.

"He's been transferred to an ICU room and there will be a family meeting with the medical staff shortly. After that, you can visit him."

The doctor leaves so Sam's family and I stare at each other. It suddenly seems wiser for me to keep moving, so I go to the other waiting area but find it's full of police officers. When I return to the family room, Nick and Angela are on the phone. Sam's best friend, Stan, is called in Vancouver.

Then Cassie, a close of friend of ours, races in, pushing her daughter in a stroller. One of Sam's former partners, Matt, kneels in front of me, looking into my eyes for the truth. Another girl-friend of mine, a police officer, calls me from Saskatchewan; the word is spreading quickly in the police world. My mother arrives and then my father. My brother, Ed, in Ontario is called. Sam's aunts, uncles and cousins start to appear. My close friends begin to trickle in. Sam's buddies show up in small groups. Police officers now line the hallways.

At 10:30 a.m., Sam's immediate family, my parents, Tom and I are taken to a conference room. The intensive care doctor explains Sam's condition in more detail.

"Sam has suffered an extremely serious brain injury," he says. "And although his condition is still stable, surgery is not an option."

I nod slowly.

"And as you may know, when an organ is injured, it swells. But since the brain is encased within the skull, it doesn't have anywhere to swell *to*."

He is speaking very quietly so I lean forward to hear him better.

"And when an organ's blood supply gets cut off," he continues, "it dies."

I swallow.

"In Sam's case, his head struck the ground so hard that his brain hemorrhaged and there's nothing we can do to stop that."

The room is quiet. My stomach churns. The doctor tells us there will be another family meeting in an hour.

Then I'm taken on my own to see Sam in his ICU room. The nurse walks me to the foot of his bed and remains there while I go to his side. I lean over and kiss him gently on the forehead. He is so still.

"Oh hon," I whisper, "this isn't looking good."

"Adri?" I hear Angela's voice behind me.

I turn to see her and Nick standing in the doorway, holding on to their parents. But they break free and run to Sam. Sam's dad sobs as he stands over his son, shaking his fists to God. His mom lays her head on Sam's chest and cries out his name.

Thankfully, the medical staff need to work on Sam so we're taken back to the family room but I choose to stay in the larger area that's now packed with people.

"There's still hope for a miracle," a well-meaning visitor whispers in my ear.

At hearing these words, I do feel a surge of hope – even though I understand the physical reality and have seen Sam with my own eyes. But you know, an old-fashioned Jesus-raising-the-dead style miracle *would* be lovely right about now. Maybe Sam's brain injury can somehow be reversed. Where's my faith?

In the same place *I* need to be. My stomach is so upset I've got to find a bathroom. I leave the waiting area but only make it as far as the hallway because I see one of Sam's older teammates leaning against the wall. We look at each other.

"There's still hope," I tell him.

He takes my hand but doesn't say anything. The pain in my stomach subsides a little so I stay here with him, which is where the social worker finds me a couple of minutes later.

"Would you like to come with me, Adri?"

No thanks. I'll just stay right here because even though I know damn well the shittiest news of my life is coming, since I haven't yet technically *heard* it, the chance still exists that all this could somehow get turned around.

But the older officer releases my hand and I know I must go.

The social worker and I walk down another corridor together, this time towards Sam's intensive care room. He asks me how I'm holding up.

"Not very good."

We stop outside an office and he turns to face me. He looks so sad.

"Sam's doctor would like to speak to you," he says.

"Oh?" I thought I'd be seeing the doctor with Sam's family.

Inside the office, he pulls out a chair for me. "I'm going to have you wait here, OK?"

So I sit down and watch him walk out the door. Now that I'm finally alone, it occurs to me that this might be a good time to have a quick chat with God, just in case He does exist. But I don't pray for Sam's brain to be healed. I don't put in a request for a miracle. I simply ask for the strength to handle whatever news is coming my way – be it a seriously brain-injured husband or a rapidly dying one.

The doctor comes in with two nurses in tow. He sits in front of me, takes both my hands in his, looks into my eyes and says: "Adri, I am very sorry to tell you this but your husband is brain dead."

When my fear of losing Sam officially becomes my reality, the impact is akin to a sledgehammer being taken to my soul. And yet I say and do absolutely nothing. For possibly the first time ever, I am speechless. Thus it is the doctor who speaks again and the news isn't getting any better, at least not for Sam and me.

"I know this is an extremely difficult time for you but the reality is that Sam is a healthy thirty-two year old."

I give him a look of suspicion, feeling rather vulnerable – like a gazelle separated from the herd.

"And although he's brain dead," the doctor continues, "the rest of Sam's organs are in excellent condition and as such, he's a suitable candidate for organ donation."

It begins to sink in that although this possibility is new to *me*, the medical personnel have obviously been perceiving Sam's injury a little differently.

"Would you consider authorizing the removal of Sam's organs?"

You're fucking kidding me, right? I want to punch him in the face. I want to kill whoever is responsible for Sam's death. But the sensation that two of me exist clicks into place again. There's the person whom others can see, and then there is my terrorized inner self – the real me – whom I cannot allow others to observe.

I lean back, trying to remember what Sam and I had discussed about organ donation. I think he was OK with being an organ donor, should such a circumstance arise. But now that it's actually happening, I'm wary. How can I know with absolute certainty that I'm being told the truth about the seriousness of Sam's injury?

"Are you *sure* Sam can't be saved?" I ask.

"Adri," he says softly, "he's already gone."

I hang my head and cry. One of the nurses places her hand on my shoulder.

I look up. "Why are you telling me all this without anyone else here?"

"We'll be informing the others at the next family meeting," he says. "But because you're Sam's wife, you're legally responsible for making decisions on his behalf now."

I feel a lot older than thirty-two. "You can remove Sam's organs," I say, as a little piece of my self disintegrates alongside the authorized dismemberment of Sam.

The doctor explains the organ donation process and I try to listen carefully. I gather I'll have about six hours to spend with Sam as they get everything in place, preparing his body for surgery and finding appropriate recipients.

By the time I'm released from the room where my heart and soul have been ever so politely smashed to pieces, I *really* have to use the bathroom. I ask a nurse where it is.

"It's just down the hall. Let me show you."

"I can find it."

"No really," she says, "I'm coming with you."

Not only does she take me to the staff bathroom instead of

a public one, she waits outside the door. Two minutes later, she asks me how I'm doing.

"Fine," I say, baffled as to why she's so interested in my bathroom activities.

It's not until I'm washing my hands that it dawns on me she's probably concerned I might harm myself. But the truth is I'm not having suicidal thoughts – just really weird ones. I get the sense that Sam is *with* me – I mean, right here in the bathroom.

Eleven

Although Sam hasn't changed since I first saw him in his ICU room, everything else has. The only sounds are the beeping of the computer monitor and the drip, drip, drip of his IV's. I walk over and gently take his hand. "What am I gonna do without you?"

I feel a tiny amount of tension, as if he's trying to hold my hand. Is this possible if a person is brain dead?

Then I see a bit of blood has trickled from his left ear onto the pillow. No.

Not wanting anyone else to see the blood because Sam is such a private guy, I cover it up with a piece of gauze. I place my hand on his forehead. It's too hot.

"I noticed his shoulders are peeling."

I look up to see the nurse watching me. "Was he somewhere warm?" she asks.

"Yeah. We were in Vegas and he wouldn't wear any sunscreen."

She tilts her head. "So you guys were just on holidays?"

I swallow. "Uh huh. We had an awesome trip."

"You're very lucky."

I stare at her.

"Those memories will carry you far." She walks over and takes my hand. "This will undoubtedly be the most difficult day of your life but it's also a very special time for you and Sam.

Many people don't get the opportunity to say goodbye while the person is still alive to hear."

"But *can* he hear me?"

"It's possible. They say hearing is the last sense to go."

I ask her if they've found Sam's cross and St Jude medal yet. They haven't.

Another nurse comes in to ask me if it's all right if Sam's sister comes in. Visitors are being kept away until an official announcement is made. But I give her the OK.

When Angela comes into the room, I avoid eye contact so she goes to Sam's other side. But when I lean in and kiss him on the lips, his chest goes into spasm.

We look at each other and her face lights up. "That's a good sign, Adri!"

I shake my head. "I don't know what it means but Sam isn't gonna make it."

"*What?*"

"He's already brain-dead," I say. "The doctor just told me. I'm sorry. I hope it's OK I told you but I just can't do this alone."

She walks around and hugs me and we both start bawling. But then Sam's parents, having managed to sneak past the nurse's station, appear in the hallway. Arms locked together, they seem so small to me, like little dolls standing side by side. I look at Angela and she shakes her head ever so slightly. It's not our place to tell Sam's parents.

So I take a step back to let them pass and Angela does the same. His mom cries out Sam's name and kisses his forehead, as his dad rests his head on Sam's chest. I want to tell them to be careful and not knock anything out of place. Sam has another spasm.

His parents look at me. I look at Angela. Then she gently leads them, sobbing, from the room. When she returns a few minutes later, the organ transplant coordinator is with her so all three of us go to the office.

"First of all," the coordinator begins, "I'd like to thank you for making this decision on Sam's behalf. Hopefully, it will help for you to know that through Sam's death, he will directly impact other people's lives."

Rationally, I understand this. Honestly, I want to tell her to fuck off and go find somebody else's husband to mine for body parts.

"We need to discuss which of Sam's organs you wish to be removed."

I give her a blank stare. "What are my options?"

"We can remove and donate internal organs such as the heart, liver, kidney, pancreas and perhaps lungs."

"OK." I could be choosing air conditioning and power windows.

"And how about the skin, tissues and kneecaps?"

I swallow rapidly, trying to not throw up. I look to Angela for clarification, as she knows the Greek Orthodox customs.

"I think you better stick with the internal organs," she says, "because it'll have to be an open casket."

I abhor this custom. But the thought of a skinned Sam upsets me more.

"Just organs," I tell the coordinator. No to the leather seats.

"And do you wish to have Sam's organs donated to medical research, if transplant is not possible?"

Sam would flip if I started handing out his body parts to med students. "No."

"You're a strong woman," the coordinator says to me when we're done.

So my prayer *was* answered. Big of Him.

Sam's sister then goes to The Family Meeting while I go tell Sam about my recycling decisions. I place my hand on his forehead. It's on fire. I ask the nurse why.

"He's likely developing pneumonia."

"Is he in pain?"

"No. He can't feel a thing."

"Then why does he have a spasm when I kiss him or his parent's touch him?"

She opens her mouth then closes it again. "Well . . ."

"Goo?"

I whip around to see my middle brother, Harry, standing in the doorway. Goo is my childhood nickname.

Harry comes in and gives me a bear hug. Then he looks down at Sam. "Oh," he says. "Oh, big fella."

He looks at me again, wide-eyed. "The doctor just told us about Sam and it was total chaos. I've never seen anything like it."

"What happened?"

"Sam's parents collapsed on the floor. His aunt screamed. His brother punched a hole in the wall. Family members rushed to help other family members and the whole time, there was all this . . . *wailing.* It didn't even sound human, Adri."

The doctor knew exactly what he was doing, speaking to me on my own, away from the herd. If I'd been in that family room and witnessed such demonstrative grief, I wouldn't have been in any shape to make a rational decision about organ donation.

"And just to give you a heads-up," Harry says, "everybody in that conference room *and* the waiting room are now on their way here to say goodbye to Sam."

Twelve

If there is one thing Sam hates – more than my mother's long-winded messages on our answering machine – it's a *scene.* Turning his last day on earth into a circus would infuriate him, never mind the logistics. Due to the hundred plus people, the nurses quickly establish a three-visitors-at-a-time rule, in addition to me.

My mom is one of the first to visit. She hugs me then leans in and whispers something in Sam's ear. His chest shakes with another spasm. I want to scream at her to get away from him. But I know damn well the message is for me.

As much as I recognize the need for people to see Sam one last time, it makes an excruciating experience even more exhausting. For the next few hours, I hug each visitor but soon realize I can't keep this up. As the day progresses, I focus all my energy on Sam. And on us.

In the quieter moments, I gently trace the three small moles in a row on his forearm. I touch the crescent-shaped scar on the back of his hand. "Remember the burning shrimp, Sammy?" I whisper.

As a kid, he'd put his hand through an iron bar while punching his brother. He'd missed his brother and got the bed frame instead. When I first saw the scar, back when we were twenty, I'd told him it looked like he'd had a run-in with a deep-fried shrimp.

I run my fingers through his hair and gently scratch his scalp. Now, however, I can only touch the top of his head because . . .

"What the hell were you doing? Why didn't you look where you were stepping?"

But Sam had always said that coming home to me at the end of every shift was his top priority. So what went wrong?

In the late afternoon, I find myself singing to him the Sunshine Song, taught to me in the summer by the daughter of my best girlfriend, Jodie.

"You are my sunshine," I sob, "my only sunshine . . ."

Drip.

"You make me happy when skies are gray . . ."

Beep.

"You'll never know, dear, how much I love you . . ."

Drip.

"So please don't take my sunshine away."

Around 6:00 o'clock, Stan and his expectant wife, Megan, arrive from Vancouver. We stand, arms around each other, staring down at Sam and I recall a game the four of us had played on the Sea to Sky highway enroute to Whistler, B.C. years ago. We had to come up with one word that described each person. I don't remember anyone else's answers except Stan's word to describe Sam: solid.

I look at him now. A white sheet drapes his frame like a bad toga costume. Wires and tubes sprout out from his neck and chest. A catheter pisses for him while a respirator does his breathing. What will solid mean when there is, physically, no more Sam?

At 7:00 p.m., eleven hours after I first saw him in the ER, I watch a nurse lift up his eyelids one at a time to shine a light in. One pupil is a tiny speck; the other fully dilated. I fold into the nearest chair.

Around 9:00 p.m., my eldest brother, Ed, arrives from Northern Ontario. Since he's missed the family meeting, he isn't as up to par on Sam's medical condition as the rest of us. He asks a nurse – not one of Sam's regular ones – if they're absolutely sure there's no hope left.

She glances at her clipboard then back at Ed. "Well, I personally haven't read his entire chart but it says right here that his gray and white matter have mixed – so no, there's no hope."

When she sees the expression on my face, she back-peddles. "I'm not telling you anything you don't already know, am I?"

"Oh no, no," I reply, waving my hand.

I understand Sam's head hit the concrete hard enough to kill him but until now, it hadn't registered that his brain is a goddamn tossed salad.

Then the organ transplant coordinator comes in. 'Oh fuck,' I think, '*now* what do you want?' But she hands me a teddy bear. I read his nametag: Hope.

"I just thought you might need someone to hug," she says.

I throw my arms around her.

Just after 10:00, the doctor tells me an operating room hasn't yet come available and it might still be a couple of hours. Good: more time with Sam.

"And because of the pneumonia," he adds, "we're concerned about the fluid building up in one of Sam's lungs. We'd like to do a procedure to try and drain that."

"Can I stay in here?"

"I don't think that's a good idea. We're going to have to make an incision in his side, so it's probably best if you wait in the hall."

The poor guy is getting sliced and diced, poked and prodded. From a medical perspective, he's already a collection of body parts versus a human whole.

When I walk out into the hallway, my youngest brother,

Dale, is waiting for me. We walk towards the window together.

"I can't believe this is happening," I say, looking out over the city Sam had been so goddamn determined to serve. "All that schooling and volunteering and working at jobs he hated and then all those rejections by the different police services . . ."

I shake my head at the irony. He'd devoted eight years of his life – *our* life – trying to get on with this stupid police service before they actually hired him. Now, after only four years, he's somehow managed to die in the line of duty. This is Canada; very few officers pass away on the job and as far as I can tell, it sounds like a freak accident.

"At least he went doing what he loved," Dale says.

I turn to him.

"Sam never gave up," he continues. "He was the most determined person I've ever met."

I jerk my head towards Sam's ICU room. "Yeah and look what *that* got him."

Dale is quiet a moment. "The chief told me today that Sam was one of her stars."

"Was," I reply, "is the operative word here."

"No," says Dale, shaking his head. "I'd say *star* is."

When I'm allowed back in after quiet time, it's nearly 11:00 so I figure I better come up with some sort of strategy: an Ops plan for widowhood. I know I can physically survive without Sam for seven months because we've been apart that length of time before. In 1992 – after we'd been dating three years and I'd just graduated from university – I'd gone backpacking on my own and made it as far as Hong Kong before I'd phoned Sam, sobbing about having made a mistake in leaving him behind.

"Bullshit," he'd said. "You've always wanted to do this, so do it – and don't come home until you're ready. If we're meant to be together, then this time apart will let us know."

"Don't you miss me?"

"It's been *two* days. Besides, it was nice watching Monday Night Football with the boys again."

"Oh."

"I'm kidding!" he'd said. "Just relax and enjoy your trip. You're lucky to have this opportunity so quit whining and have some fun."

I reach over and take Sam's hand. No tension remains. "I'll stick around for seven months," I tell him, "but after that I'm not making any promises."

Just after midnight, an operating room becomes available. I watch as a group of nurses and technicians prepare Sam's body for the transfer. One person temporarily detaches him from the respirator while another manually forces air into his lungs through a device that looks like a plunger. I want to scream. He's leaving me and there's not a goddamn thing I can do about it.

They wheel Sam out of his room and down the hall. I follow behind, right into the OR. When I turn around and see that several family members have followed us in, I scream at them instead: "Get out! Leave us alone!"

The medical personnel stare at me. But my crew of supporters high-tail it out of the operating room. I walk up to Sam, lean over and kiss him on the lips. "I love you."

Then I take a deep breath, give him one last wave, turn around and walk out into the hallway full of family and friends. I start to thank people for staying but Dale puts his arm around me. "I think that's enough for today. Let's get you home."

So in silence we walk through the hospital corridors and out into the night.

Thirteen

When Dale pulls up beside our little blue house on the corner, my stomach is in knots. How am I going to face, without Sam, all that represents our life together?

I walk in the back door and am enthusiastically greeted by Sasha. I kneel on the kitchen floor and hug her tightly; our family of three reduced to two.

During the day, it had been decided that Ed, Harry and his wife, Katrina, will stay with me – the crisis-workers assigned to my case. Katrina makes tea with a shot of Tia Maria then passes around a plate of Sam's chocolate-covered granola bars. I sit in front of the fireplace, glaring at the stairs.

"How am I gonna sleep in our bed?" I ask.

"Just do the best you can," says Katrina.

But walking into our bedroom is like seeing Sam in the ICU after first being told of his brain death. Our bed, my vanity, and the pictures on the wall all look the same and of course, are the same. But everything else has changed. Sam will never sleep beside me again, or empty the change from his pockets onto the counter, or pray to the picture of the Saint tucked in the corner of the mirror before climbing into bed.

I take a deep breath and open the closet doors but stumble backwards at the sight of his clothes. I hold up to my face his gray dress shirt, worn to the wedding in Disneyland last week, and breathe in his scent as if it can sustain me. I pull out the flowered Hawaiian shirt he liked to barbeque in and his blue plaid boxer shorts then shut the doors again.

Sasha lies on the bed, watching me closely as I brush my teeth with Sam's electric toothbrush. I then put on his shirt and shorts, take his wedding ring from my vanity and place it on his chain around my neck. He never wore his wedding ring to work because he didn't want the 'shitrats' to know he was married.

I climb into his side of the bed and put my head on his pillow, clutching his ring tightly. Then, like a wolf in her den or a Canada Goose in her nest, I begin mourning the death of my mate. And just to be on the safe side, I throw in a prayer to the God Sam believed in.

When I close my eyes, the events of the day replay themselves again and again:

Sam fell; your husband is brain dead; heart, liver and kidneys?

Trauma unit; your husband is brain dead; skin, tissues and kneecaps?

He's in rough shape; your husband is brain dead; open casket?

I don't know how to stop the negative thoughts so I come up with a nicer one.

"Come to me in my dreams," I whisper into the darkness. "And maybe you could turn on your watch light or something . . . you know, as a sign that you're OK."

I awake at 6:00 a.m. Saturday morning to see a large reddish-orange light framing the edges of the entire bedroom window. I blink a few times to make sure I'm actually awake then watch as the light slowly dissipates. Then I recall my dream. I was in an underground parkade and noticed blood spatter on the concrete a few meters away. I flew towards it, my body parallel to the ground, but when I got to the blood, my field of vision simply faded to black – like the end of an old movie.

That I actually feel a sense of peace tells me that when Sam's head hit the cement, it was simply over for him. I know now that he didn't suffer.

I fall back to sleep for an hour but when I awake the second time, the horrific hurt crashes into me. There are no mysterious lights, strange dreams or peaceful feelings to buffer the reality. All I feel is excruciating emotional pain and sheer terror.

There's a knock on my door. "Can I come in?" It's Katrina.

"Yeah."

"How did the night go?"

"Brutal."

She sits on the edge of my bed. "What can I do?"

"You could make poached eggs," I say. "Those were Sam's favourite."

"You got it."

Ed and Harry are waiting for me at the bottom of the stairs.

"Good morning, Googie," says Harry.

I smile. "Good morning."

Ed asks me how I'm doing.

"I'd love a coffee."

Then I wander over to the dining room window and look

out at our mountain ash tree. The bright red berries stand out against the yellow leaves and blue sky. It's a beautiful image.

Harry hands me my coffee.

"Thanks," I say, turning to him. "I'm glad it's a sunny day."

"You're gonna be OK, aren't you?"

I manage a smile. "Yup. Someday."

After breakfast, I'm passing by the living room window on my way upstairs when I see one of Sam's black work socks hanging from the birch tree. It's as if my life has turned into one of those kid's books – the kind where you have to find ten things wrong with a picture, like a person walking on air or a house with no door. I squint. That's not Sam's *sock*. It's a squirrel hanging upside down, eating from the birdbell. Sasha joins me at the window and when she catches sight of the squirrel, barks ferociously, tail wagging. Sam always got a kick out of Sasha's behavior towards squirrels. I smile.

Then I remember that according to the clipboard of fun, I was supposed to work dayshift today and was going to duck out early so that my mom and I could take Sasha to be blessed at the annual 'blessing of the animals' ceremony held in honour of St Francis of Assisi – the patron saint of animals – at the Anglican Church where Sam and I were married.

Plan B.

I go upstairs. In Sam's shower, I use his shampoo and soap – personal items he'll never touch again. I run the water good and hot just like Sam did and the sorrow surges to the surface. Sobbing, I wonder how I'll ever get through this. I step out of the shower and am reaching for Sam's towel when I realize that's one of the last things I'd seen him touch, so I know I can't disturb it. I reach instead for my own towel which is when I notice my pink packet of birth control pills on the counter.

"I THINK I'M GONNA NEED SOME HELP IN HERE!"

Moments later, Katrina finds me in the bathroom trying to put on my bathrobe but my hands are shaking so badly, I can't tie it up.

"What's wrong?" she asks.

I push past her and slump onto the bed. "I can't fucking handle this."

"What happened?"

I open up my hand.

She looks at the birth control pills. "Uh oh."

"He'll never touch me again." I don't recognize my voice.

"Adri . . ."

"We'll never make love again."

She bites her lip.

"We're never going to be parents," I say. "I knew we probably wouldn't have kids but this makes it pretty fucking final."

Then she holds me as I cry. And cry and cry.

Fourteen

Today, I put on my jean overalls and a little grey t-shirt. No black for this widow; life is dark enough.

The first phone call of the day is from the organ transplant coordinator. I sit on Sam's Perch and ask her how the surgery went.

"Excellent. The doctor didn't finish until early this morning. He was able to remove Sam's heart, both his kidneys and his pancreatic islets for transplant."

"That's pretty good, eh?"

"I'll say. The transplant surgeries were also successful. Sam saved the life of the fifty-three year old man who received his heart, and greatly improved the lives of three other people. You should be very proud, Adri."

Pride is rather low on the list of what I'm feeling at the moment. Anger, hatred, sorrow, resentment, disgust and fear rank significantly higher.

I recall the late night incision in Sam's side. "What about his lungs?" I ask.

"Unfortunately, no. One was badly bruised from the fall and the other had pneumonia. Sam's liver wasn't suitable either."

"Why not?"

"Well it was healthy," she says, "but it had significant fatty deposits, which was probably dietary."

"That'd be his mom's Greek cooking," I say with a small laugh.

Then I ask her what time Sam's heart was removed.

"Oh well, let's see. His heart was obviously the last to go so I'd say that was around . . ." There is a rustling of papers. "Six a.m."

The next call is from an ICU nurse. They found Sam's cross and medal.

"Any idea where they'd disappeared to?" I ask.

"They weren't found until after his transplant surgery, so I guess they must have been stuck to his back the whole time."

"But you guys were keeping an eye out for them all day," I reply. "Surely someone must have looked *underneath* him at some point. I mean, Sam must have been moved at least three times yesterday."

"I wasn't working, Adri. But I could find out more if you like."

"Nah." I wave at the fireplace. "I'm just glad they're found. Thank you."

Two of Sam's buddies had given him the St. Jude medal the day he'd graduated from police recruit class. They'd got the idea from the movie, *The Untouchables*, and had told Sam that St. Jude is the patron saint for police officers and lost causes. He'd placed the medal on his chain, next to the tiny cross he'd received the day he was baptized and had rarely been without the two pendants next to his heart since.

Even though Sam hadn't attended church regularly since he was a kid, his belief in God, Jesus and the Saints had been unwavering. I'd asked him once why he refused to go to church except for weddings and funerals.

"Because when I was little," he'd said, "I realized that many of the people going to church were more interested in the clothes they wore and the cars they drove than in being good, decent people."

"Isn't that a bit over-generalizing?"

"Of course it is. Plenty of great people go to church as well."

"But?"

"I just don't feel I have to go to church to be with God, Adri."

The doorbell rings. Upstairs, Tom is at the front door. He looks rough. When he holds out to me a pretty basket of autumn flowers and miniature pumpkins, I stare at it.

When a person dies, Adri, you get flowers.

"Uh . . . thanks," I say, taking the basket.

Then he hugs me but I'm disoriented and I want to call out to Sam that Tom has dropped by. Since I can't do this in the new reality, I tell Tom that the hospital staff found Sam's pendants. He says he'll send an officer over right away to pick them up.

So I put the basket on the coffee table and am introducing Tom to my family, when the phone rings again. I take the call downstairs. Minutes later, I hear a crash.

"Adri!" Harry yells down the stairs. "You better get up here right away."

I run up to find Tom passed out on our front step, bleeding from his forehead.

"What the heck happened?" I ask my brothers.

"I'm not sure," replies a baffled Ed. "He went outside to answer his cell phone and then I guess he fell."

Tom opens his eyes and tries to sit up, when a police car pulls up in front of the house and two officers get out. When they see what's happening, they race up the walk.

"What happened?" the shorter officer asks me.

"I think he . . . " I am about to say 'fainted' but then realize a guy might not appreciate this choice of words. "Passed out."

"You must be Adri," the officer says.

I nod and am about to shake his hand when I hear these horrible wracking sobs coming from Tom. He's sitting up now but his whole body is shaking. So I sit beside him and put my arm around his shoulders, which is when I hear a distant voice calling out, "Hello, hello . . . is anybody there?" The voice seems to be coming from our cedar bush and frankly, at this point, a talking bush wouldn't surprise me.

I look at the taller officer, standing open-mouthed in front of me, and point to the ground beneath the cedar bush where Tom's cell phone obviously landed after he fell. "You might want to answer that."

The officer nods, picks up the phone and explains to whoever is on the line what's happening. Meanwhile, the shorter officer introduces himself and the tall guy as the police chaplains.

"Nice to meet you," I say. "But I better get an icepack for Tom."

When I return from the kitchen, I sit beside Tom on the step and hold the compress to his forehead. The shorter chaplain sits on his other side and asks him what his name and date of birth are. But as Tom is answering his questions, I happen to glance up at the sky and notice how the rays of sun shine through the fluttery leaves of our birch tree. I am again struck by the beauty. For just a split second, I even feel *happy* . . . and safe. And then just like that, I'm at the top of Splash Mountain again, floating along in the log car with Sam.

I shake my head and see that my brothers are now scattered across the front yard. My teenage half-brother, Anthony, from my dad's second marriage, is on the sidewalk watching for the ambulance. Dale and Harry stand beneath the birch tree. Ed is stationed under the fir, staring slack-jawed at the unfolding drama of his little sister's life.

The paramedics arrive and the tall chaplain goes with Tom to the hospital, leaving the shorter chaplain behind with me. We all watch as the ambulance pulls away.

I turn to the chaplain. "I hope he'll be all right."

"Me too. The shock and exhaustion are obviously taking their toll."

It hadn't occurred to me until now that because Sam fell at the end of his nightshift, Tom, the rest of his team and the other officers at the scene have likely been awake and answering questions for at least thirty-six hours.

Fifteen

In our living room, my family takes their seats while the chaplain sits beside me on the couch. I pull my knees up to my chest, tightly wrapping my arms around them.

"I'm very sorry about Sam," he begins.

"Thanks. I still don't know much about what happened."

"That's why Tom was here. He was going bring you up to speed about the investigation."

Plan C.

I stare at the chaplain. "You knew Sam, didn't you?"

"Yes."

"He told me once you were a good guy."

The chaplain smiles. I unlock my arms and sit cross-legged.

"We're going to have to talk about Sam's funeral," he says.

"Oh?" Just like the basket of flowers, this first mention of Sam's funeral surprises me. I don't know why else the chaplain would be sitting in my living room and yet it strikes me as odd that he's here to talk about funeral arrangements.

"Since Sam died in the line of duty, the police service is going to cover all costs for his funeral."

Again, I'm surprised. "That's good."

I have no idea how much a funeral costs. I don't know much at all about funerals.

"Adri, do you have a copy of Sam's will? We just want to make sure we're in accordance with his wishes."

"Yeah."

Thanks to Ed – the financial guru in the family – harping to Sam and me about the importance of financial and estate planning for the past decade, we have wills. I go downstairs to my office and retrieve Sam's from the file. But before heading back up, I quickly flip to the part about organ donation and read, much to my relief considering Sam's heart is already beating in another man, that he *had* wanted to donate his organs for transplant.

Upstairs again, I read out loud: "If Sam passed away on duty, he wanted a police funeral. If it was off duty, he wanted the service to be Greek Orthodox."

That's odd. Why would we have put the latter clause in Sam's will when we knew it couldn't happen?

"With your permission," says the chaplain, "we're hoping to give Sam a full police funeral."

"Absolutely."

"And Sam's priest has spoken to me as well."

My eyes narrow. "Oh really?"

"Yes. And they're prepared to also have a Greek Orthodox Service."

"Well, isn't *that* interesting."

"Why?"

"Because when Sam and I made the decision to get married in the Anglican Church, he was specifically told that he wouldn't be allowed to be buried by the Greek Orthodox Church."

"That doesn't seem to be an issue now."

"Well, it sure as hell *was* an issue four years ago! Between his goddamn church and my mother, planning our wedding nearly tore us and our families apart."

The living room is very quiet. I point my finger at the chaplain. "You wouldn't believe the shit his church put us through."

The room goes a notch quieter.

"Sam was devastated at losing the right to a funeral in his own church," I continue. "Do you know how hard that was on him?"

"I can only imagine."

I stand up. "This is bullshit. We were told in no uncertain terms that when he died, *his church would not bury him*. So what's changed now?"

The chaplain waits a moment before replying. "Perhaps what's more important right now is that we focus on what *Sam* would want for his funeral."

I sit back down.

He nods towards the will in my hands. "And would he want a police funeral and a Greek Orthodox service?"

"*Want* isn't the word Sam would be using at the moment."

"Fair enough." The chaplain tries a different approach. "I

can't fathom what you're going through right now but you and
Sam are both Christians, correct?"

I shrug. "That's a loaded question."

Although my faith is a meandering stream, Sam had been
very black and white about his Christian beliefs: you either believed in something or you didn't.

"In light of what's gone on," the chaplain says, "you may
have to consider forgiveness. You've got enough on your plate
without having to deal with anger, resentment and bitterness
about things in the past."

"That's not easy."

"No, it's not," he says. "But it is possible."

"It's also why nothing changes."

He nods slowly. "And yet perhaps there is a time and place
for effecting change."

And this, I gather, isn't it. I let out a sigh and a quasi sense of
calm comes over me. Is this what forgiveness feels like? Regardless, I agree to the dual service.

The chaplain then asks me if I'd like to talk further about
Sam's death.

It takes me a moment to realize what he might be referring
to. "What? Like the God-stuff, you mean?"

He smiles. "That's right."

"Nah." I give him the wave. "Maybe next week."

"No," Harry says, breaking the family silence. "She'll talk
to you today."

My family is usually keen to speak their mind, especially
on Adri-related matters, but this has not been the case over the
past twenty-four hours. However, I now watch as each person
stands up and walks into the kitchen. I hear the back door open
and close.

With my herd gone, I feel rather like I did in the doctor's office yesterday, prior to receiving the news about the stellar state
of Sam's organs – and that since he was done with them, perhaps
I should share.

"Can I ask you a personal question?" the chaplain begins.

"Uh huh."

"What are you thinking about Sam right now?"

Hmmm . . . let's see. Well, wherever he is at the moment, he's one pissed off Greek. And I'm pretty sure he was in the hospital bathroom with me yesterday because if there's one place on the planet where Sam's soul would be sorting things out, it would be a toilet. I know he felt me kiss him in the ICU and managed to hold my hand, brain-dead and all. He's very concerned that I'll let my mother control my life now that he's not here to be the buffer. I suspect the squirrel at the birdbell was some sort of sign. And I think Tom falling and hitting his head the day after Sam fell and hit *his* head is significant, as is the fact that one of the happiest days of my life and the absolute worst happened exactly one week apart.

I shrug. "Stuff."

"What does the word hope mean to you?"

"I dunno. I guess just that one day things will get better."

"Yes . . ."

"Yesterday morning," I continue, figuring the chaplain is looking for more of a God-related answer, "I had a fleeting hope for some sort of biblical style miracle – like Sam's brain injury being reversed. But I knew that was impossible so I let it go."

He nods slowly.

"And since the transplant surgeries were a success, I guess there's a kind of hope that Sam lives on in the donor recipients."

"Sam will also live on in you," says the chaplain, "and in many of us because of the good man he was. And for what it's worth, Adri, *I* believe . . ."

Wait for it.

"Sam's in good hands because he's with Jesus."

I smile politely but this guy's used to skepticism. He doesn't preach in a church to the converted; he deals with disillusioned cops all day, most often in times of crisis.

"I believe Sam *is* OK," he says. "To me, the word hope has a capital 'h' because Jesus said we would all see each other again one day in heaven."

I fold my arms across my chest. "Uh huh."

"Jesus died on the cross for our salvation. He died so that

our souls and spirits would live forever."

I rack my brain, trying to remember all this from Sunday school.

"Sam's body is only the shell that housed his soul and spirit. Sam is waiting for you in heaven. I really believe that."

"Too bad the women in my family live 'til they're ninety-seven."

I get the raised eyebrows.

"That means I have SIXTY-FIVE MORE YEARS without him!"

"Oh," he says. "But time is different in eternity than it is on earth. Even if you do live many more years, in heaven that's like a handful of dust." He puts his hand out, palm up, and blows imaginary particles into the air. "It's gone in an instant."

"For *him*, yeah."

"Trust me, your time here will go by very quickly."

I glance at Sam's digital watch on my wrist. The blinking numbers mark the passing seconds.

"Maybe don't think of this as good-bye," he says. "Think of this as 'see ya later.'"

I lean back against the couch. That *does* sound better.

"Adri, I know you have a strong faith . . ."

I do: I just don't know what *in*. I believe one day, all this will make sense but since I don't understand how I can know this, I begin to doubt my undefined faith.

"I believe God has a purpose for each of us," the chaplain finishes. "He has one for Sam and He has one for you too."

Well then, I'd best discover what these are. For what's the point of there *being* a purpose if it remains unknown?

Sixteen

After the chaplain leaves, I retreat to the serenity of our blue bedroom. Downstairs, the phone and doorbell continue to ring so I close the door, open the window and lie on our bed. Sasha curls up beside me. The late September sun streams through the blinds, casting horizontal beams of light across the duvet cover. I think about the chaplain's words. Maybe I *should* grab onto the Hope-with-a-capital-h life preserver because believing I'm going to see Sam again in heaven makes me feel a hell of a lot better than the reality that his body now has no heart in it.

There's a knock at my door. "Goo, can I come in?"

"Yeah."

Harry comes in and hands me a white envelope. "An officer just dropped this off for you."

I open it up. Sam's cross and St. Jude medal are sticky-taped to a piece of paper with my name written on it; dried blood is still stuck to his pendants. I breathe in sharply.

"I guess these are mine now," I say, gently peeling off the pendants and placing them on the chain around my neck.

"Oh Googie . . ."

I bring the cross and medal to my lips and kiss them.

Harry tilts his head to one side, watching me. "Maybe the big fella kept them for as long as he needed them?"

"Maybe."

Then I turn the medal over and read the inscription on the back. "Pray for us."

"What?"

"That's the wording on the St. Jude medal. Jude is the patron saint of police officers and lost causes."

"Oh."

"So where the hell were they yesterday?" I ask. "On a goddamn coffee break?"

"I'm sorry?"

"Jesus and Jude! Great protection they turned out to be – useless fucks."

Harry's mouth drops open. I lie back and pull a pillow over my head.

"Ummmm . . . Adri?"

"*What*?"

"I hate to bother you but I think we better get you over to Sam's parents' place."

I pull the pillow off. "Why?"

His eyes widen. "Because his mom and dad really need to see you."

So my dad drives my mom, Anthony and me the twenty minutes to the house where Sam grew up. Not five minutes into the drive, I hear my mother ask Anthony about *military school.*

"You're fucking kidding me, right?" I snap from the back seat.

She turns around. "I'm sorry, Adri. I was just trying . . ."

"Not now, mother. That's completely inappropriate."

In the rear-view mirror, I catch my dad's tiny smile. Nobody says a word for the rest of the drive. When my father pulls up in front of Sam's parent's place, both sides of the street are lined with vehicles. "Oh for God's sakes," I say, "look at all the cars."

Still no one says a word.

"Surely they can't all be visitors." I try again.

"Er, they're probably Sam's relatives," my dad says.

"Well, I'M not going in there and talking to everyone!"

Luckily, Nick and Angela immediately come out to the car. I tell them I'm not talking to a bunch of people right now.

Nick nods. "We'll meet in the backyard."

It seems to me that Sam's brother and sister are handling this pretty well. When I walk in the back gate, I see why. Sam's parents, dressed completely in black, are sitting on white lawn chairs in the middle of the yard. With her arms folded tightly across her chest, his mom rocks back and forth, sobbing loudly, as her husband holds her. Nick and Angela are having to place their own sorrow aside to care for their parents.

So what is one to say to a grieving mother? Wait, I know! I walk straight over to Sam's mom, hug her and announce: "Don't worry. Sam is in heaven and one day we'll all be together again."

This goes over like a lead balloon.

"I know that!" she screams. "But he's my son and I WANT HIM HERE."

My first thought? If *I* can find some solace in Christianity after a single conversation, why isn't a strong believer like Sam's mom able to do so?

I shut my mouth and hold her as she sobs. Then I look up and see a squirrel scurrying along the top of the fence with what appears to be a peanut in its mouth. I catch myself smiling because Sam loved nuts but they'd upset his stomach. Now that he's free from the confines of his body, he can eat as many as he wants . . .

Speaking of nuts, you better get a grip on yourself, Adri: it's a *squirrel.*

The gate opens and the two police chaplains and Tom, now sporting a bandage above his right eye, walk in the backyard. I ask Tom how he's doing.

"I am *so* sorry, Adri . . . I don't know what happened at your place."

You were removed from the scene so the chaplain could tell me about Hope.

"I'm just glad you're OK," is what I say.

We all sit in a circle of lawn chairs beneath the apple trees; a garden party of grief. After a prayer by the Hope Chaplain (a nicer undercover name than the Shorter Chaplain), Sam's family is told about the police component of the funeral. But I don't think his parents catch much because Sam's mom rocks and sobs throughout the meeting and his dad's attention is on her.

Afterwards, Nick and Angela pull me aside. "We saw something strange this morning," says Nick.

"What?"

He tells me how they saw the first letter of their brother's name in a cloud.

"Huh?"

"I mean, it was the same *shape*," Nick says sheepishly. "Except that the letter was backwards."

I don't feel so silly about my squirrel thoughts but cloud-shapes are not my concern at the moment. I nod towards their mom. "Is she going to be OK?"

"She's definitely better with you here, Adri," says Angela.

"That's *better?*"

Nick nods. "And thank God her best friend came up right away."

"From San Diego?" I ask.

"Yeah."

"Sam and I just saw her last week – she showed us her prayer room."

"Oh, we've heard all about your visit," says Angela.

Two minutes later, the Greek lady from San Diego is in the backyard, hugging me. "I just don't understand how this could happen," she says.

For privacy, the two of us go to the side of the house and sit by the yellow daisies. I ask her if she believes Sam is in heaven.

"Absolutely. But I don't understand *why* God would have taken him."

"That's what I'm trying to figure out."

"Perhaps we're not meant to know God's plan, Adri."

"If indeed there is one."

She places her hand on my arm. "There is."

"How do you know that?"

"Because there *has* to be."

I raise an eyebrow. Then she asks me if I've heard about the Greek Orthodox forty-day ceremony."

"No."

"Well, we believe that starting on the ninth day after a person passes away, Michael the Archangel takes the soul on a journey and shows him all the good and bad deeds he's done throughout his lifetime. It's a time of learning and then, on the fortieth day, God tells him what his work in heaven will be."

"Are you saying that Sam's soul *leaves* after forty days?"

"No, no!" She shakes her head. "Sam's soul will always be with you. Just because he's working in heaven doesn't mean he can't also be watching over all of us."

"What's your take on the Second Coming?"

She looks as surprised at my question as I am hearing myself ask it. "On Judgement Day," she replies, "Jesus will be coming back as our Saviour."

"To . . ."

"Judge the living and the dead."

"The dead? How's that gonna work?"

"Well, the deceased souls are in a sort of temporary heaven right now, waiting for Jesus to come back to earth. Then, after the Second Coming, God will decide who goes to heaven and who goes to hell for all eternity."

I picture billions of souls, flipping through magazines in heaven's waiting room. "That's getting kinda complicated," I say. Never mind ridiculous.

"Look," she says, "what I've told you are *my* Orthodox beliefs. You need to follow your own heart on this. You and Sam were very much in love . . ."

"*Are.*"

"Are. And that's what really matters."

Except that my heart is currently shattered into thousands of pieces, so which one do I pick up first?

". . . so you could do that too, if you like."

I look to the Greek lady. "I'm sorry?"

"I was just saying that Sam's parents have put a glass of water out for Sam's soul to drink so you could do that, as well."

"Why water?"

"I don't know. But it's connected to the soul somehow."

Seventeen

We arrive home to find that food and flowers, gifts and cards have been dropped off in droves. Containers of baked goods are piling up on the kitchen table.

For dinner, Dale has ordered Chinese food from our favorite restaurant. I sit at our dining room table and try to eat but all I can think of is the first night Sam and I spent in this house. We'd ordered dinner from this same restaurant and eaten it at this table, planning the next chapter of our life together – which wasn't supposed to end three years later. I stand up and slide my dinner into Sasha's dish.

"Goo," Harry says, "you have to eat."

I force a smile. "Never thought I'd hear those words."

I take a chocolate chip cookie from the stack of baking and

then open the china cabinet where the liquor is stashed. I pour myself a glass of sherry – an evening ritual Sam and I enjoyed on occasion. When I wander into the living room, a dozen eyeballs watch my every move.

I sit on the couch and sip my sherry, glaring at the stairs. Katrina asks how I feel about going to bed tonight.

"I want him here."

"But that can't be," she says softly. "You know that, right?"

I nod, watching as tears well up in *her* eyes.

"I'm sorry!" she cries. "This is just so unfair."

I sigh. "Where do you think he is right now?"

"Heaven."

"Do you *really* believe that?"

"Yes."

"Good. Because I can't just be grasping at straws here. When I go upstairs, I *have* to know that Sam can somehow hear me talking to him."

"I believe Sam is here, too," Ed says from where he's sitting on the stairs. "I think his spirit lives on in you, Adri."

"Yeah . . ."

"So who knows," he continues, "maybe when you go up to bed and talk to Sam, you're actually talking to yourself."

Kaboom. I leap off the couch. "THANK YOU VERY FUCKING MUCH!" I scream, hurling a cookie at his head.

He ducks and it bounces off the wall. Sasha cowers beside me.

"Oh my God," he says. "I am SO sorry. I . . . I didn't mean that in a bad way."

I glare at him, hands on my hips. "How *else* am I supposed to take that?"

"There is a time and a place for a philosophical discussion," Katrina cuts in, "and I don't think this is it."

My devastated brother creeps off to the kitchen as Katrina begins damage control.

"Everyone has their own beliefs and that's fine. You need to listen to your *own* heart, Adri."

I down the rest of my sherry as the fear, confusion and anxiety build again.

"You and Sam shared a beautiful love," she adds. "Hold onto that."

But Ed's sentence hangs in mid-air, taunting me. How could Sam exist *in* me?

I stomp downstairs to collect some pictures of our now historical beautiful love to put in my bedroom. I find a classic Sam & Adri self-portrait taken in Banff when we were twenty-one. Two young, naïve faces smile tentatively at the camera. Sam with jet-black hair and a diamond stud in his ear, me with my toothy smile. I see a second photo taken three months ago, another self-portrait taken on the beach in Vancouver. Sam has plenty of gray hair and I've got crow's feet but our smiles are the same.

Now, after eleven and a half years, multiple break-ups, two university degrees, a few trips, dozens of jobs, some spectacular fights, lots of awesome sex, a wedding, a police graduation, a broken ankle, and countless conversations over coffee, it's all over. These photos are the bookends of our life together. The present has become hell on earth and my future looms ahead like a sixty-five year prison sentence, so the past is looking damn appealing. I grab my precious pictures and go into our bedroom to begin building a photographic shrine to Sam.

I'm already in bed when I think, what the heck? I run back downstairs, fill a sherry glass full of water for Sam's soul to sip, then take it into my room and place it among the photos.

Waking up Sunday morning is, to my astonishment, even more painful than yesterday. By 5:30 a.m., the precious Hope is gone. Sam is dead; I am a widow. That I will perhaps see him again in heaven does nothing to comfort me. I lie sprawled out on my bed; a starfish clinging to a rock, waiting for the tide to return.

I fantasize about what this morning *should* have held, had our lives continued on their probable path. Since Sam would have worked the night shift, he would've still been sleeping. So I'd be getting up and having a coffee. Then I would've puttered around the house and maybe worked a little in my office. Writing? Sam would have woken up around noon and we'd have hung out in the living room, reading the newspaper – me in my big blue chair, him on the couch.

"Hey, Adri" he would've said, "pass me the city section, will ya?"

I'd have handed it to him, making a cheeky comment like, "There's more to life than what happens on the streets of *this* town you know."

"You read what you want," he'd have said, "and I'll read what I want."

I'd have leapt off my chair and tackled him on the couch. Sasha would've jumped up to join in and we'd have tossed her the tennis ball a few times. Then Sam would have gone downstairs to The Perch and watched TV while I yakked on the phone. Around 2:00 p.m., we'd have hit the off-leash park and then stopped in at the grocery store to pick up roast chicken and potato salad for dinner . . .

The knock on the door comes. Katrina takes one look at me, lying on my back as tears stream onto a drenched pillow. "Uh oh."

"This isn't how it was supposed to be."

She sits on the end of my bed.

"How am I gonna do this?" I ask.

"Do what?"

"Live without him."

She shakes her head. "You *have* to take this one day at a time."

"I can't even get out of bed."

"You don't have to. You can lie there all day if you like."

"Good." I scowl at the ceiling, gripping Sam's pendants. Except that if I continue lying here thinking about how life is supposed to be, they'll have to commit me by noon.

The doorbell rings.

"Who the hell is here at this time of day?" I snap.

"Uh well, yesterday, you asked . . ."

From downstairs, I recognize Jodie's voice.

"Oh right." Yesterday, I'd asked my best friend, Jodie, to shop for me. Between the lessons on Hope and heaven, I'd somehow squeezed in fashion: what to wear to Sam's funeral?

Now there are two women sitting on the end of my bed staring at me, still sprawled out on my back. I struggle to sit up but my body feels like a sack of wet sand.

"Do you guys *really* believe Sam's in a better place?" I ask.

They both nod.

"But what if we're just fooling ourselves?" I say. "What if when you die, it's all just fucking over?"

Jodie winces.

"I think you *do* believe Sam is in a better place," Katrina says, "and you're just torturing yourself by doubting everything."

"How do we really know, though?" I ask.

"We don't. That's what faith is, Adri. You're either a believer or you're not."

I point to the shopping bags and ask Jodie how she did with the hat and shoes.

From one bag, she produces a fetching black hat with a chiffon bow. "I bought you a couple of each so you'd have a choice."

I get out of bed and try on the first hat. "I love it."

Jodie pulls out a pair of black Mary Jane heels. I put them on. "These are they."

Katrina asks me what dress I'll wear.

I pull the black one out of my closet. "I just wore this to the wedding in Disneyland. That'll teach me to wear black to a wedding."

"You're going to look simply beautiful for Sam," is her response.

I look in the mirror and let out a snort. In his flowered shirt, plaid boxer shorts, a fancy black hat and high-heels, my eyes tiny slits from hours of crying and all the sorrow, fear, doubt, anger, confusion and self-pity simmering below the surface, I am miles from beautiful – outside and in.

Eighteen

Next on today's agenda is the Writing of the Obituary. Amidst a house full of family, constantly ringing phone and chiming doorbell, I sit down at my computer. I want to write "I HOPE YOU APPRECIATE THAT MY HUSBAND GAVE HIS LIFE PROTECTING YOUR PRECIOUS CITY" but this wouldn't be socially acceptable. Thus I write a normal obituary for a man who was from ordinary.

For the photo, I choose the self-portrait of Sam and me taken in Vancouver three months ago. "You don't think," I ask Katrina, "that by using a picture of the two of us, people will think we *both* died, do you?"

"No. And besides, it's important that you show Sam the person instead of Sam the police officer because the papers are already filled with those pictures."

I haven't seen a newspaper yet and I have no urge to.

"So that photo," she finishes, "is a powerful reminder that Sam was also *your* husband."

Oh, I won't let them forget.

I go upstairs, take my excruciating shower then get dressed. Today, I wear black.

After lunch, Tom picks me, my dad and Katrina up to drive us to the funeral home. Arrangements must be made. En route, Tom explains he's the family liaison officer and therefore responsible for keeping me in the loop for all police-related matters.

"Well, I'm glad they chose you," I say, "and not some stranger."

We're stopped at a red light so he turns to look at me. "I requested to do this."

The light turns green so he resumes driving.

"So did they catch the bad guy?" I ask. "The one Sam was searching for?"

Tom shakes his head. "They're pretty sure it was a false alarm."

And I'm pretty sure that's gonna be a huge problem.

Other than the crackle of the police radio, the car is silent; the tension inside palpable. I stare out the window.

"Hmmm . . ." I say. "Isn't that interesting?"

For lining both sides of the street are hundreds of people holding signs that read: *Abortion Kills Children.*

Are *you* gonna raise the unwanted kids? I think to myself, echoing my mother's perspective on the matter. No? Then take your stupid signs and go home.

"We've got a ten day old child with severe head injuries . . ."

All four of us stare at the police radio, from which the female dispatcher speaks.

"Did you say ten day or ten month?" we hear a male officer ask.

"Ten *day*," replies dispatch. "The father threw him to the floor and he landed on his head."

Again with the head injuries. I turn to Tom and open my mouth a few times, goldfish-style.

"I'm sorry," he says, reaching over and turning off the radio.

I give him my don't-you-worry-about-it wave. "That's OK."

But it's not. Nothing whatsoever is OK. Sam is gone and I'm left behind to find my own way in this screwed-up world. He'd cared deeply about what was wrong in society. Does his death mean the end of his commitment to trying to make it better? Is it me who has to deal with the crap now? Why does Sam get to float around some fluffy-clouded, pearly-gated heaven while I'm stuck in hellville? How am I gonna find peace on a planet where mothers abort their fetuses, fathers throw their sons on their heads, and decent guys don't make it home from work? I wish Tom could reach over and turn off my mind like he did the radio.

At the funeral home, Nick and Angela are waiting for us. The funeral director takes us to his office, sits behind a massive oak desk and pulls out a pad of paper. "The first order of business is the obituary. Did you get a chance to start that, Adri?"

I pull out a piece of paper covered in red scribbles. "Yeah."

He suggests I read to him what I've written, then he'll write it down and his assistant will type it up. To me, this seems ineffective – but obituaries are his business, not mine. So I read him the first line and watch in irritation as he slowly writes it out.

"Listen," I say, "How about you let *me* type it. Is there a computer I can use?"

Thus I spend the next two hours retyping, and therefore rewriting, Sam's obituary in a back office. I type a line, sprint back to the herd for advice then race down the hallway again. I can see Sam shaking his head at me for running through a funeral home. After I finish, I plop in the chair in front of the funeral director. "Now what?" I ask.

"Well, we were just discussing the decisions you'll have to make."

"Such as?"

"Choosing a casket, flowers, where the reception will be held, the funeral service pamphlet, the burial plot . . ."

"Oh my God!" I say. Did I just fall off the turnip truck? It sounds like a wedding we're planning – only they bury the groom when it's over.

Misinterpreting my response, the funeral director sighs. "There are some tough decisions ahead but you *will* get through it." Then he slides a folder across the desk towards me. "And here's some information on grieving as well as some more, er, practical suggestions."

"Such as . . ."

"Oh, places to record who gave you what food, baking, cards, flowers . . ."

I fold my arms across my chest. I was brought up to thank people for their kindness but two days after Sam's death the whole idea pisses me off. Am I to thank people for *caring* that my husband's head was smashed open like a goddamn pumpkin?

Katrina grabs the folder. "I'll take that," she says to the Director. "I'm sure it'll come in handy."

To line the bottom of a bird cage, maybe.

"If you're finished here," Tom says from the doorway, "then

we better keep moving because we've got that meeting at Sam's church tonight."

My hackles go up. If choosing flowers for Sam's casket and reading up on grief etiquette don't kill me, dealing with the Greek Orthodox Church will.

We all file into the hall and I assume we're heading home. Not *quite*.

Angela turns to me. "Would you like to see Sam?"

I slump against the nearest wall. "*Sam*? Where's he?"

Apparently neither the church nor the grief folder will have the honours of finishing me off. Seeing Sam's dead body for the first time will likely do the trick.

Angela looks at me as if I *have* just fallen off the turnip truck. "In the basement."

Why have I not yet considered the whereabouts of Sam's body?

"Mom's anointing him with oil right now," says Angela.

"WHAT?" I cry.

"It's a Greek Orthodox thing."

Bile rises in my throat.

"A purification ritual," she adds. "It's really important to my parents."

I swallow to keep down the vomit and the fury. But would *Sam* have wanted his mother rubbing oil on his naked body? I think not.

"You might want to see Sam before the prayer service," Angela says, "because that'll probably be pretty crazy."

I have no clue what she's referring to and I'm not about to ask. If I open my mouth right now, I will regret what comes out.

Nineteen

We take the elevator to the basement of the funeral home. As the doors open, I see Sam's mom sort of . . . floating towards me. I mean, she's walking but she looks lighter somehow and has a quasi-serene expression on her face.

"Are you OK?" I ask.

She takes my hand. "I just saw Sam and he looks *so* peaceful."

That's because he's DEAD.

"I gave him his first bath, Adri, and now I've given him his last."

I don't know what to say to this.

"God gave me my angel and now I've sent him back."

There is nothing to say. My anger dissipates and I'm left with raw empathy for a mother who just bathed her thirty-two year old son's dead body.

"Go see him," she whispers, "his body is warmer than it should be."

I grab the hand of the unsuspecting Hope Chaplain, who happens to be standing nearest me. "Come with me," I say.

This takes us both by surprise. So as I'm dragging him through the doorway, he tries to shift the notebook he's holding from the hand I've grabbed to his free one, which means we end up doing a sort of untangling-dance into the room where Sam is lying on yet another stainless steel gurney. So much for a grand entrance. Seeing Sam all by himself in such sterile surroundings – not to mention dead as a doornail – shocks me. I double over as if punched in the stomach and since the chaplain is still firmly attached, crush his hand in the process.

Then the futility of a dramatic breakdown hits me; theatrics won't change the facts. I release the chaplain, stand up properly and walk the several steps towards Sam – and towards growing up. My husband is now a body without a soul, a car without a driver. Unlike in the emergency room on Friday morning when I first saw him, I know now how the story ends – for Sam anyway. Nothing I do, say, think, feel or believe is going to change the reality that he is now a corpse. I can either accept this as truth or seek refuge from it within the labyrinth of my mind.

I once read that some primates have been observed dragging the dead body of a family member around for a few days after the animal has died. At first, a dead husband does seem better than no husband at all. But when I lean over to kiss his lips, I smell formaldehyde. And his skin is the color of a Ken-doll. When I place my hand on his forehead, it feels stretched too tight. But the fever is gone. Then I see the stitches at the base of his neck and consider pulling the sheet down to look at his incision. No. I will choose to remember Sam's chest the way it looked last week when we'd hung out in our hotel bed till noon, eating leftover fried chicken and boysenberry pie – not as the exit point for his heart.

"May I pray?" the chaplain asks.

"Sure."

"Dear Lord Jesus, please bless Sam's soul and care for him in the place you have prepared in your Heavenly Father's home . . ."

Is Sam waiting somewhere else – or is his soul still right here on earth? It doesn't seem to me that a soul, if such a thing really exists, can be in two places at once.

I think again of the infant whose father had thrown him on his head. Why had I heard that on the radio? Is it a blessing that Sam doesn't have to deal with such sad stuff anymore? Does the soul cease to care once released from the confines of the body? Does the essence of a person end with death?

Sam's compassion had been a driving force behind his determination to become a police officer in the first place. Years ago, his mom had told me that when Sam was seven, he'd seen a homeless person on a park bench and had been so upset she'd had to take him to talk to the priest.

"Sam cried for days," his mom had said, "there was no consoling him. He just couldn't understand why some people didn't have homes."

I recall the homeless woman Sam and I had passed on Santa Monica Beach last Monday. Could she have been a . . . signpost of sorts, marking the end of our vacation and happy times together, as well as symbolizing the return to Sam's caring childhood self? For once the adult Sam had faced the reality of police work, he'd changed. He began to perceive that his potential for making a significant difference to complex societal problems was minimal.

"It's frustrating," he'd said, "because most offenders just get their wrists slapped for breaking the law. The consequences for their actions are minimal so they just go out and re-offend."

"But you're doing the best you can within the legal system," I'd reminded him.

"A fundamentally flawed one," had been his response, "that often protects the rights of criminals over victims. Young offenders are a perfect example."

"Sam . . ."

"Most of the time, I feel more like a babysitter than a cop, Adri. When I take a young offender home to his or her parents, half the time they refuse to accept responsibility for their kid's criminal behavior. And even when parents do admit their little angel screwed up, they usually ask *me* to discipline them."

It's not that Sam had stopped caring but in the last two years, he'd definitely refocused his efforts into an area of police work through which he believed he could make a difference: undercover work. He'd also been putting a great deal of effort into getting *me* back on the writing track, which had entailed some tough love on his part.

I open my eyes and look down at Sam on the gurney. You were yanked from the game, my friend.

The chaplain opens his eyes. "Amen."

"Amen," I say.

Then I kiss Sam on the forehead, give him my little wave and walk out.

I, however, am very much still *in* the game and this evening's opponent is the Greek Orthodox Church. After dinner, Tom delivers me, my dad and Katrina to Sam's church where the Tall Chaplain meets us in the foyer.

"They're just inside the hall," he says, referring to the Hope Chaplain and Sam's priest, "talking about Sam's eulogy."

"What about it?" I ask, folding my arms across my chest. "Stan's gonna do it."

The chaplain clears his throat. "Well, in the Greek Orthodox tradition, they don't usually allow that. I think only the priest speaks."

"Well," I say, "in MY tradition, that's just too damn bad because Sam made it *very* clear that Stan is to give his eulogy."

Our wedding planning fiasco comes crashing back and I recall another stipulation his church would've placed on us, had we been married here: Stan couldn't have been his Best Man simply because he wasn't Greek Orthodox.

"I'm sure it'll all work out," the Tall Chaplain says.

There's only one way this *can* work out – so this church is gonna learn how to operate with some goddamn flexibility very quickly.

The Hope Chaplain comes out of the hall and confirms the priest has agreed to allow Stan to give the eulogy. Damn rights.

Then, through the front doors of the church walk three very official-looking men, gripping their clipboards in front of them like shields. They're introduced to me as the staff sergeants and inspectors in charge of planning Sam's funeral. Sam made the ultimate sacrifice and it's these senior officers' jobs to make sure his final tribute is one of respect. This I understand. It's the way these men are looking at *me* that is of concern: I am a deer in headlights. Sam isn't the only one paying the price for his dedication and these officers know it. Many deer don't make it off the road in time.

Inside the hall, the police sit at one end of the table, family members at the other, and the Orthodox priest, two police chaplains – God's reps – and I take the middle.

The chief of police walks in and everyone stands up. She shakes her head so we sit back down. She walks over, gives me a hug and then takes a seat beside her officers.

The meeting is a tennis match as police protocol, family requests and religious traditions are lobbed back and forth over the net. I'm just the ball girl struggling to follow the game.

"How are we going to drape the Canadian flag over the casket if it's *open*?" someone asks.

"Does it have to be open?" asks another, whom I could kiss with gratitude.

"Yes," Sam's priest assures us, "it has to be open."

No kisses for him. I keep my mouth shut. This isn't a battle I can win.

Will the piper be piping both before and after the service? How many people will be attending from the Greek community? Where will Sam's teammates and recruit classmates sit? How long will it take for people to pay their last respects? Who will be giving speeches? Will communion be offered? Will it be OK for me to receive Sam's hat, badge and Canada flag while Sam's parents receive a provincial flag and special plaque? Will the police helicopter do a fly-over? Will alcohol be served at the reception? What songs will the police choir sing?

"A *choir*?"

Play stops. All eyes turn to me.

The officer who suggested it clears his throat. "Well yes, Adri, there's a police choir that could sing a few songs . . . perhaps from the balcony of the church."

I scrunch up my nose. "Ummm, actually Sam wasn't too keen on stuff like that."

My objection is met with nods from around the table. Play resumes.

I appreciate the effort going into Sam's funeral but if I learned nothing else from our wedding fiasco, I did take away this valuable lesson: despite the disagreements between the Orthodox Church and our families, the day itself had come and gone and our wedding had been lovely. In the end, it was our marriage, not the ceremony, where our most worthwhile efforts had been directed. Likewise, Sam's funeral will come and go. My job will be to come to terms with Sam's *death* – and my own life without him in it.

After the meeting ends, the chief comes up to me. "Are you OK with all this?"

"I guess so."

"As you heard, I'll be giving you Sam's hat and badge during the service and I . . . I just want to prepare you for how difficult that is going to be."

I nod. "All right."

She takes my hand and looks me in the eye. "That moment is going to be *extremely* tough on you, Adri."

Twenty

Monday morning, I wake to the sun streaming through my win-dow and a sickening sense of dread creeping over my heart. Sam's been by my side for nearly a dozen years; listening to me when I complained, laughing when I was being an idiot, boosting my confidence when I was down, hugging me when I was upset. How am I going to get through his death – without him?

The familiar knock on the door comes.

I feel like one of those dying birds you see on TV after an oil tanker spill; volunteers gently trying to wipe away the sludge from her feathers.

"Hi Googie." It's Harry.

Katrina pops her head around him. "Dare I ask?"

"Tell me again," I say, "how I'm supposed to do this without Sam."

She starts back at square one. "You've *got* to take it one day at a time. You cannot focus on the future right now."

"Well it's a little hard not to." I struggle to sit up in bed as my six foot four, two-hundred-and-fifty-pound brother tiptoes out the door.

"Let's just get you through these days, OK?" She sits on my bed. "You have some big decisions ahead, so try and concentrate on those."

But managing my mind is not going to be easy. After the usual agonizing shower, I head into the kitchen for coffee.

Katrina follows me in. "I made my bed, Adri."

I smile politely.

Harry explains: "She *never* makes the bed at home."

"It's just that I know how important a tidy house was to Sam," she says.

"And I'm trying to keep the kitchen clean," adds Ed, theatri-cally wiping the counter with a dishrag.

I laugh. They're right – Sam needed order. He couldn't sleep if there were dishes in the sink or newspapers lying around.

Today's paper, in fact, is already neatly placed at the corner of the kitchen table. An extreme close-up of Sam's scowling face stares up at me. Obviously taken from the police archives, not mine, it's one of the worst pictures of Sam I've ever seen.

Ed opens the paper to Sam's obituary and hands it to me. "That's an excellent piece of writing," he says kindly. "Although it's the first obituary I've ever read with multiple exclamation marks in it."

After poached eggs and toast, Tom takes me, my dad and Katrina back to the funeral home where we meet up again with Nick and Angela. All six of us follow closely behind the funeral director, like a group of ducklings following their mama, until he stops outside a closed door and we damn near run into him.

He turns around to face us. "This is our first stop and I like to warn people that it can be a . . . bit of a shock."

We nod bravely.

"Because this," he says, reaching for the door handle, "is the casket room."

Sure enough, it's a room full of coffins. So up and down the aisles we stroll, passing shiny black caskets, ornately carved oak ones and small white versions for children. They have a casket for everyone – except *my* husband.

"Have you got anything in pine?" I ask.

I wouldn't have thought a room full of caskets could get any quieter, but it did.

The director clears his throat. "Uh yes, but we keep those in another room."

Everyone stares at me.

"Would you like to see those?" he asks.

My dad leans over and whispers in my ear, "I don't mean to be rude, but pine caskets are usually for . . . well, they're less expensive."

"So?" I say loudly. "Sam liked pine. We have pine furniture."

My dad's eyes widen, perhaps at the inferred connection between one's casket and one's china cabinet. "You do whatever you want, Adri, it's your decision. It's just that you don't usually see a pine casket for such a . . ." He clears his throat. "Public funeral."

Fine. We have maple hardwood floors. Our neighbourhood is named after the maple tree. The symbol for Canada is the maple leaf.

"Have you got a maple casket?" I ask the funeral director.

"We sure do," he replies, visibly relieved.

So I choose a beautiful maple casket. It's simple, with no twirls and swirls, and has the least flouncy of the satin linings. I don't want Sam looking like a doll lying there in ruffles.

Then the director asks me if I'd like Sam's casket placed in a vault.

I picture some sort of mammoth safety deposit box for bodies. "Pardon me?"

He explains that a vault is a concrete container in the ground.

"Why would we do that?" I ask, genuinely puzzled.

"Personal preference," he says. "Or a religious belief."

But why would we want to delay the inevitable? Encasing Sam's casket in concrete would certainly make him . . . you know, last longer. But I can't fathom *why* we would do that. I turn to Angela. "Do other Greeks have this vault-thing?"

She shakes her head.

"There's your answer," I tell the funeral director.

Next, he shows us a selection of guest books.

Dear Adri, Considering the dreadful circumstances, Sam's funeral was simply lovely and you both looked smashing! I wish you all the best in your new life as a widow.

"And this is a nice idea," the director continues, showing me a piece of paper with questions on it. "You can write down Sam's particulars, as well as a message for him. Then there's a drawer inside his casket where you can tuck . . ." He stops speaking, likely noticing the look of disgust on my face. Once Sam's settled into his grave, he's not gonna read my note. He barely read when he was alive, for God's sake.

"Ummm . . . what other decisions have to be made today?" Katrina asks him.

"The flowers have to be ordered."

"Tulips!" I say. "Sam always gave me tulips."

More raised eyebrows. Apparently, this is a hell of a lot of tulips for *October*.

As a compromise, Angela suggests white roses for his casket and a special bouquet of tulips just from me. Whatever. I know Sam wouldn't give a rat's ass about flowers. How he fell to his death during a routine investigation would take top priority.

When we're released from this wretched place, Tom promptly takes us to another. At the cemetery, we are directed to the section where Sam's uncle is buried.

"East or west?" the cemetery guy asks me.

"Excuse me?"

"Would you like your husband's burial plot to face east or west?"

This seems to me an odd question. "Well let's see," I say, "I guess west would be better because Sam wasn't much of a morning person."

Nick leans in to me. "I think he asked you that because of a religious belief."

I turn to him. "*Now* what?"

"Well, some Christians believe that when Jesus comes back . . ."

Everyone leans towards Nick, cemetery guy included.

". . . He'll come back from the east," he finishes.

I shrug. "And this has what to do with choosing Sam's grave?"

Nick shifts from one foot to the other. "The idea is that you want to be buried facing east so that when Jesus returns, you'll be able to see him."

"That's ridiculous!" I say.

He shrugs. "I just thought you'd want to know."

I sense it's taking every ounce of willpower for my dad, an atheist, to keep out of this conversation because he's practically vibrating beside me.

"What I was going to suggest," says the cemetery guy, "is that Sam be buried on the other side of his uncle."

So he walks us over to Sam's uncle's grave. When I read the name on his headstone, I let out a little gasp. It's the exact same name as Sam's. I'd forgotten this. Had his uncle's funeral been foreshadowing?

I walk around to the other side. I look down and see that the plot number is 130. Sam's lucky number is thirteen. His birthday is May 13th. So far, so good. Then I turn so that I'm facing west, the same direction Sam would be if we go with this plot, and close my eyes – just to get a feel for the place.

When I open them again, I turn my head to the right and there, four plots over, is a headstone with a yellow Winnie the Pooh engraved on it. Clunk goes the coin. At Disneyland, Pooh Grandma had fallen right in front of Sam and hit *her* head. That had been exactly one week before his fall.

I stamp my feet on the earth. "This is it. This is Sam's new home."

And if I'm wrong, Sam can just damn well turn around to see Jesus.

Twenty-one

Back at his former home, I pour myself a glass of milk and pluck a handful of oatmeal chocolate chip cookies from the growing pile of baking. My husband died and they give me cookies.

I go downstairs and begin writing Sam a good-bye poem for the back of his funeral service pamphlet. I'm making decent headway when a phone call comes in. I'm not taking many calls but do I take this one. It's Charlie – another of Sam's recruit classmates and one of the two guys Sam often met for lunch. He tells me about a pin their class has had made in memory of Sam. The pins are being sold to police officers but instead of paying cash, they're donating their court time to a fund set up in Sam's name. So depending on the officer's rate of pay and the number of court hours donated, this means that individual donations are anywhere from twenty bucks to hundreds of dollars.

"And we're hoping that later on," Charlie says, "you'll be involved in deciding how to use the money."

"I'd like that."

He is quiet a moment. "There's something else, Adri."

"Yeah?" I say, nervously reaching for Sam's pendants.

"I just wanted to tell you that, uh . . . well that Sam loved you very much."

"Oh." I wasn't expecting this comment – or how much it hurt to hear.

"He loved your smile," Charlie continues. "Sam told me once how you liked to go the dentist because they were always complimenting you on your teeth."

I laugh. "He told you *that*?"

"Yeah. He talked about you all the time."

When I hang up, I realize I'm smiling . . . I mean genuinely smiling instead of the forced mechanical grin I have acquired.

After dinner, the same senior officers from last night come over for a second funeral-planning meeting. They sit on three chairs, lined up all in a row in front of the fireplace.

"We have a few more items to run by you," Officer A starts off. "First of all, about the choir . . ."

I roll my eyes.

"We got the feeling yesterday you weren't too keen on that."

"Oh, it's not me," I say as cheerfully as possible. "It's Sam. He hated touchy-feely stuff like that."

"OK, so no choir."

A small victory but one nonetheless.

"Now about the media," Officer B, seated in the middle, says, "we need to know what components of Sam's funeral you want and don't want filmed."

"I hadn't thought about it."

"This will be a newsworthy event so we have to be very clear ahead of time."

I nod. He tilts his head forward slightly. So I nod again.

"Do you want the media at Sam's interment?" he asks.

I stare at him, having no idea what that word means.

"The interment is the graveside service, Adri," explains the Hope Chaplain.

I jump up. "*What*? They're going to film Sam's coffin going into the ground?"

"Not necessarily," replies Officer A. "That's up to you. It's just that if we don't cooperate with the media and give them proper direction, then there's the chance that an inappropriate photograph of you or Sam's family might get taken."

"Fine," I say. "No media at Sam's grave."

"Done. OK, next is the seating arrangements."

I shrug. "People walk in and take their seats – how difficult can that be?"

The officers look at each other then back at me. "There will be police officers here from all over Canada," says Officer B. "There could easily be two thousand people."

I nearly choke on my gum. What rock have I just crawled out from underneath? I had no clue Sam's funeral could be anywhere near this big.

"There'll be seating in the main part of the church," Officer B continues, "as well as in the gymnasium and in a tent outside."

"Where are you going to put Sam and Adri's friends?" Katrina asks. "How can we make sure they don't get put in the tent while a bunch of strangers are in the church?"

"Ushers," replies Officer C. "We'll need ushers."

It's sounding like a wedding again.

"Now, about the funeral procession," says Officer A.

I look at him. "The what?"

"After Sam's funeral, when all the cars drive to the cemetery together . . ."

Officer C pulls out a pad of paper and draws a little diagram for me. "This," he says, pointing to his sketch of a long car, "will be Sam's hearse." Then he draws another car behind the hearse. "And this will be you and Sam's family."

I lean in and look at the drawing. "Uh huh."

"Then there will be police officers," he continues, drawing little stick men all in a row, "lining the streets and saluting Sam as he passes . . ."

"Oh my God! I cry. "It's a parade!"

Officer C stops sketching. The room falls silent. Everyone stares at me.

"Yeah kinda," Officer B says. "But it's called a procession."

"I know THAT," I snap. "But Sam and I were in the *Disneyland* parade a week before he died. We were walking behind Mickey Mouse, waving to the crowd and . . ."

Officer B clears his throat. Officer C shifts in his chair and puts the cap back on his pen. Officer A stares at the floor.

"And the crowd," I finish, "waved back at us."

I look to my family for backup but Ed's mouth is hanging open. Harry's eyes are enormous. Dale hangs his head. Even my mother has nothing to say.

But *how* could Sam be in a parade at the Happiest Place on Earth one week and his own funeral procession the next?

"That's, uh, that's quite something," Officer A says softly. "So the procession sounds all right to you then, Adri?"

I nod and keep my mouth shut for the rest of the meeting.

Twenty-two

By the time Katrina knocks on my door Tuesday morning, I've been awake for hours, my mind struggling to regain that elusive Hope. The Pooh headstone and Disneyland parade connections from yesterday now seem childish and silly. Whereas two thousand years of Christianity can't be wrong. And since Sam is in heaven waiting for me, the sooner I die, the quicker we'll be together. I don't give a flying fuck in a rolling donut about eternal time passing quickly. All that matters to me is time here on earth and I'm NOT waiting sixty-five years to see him again. I promised Sam I'd hang around for seven months so that'll take me to the end of April . . .

". . . time, it'll get easier," says Katrina from the foot of my bed.

"Huh?"

"I was just saying that maybe with time, this will get a bit easier."

"But I don't WANT it to get easier! I don't want to get *over* him!"

"No, no," she recants, "that's not what I meant. I don't think you'll ever get *over* Sam. You two had something incredibly special."

"We still do."

"I know. It's just that time is a strong healer so one day you might find that the sorrow you feel now will be replaced by wonderful memories."

"I highly doubt *memories* will ever sustain me," I say snottily.

"Adri . . ."

I throw back the covers. "I'm taking Sasha to the dog-park."

I put on a pair of jeans and the sweatshirt Sam bought me in Disneyland and go downstairs, determined to bring a sense of normalcy to my day.

"Are you sure you don't want one of us to come along?" Ed asks, pouring my coffee into a go-mug.

"Nope." I tie up my runners. "I need some time on my own."

As I'm walking out the back door, I overhear Katrina telling my brothers, "Don't worry, she has to start letting some of that hurt *out*."

I'll be fine – just six months and twenty-five days to go. I pop open the back hatch of the Jeep and Sasha jumps in. We make it a block before a Savage Garden song comes on the radio: *I wanna stand with you on a mountain, I wanna bathe with you in the sea, I wanna lie like this forever until the sky falls down on me.*

"FUCK!" I scream, pounding the steering wheel with my fist. I pull over to the side of the road and slump against the steering column as deep wracking sobs shake my entire body.

This is the first time since hearing of Sam's fall that I'm completely alone – no one can rush over and comfort me nor tell me the spiritual answer I want to hear. With no audience, the expression of my grief is, at last, real, raw and untamed. From the back seat, Sasha creeps up and nuzzles her nose into my face. I hug her tightly.

When I open my eyes, I notice a man raking his leaves and a woman walking her poodle. My world has stopped turning, why hasn't everybody else's?

At the park, Sam's absence is overwhelming. Everything has happened so fast. But maybe that's for the best. For as much I was prepared to handle the responsibility of spending the rest of my life caring for a severely brain-injured husband, perhaps it's better for both me and Sam that he died quickly from his injuries. Or is it wrong for me to think this?

In the late afternoon, I have a bubble bath to try and relax before this evening's prayer service – the 'pretty crazy' one Angela alluded to. But I am beyond anxious.

At 6:00 p.m., Tom picks me up and takes me to the funeral home because I've been told to arrive early for a private family time before the service. I go into the chapel on my own to see Sam. He's now in his full police uniform – the one that officers wear only for graduation, weddings and funerals. Though not a doll in ruffles, he does resemble an over-sized toy soldier crammed into a casket. His white gloved-hands are neatly folded over each other, as they never were in life. I notice his lips are chapped so I pull out some lip balm from my purse and gently rub it on. Then I lean in and kiss his waxy forehead and am greeted by the smell of formaldehyde. It's Sam but it isn't.

A few minutes later, his family joins me to pay their respects to Sam. Then the Greek Priest comes in and says a brief prayer. What else we're supposed to be doing during private family time isn't clear so we all squish into the front pew together and stare at Sam's dead body for over an hour. My anxiety builds exponentially.

The chapel is nearly full of mourners by the time I excuse

myself to go to the bathroom. I'm in the hallway when an older lady who works for the funeral home asks me if I'm OK.

"I'm hungry," I say, not hungry whatsoever.

She smiles. "There's some pizza downstairs."

I follow her down to the staff lunchroom and sit at the kitchen table while she heats a piece of pizza in the microwave. Then she walks over to the fridge. "And we also have some peach juice here, if you like."

Peach juice? Where else was I offered that recently?

"And then I think you better get back upstairs," she says, "because the service will be starting soon."

I eat a couple of bites of pizza then go back to the chapel. The Tall Chaplain, clearly concerned, takes my arm and leads me to the front of the room where several members of Sam's recruit class present me with a large blue picture of Sam in uniform. He's standing on a hill with the downtown skyline behind him and on top of the photograph is a poem about the importance of police officers not becoming mean, tarnished or afraid. Oh boy. I take the picture and return to my post between Sam's parents. The prayer service begins immediately.

Since most of the words spoken by the priest are in Greek, I figure that although my body has to be in this chapel, my mind does not. So I close my eyes and I can see Sam on Santa Monica Beach, waiting for me on the sand. But a sickly sweet smell brings me back to the task at hand. I open my eyes to see the priest waving a brass container of incense towards Sam's casket. The overpowering stench nearly gags me. STOP IT! Sam hates the smell of that shit.

San Diego! The lady with the prayer room – *that's* where we had peach juice . . .

"I'm sorry for your loss, dear."

I blink. A stranger is now standing in front of me. She leans over and kisses me on both cheeks. Not knowing what else to do, I stand up.

"Be strong dear," says the next lady in line, also hugging and kissing me.

Apparently, the formal portion of the program is over and

the 'pretty crazy' part is underway. When it finally occurs to me that I'm in a *receiving* line three feet from Sam's dead body, it's too late to flee.

"It's God's plan," whispers the next woman, kissing me on both cheeks. I seriously consider exposing her a third cheek to kiss.

As both my life and Sam's quite literally pass before my eyes, I am kissed and hugged by hundreds of people. But each familiar face brings with it a memory. My childhood friends, Sam's university buddies, members of my family, a former co-worker of mine, members of Sam's extended family . . .

Then there's a lull in the line and I catch a glimpse of Sam in his casket, white-gloved hands still neatly folded. Then more faces, more memories: my university friends, one of Sam's old partners, a recruit classmate, an old friend, a teammate. Interspersed with faces from our past and present are complete strangers: police officers from all over the country, members of the Greek community I've never met and God knows who else.

I don't think the human body is built to sustain the mental and emotional impact of re-living hundreds of memories within such a short timeframe and under such heart-wrenching conditions. But what do I know? I tell myself this receiving line tradition must be healthy because if not, then surely someone would put a stop to it.

But after about four hundred people have expressed their sympathy and reminded me – in case I forget – to be strong, I look back over my shoulder. Katrina is scowling, clearly livid that I'm allowing myself to be put through this unnecessary torture. But I stay where I am, determined to finish what I started.

As the end of the line draws near, I must confess that my strength does seem to be waning because I start to lose consciousness. I sit down. When I look up, I catch the eye of an older police officer, one of two honour guards standing beside Sam's casket. He winks at me. I smile back in surprise and feel a surge of strength. Such a small gesture and yet it gives me more comfort than all the prayers, incense waving, stupid clichés and handshakes put together.

When the line of mourners ends, all that remain in the chapel are our families and some of Sam's buddies. Out of the corner of my eye, I see my dad walk up to Sam and stand there a moment, head bowed. Then he comes over to me.

"I'm very sorry you lost Sam, Adri."

"Thanks, Dad, I . . ."

"I'm sorry you lost Sam," he repeats, "because he gave you what I never could."

I let the tears fall as I hug my dad tighter than I have since I was a little girl. He's right; Sam was more of a father-figure to me than my own father.

"Do you know what the chief said to me back there?" Harry asks me as we're walking out of the chapel.

"What?"

"She said, 'Your little sister is one tough cookie.'"

I push open the door to the parking lot. "Maybe so, but letting myself be put through THAT makes me not a particularly smart one."

My dad shakes his head. "Only if you don't learn the lesson."

Twenty-three

Today – Wednesday October 4th – is Sam's funeral. Its also four years to the day since Sam started his classes as a police recruit. True to his orderly nature, Sam's policing career will end on the same date it began. Today is also Sasha's third birthday.

When I go downstairs to get coffee started, I notice that several inches of snow have accumulated on the front lawn. I smile. I love winter.

"Thanks for the snow," I say to the living room window.

After breakfast, I put on my black dress, followed by my fancy new hat with the chiffon bow. When I look in the mirror, I see the pasty, puffy image of a widow who's visited a few too many buffets. My slip is so snug that Anthony has to do up the clasps of my new shoes for me.

By 8:30 a.m., both police chaplains are standing in my

kitchen waiting for the rest of my family and the funeral limousines to show up. I make a comment about the snowstorm being a good sign.

"Do you have any idea," is the Hope Chaplain's response, "how much havoc it's causing on the roads out there?"

"No."

"The streets are skating rinks," he says.

"Cars are in the ditches," adds the Tall Chaplain.

"But Sam knew how much I loved the snow. Maybe he's trying to make this day a bit easier for me."

The Hope Chaplain smiles. "Well, if it *is* a gift to you, could you ask him to ease up a little? It's a mess out there."

When the limousines arrive, all seventeen of us pile into two cars then begin the slow crawl to the funeral home. I stare out the window as the panic, thankfully delayed somewhat today, begins its familiar ascent from my stomach to my chest to my head. My always being late really bothered Sam; now I can't even show up for his funeral on time.

Or maybe there's another reason for a heavy snowstorm to hit today. No more running, no more incessant busyness, no more racing around like . . . chickens with our heads cut off: this is a forced time out for reflection.

Sam is dead. He went to a break and enter call that was likely a false alarm. He stepped through a false ceiling and fell to his death. What are the chances of this? Am I the only person who thinks this scenario a bit odd?

"It's more than a hat-rack," Sam used to say to me from The Perch, tapping his temple with his index finger. "You think I'm just mindlessly watching TV, don't you?"

"Uh, *yeah*. Call me crazy but what else would you be doing?"

"I'm relaxing and thinking."

"With the TV *on*?"

"It's how I chill out."

Watching the cars inch along in traffic, I promise Sam I won't just attend his funeral today and rush right back into the rat race. I'll take the necessary time to reflect and learn from his life, his death and our relationship. Easy to say this, while held captive inside a limo during a snowstorm.

We arrive at the funeral home just as Sam's pallbearers are lifting his casket into the hearse. I am incredibly thirsty so someone gives me a bottle of water. Our limousines follow the hearse out of the parking lot and we make our way towards the Greek Orthodox Church. When our vehicle turns the last corner, I am shocked at what I see.

Hundreds of police officers and other emergency services personnel are lining the streets and church steps, patiently awaiting our arrival; blue, black and red uniforms from all over North America are a sea of colour against the snow.

"Respect isn't granted," Sam had repeatedly reminded me, "it must be earned."

My door is opened from the outside and the Tall Chaplain leans in, offering me his arm. I take it and climb out. I'm wearing my long brown swing coat – the one I vowed to Sam I would wear to lunch with my future publisher in New York City one autumn day.

I take in the scene before me. Snowflakes fall gently to the ground. Are we figurines in a glass ball God has given a good shaking to? Is He up there watching as the snow settles around our lives, curious to see if we'll learn a lesson or two?

I glance to the left and see a photographer on the roof of the house next to the church. I turn away in time to see the pallbearers removing Sam's casket, now draped in a Canadian flag, from the hearse. I tighten my grip on the chaplain's arm. Then they start to carry the casket towards the steps. Bagpipes play and a drum pounds. Boom, boom, boom; up the steps of the church the pallbearers' boots move in time to the beat of the drum. But that isn't just any police officer in that casket; that's *my* Sammy. When all this pomp and circumstance ends, how much solace will pride, honour and respect give me? I can't cuddle up in bed with virtues.

I follow Sam up the steps in my new black shoes. Past the officers, through the church doors and down the aisle we walk;

my eyes fixated on Sam's casket. As we pass row after row of people who, unlike me, get to go home to their loved ones at the end of today, my anger builds. DOES ANYBODY *GET IT*? WHO HERE WILL TAKE MORE THAN A FUCKING DATE-SQUARE FROM THIS FUNERAL?

And what, exactly, do I expect everybody else to be 'getting' from Sam's death? That life is short? That our final day often comes without warning? No. People already know all that, although this could be a reminder. What *I* want is an assurance that the end of Sam's life, and the shattering of my own, will not be in vain. I fear acceptance of Sam's death because I know that will lead to apathy. Somehow, positive change *has* to come out of this.

But just as I know Sam wouldn't appreciate a choir singing at his funeral, nor would he approve of me having a spectacular meltdown in front of our family, friends and colleagues. Thus it is in silence that I make my way down the aisle of the church that had refused to accept Sam's decision to marry me within the Anglican faith. Well, they got him now, didn't they? Media coverage and all.

Twenty-four

The only good thing about being the widow is the front row seating. So there's nothing between Sam and myself except death itself – and an expensive maple casket, which is, thankfully, closed for the time being. I take my seat between Sam's parents and we hold hands. To our right, several old men in robes begin chanting in ancient Greek.

I then watch as three police officers – Charlie, Mark and one of Sam's teammates – slowly march up to Sam's casket. Mark places Sam's police hat on the casket, above Sam's head. The teammate places Sam's badge above Sam's chest. Charlie places a folded flag and framed photograph of Sam at the other end of the casket. Then all three march slowly back to their seats as a fourth officer rests a sword on top of the items.

The priest welcomes the congregation then begins the religious portion of the service, much of it in Greek. My eyes drift from one gold panel to the next: Jesus Christ, the Virgin Mary, the twelve disciples and several Saints. Is Sam with all the gang now?

"Sam is not leaving this world to disappear," the priest says, in English. "He is leaving to live the eternal life with God."

Then he looks at Sam's mom. "Jesus said, 'Mother do not weep.'"

She stifles a sob. I squeeze her hand.

"For in the history of humanity," he continues, "there have been mothers who gave birth to tyrants, dictators and killers; mothers who gave birth to angels and saints; and then there are mothers who gave birth to heroes. And this last one is you."

Kaboom. Sam's mom *howls*.

A second priest then gives a speech entirely in Greek; his message lost to most of the congregation.

Then Stan steps up to give the eulogy.

"Adri," he says to me, as if we're the only two in the church, "from the moment he met you, Sam knew you were his soul mate. He told me so on the car ride home."

I'd been out with Jodie that night – all four us, drunk as skunks. Sam and I had even had an argument, which was a fitting start to our relationship. The connection between us had been there from the get-go; it was the details that needed working out.

"Three months ago," Stan continues, "during their last visit to Vancouver, Sam, Adri and I went for a walk through Stanley Park. And Sam said to me: 'I am a simple man. I have a wife I love dearly, a wonderful family, a great group of friends, my dog, and a career where I can make a difference.'"

Stan stops speaking to gain his composure. "Then he said, 'My life is perfect. My life is complete.'"

I, too, had heard Sam say those exact words. Maybe he *had* accomplished all he needed to. I have no doubt Sam passed away a fulfilled person but I also know he would NOT be impressed with the circumstances in which he died. He'd achieved his goal of becoming a police officer but that doesn't mean he'd be A-OK with dying on the job after only four years.

After Stan, the chief of police makes her way to the front of the church. "Our souls ache," she begins, "for the loss of a fair and kind man; a man who lived and breathed police work; who showed determination and commitment; tenacity and bravery; professionalism and confidence."

I listen carefully, trying to absorb every word.

"The loss will always be with us but the life that Sam led will become a bright and sustaining light."

I can't stop crying, nor can Sam's parents, sister and brother beside me.

"It has been said there are givers and takers in this world," the chief says. "Police officers are true givers. They give of themselves on the job and off and sometimes they give their lives to protect the lives and property of others."

My hand flies up to my face. She's cut to the heart of what's been bothering me: that people won't appreciate the ultimate sacrifice Sam made. He gave his life protecting the peace we take for granted.

After she finishes, several officers wearing pointed helmets march up and remove the Canadian flag from Sam's casket then carefully fold it up. The officer holding the flag then marches around to the opposite side of the casket, where the other officers remove the hat and badge then place them on top of the folded flag. Oh shit. *This* is the part the chief warned me about.

The first officer marches over to the chief and gives her the flag, Sam's hat and badge. When she presents them to me, I respond by throwing my arms around her – wailing like a banshee – and then slump back into the pew, empty.

I close my eyes, looking for Sam on Santa Monica beach. But what I hear is Amazing Grace being played on the bagpipes. Why don't they just rip my heart right out? It would be a lot less painful. I open my eyes to see the top part of Sam's casket being lifted up so that we can see his head and chest. Instead of rage, however, I feel a sort of peace . . . almost as if something has just *joined* me. Whatever's happening, it gives me the strength to handle viewing Sam's body one last time because frankly, I've seen this stuffed version quite enough.

Many of the same people I saw pass in front of me last night begin lining up again. Some of them even stop in front of our pew to offer us their condolences. But I'm not falling for *that* again. I fold my arms across my chest and avoid eye contact: this widow is closed for business. Instead, I watch carefully how each mourner interacts with Sam.

"Wouldn't it be cool to see what went on at your own funeral?" Sam had once asked me. "I'd be curious to see who'd be there and how they'd be reacting."

When the church has cleared out and we're down to close friends and family, I notice Ed lean in and whisper in Sam's ear. When my turn comes to say goodbye, I go to kiss Sam on the lips but the stench of formaldehyde is overpowering. His complexion seems grayer than last night, his face puffier. We've put my lover on display too long. Exactly two weeks ago today, we made love for the very last time in our Vegas hotel room. Katrina was right: my memories *will* have to sustain me from here on in. The time has come to let Sam's body go.

I tuck a letter I wrote him – a contract of sorts – into the drawer inside his casket. Although Sam won't be reading it, I still had to write it.

"Let's go big or go home," I say to him, "just like Vegas."

Then I stand up straight, give Sam one last wave and walk away. But out of the corner of my eye, I see the chief of police, now wearing a long black cape, lean over and whisper something in Sam's ear. Only then is his casket closed for the last time.

Walking down the aisle to the foyer, I see the front doors of the church are open. I quicken my pace towards the light. Outside, the scene has changed: the sun is shining and the snow is melting away.

Twenty-five

I walk down the church steps and into the waiting limousine.

After Sam's casket is loaded into the hearse, the procession begins. As our limo moves along, I look out the window at police officers, RCMP, firefighters, EMS personnel, corrections and peace officers from all over North America standing side by side, saluting Sam – and me, by default – as we pass by.

I *have* been here before: only it was the opposite end of the emotional spectrum.

"Look at them all," says Sam's mom. "I can't . . ."

She's interrupted by a loud chopping sound overhead; the police helicopter is doing the fly-over. And it hits me: *three* times on our vacation, Sam had turned down the chance to go up in a helicopter. Is today his turn?

When the helicopter has passed, I turn his mom. "What did that other priest say about Sam during the funeral – the one who spoke entirely in Greek?"

She looks surprised at my question or perhaps the timing of it. "He talked about Sam as a child who'd been concerned at a very young age about poor people."

"He knew Sam as a kid?" I ask.

She nods. "He's the priest we took Sam to when he was so upset after seeing the homeless man on a park bench."

At the cemetery, we wade through the slush to plot number 130. I somehow get separated from Sam's family but luckily, Harry appears beside me and slips his arm through mine. Then the priest begins waving the goddamn incense again and chanting in Greek while Sam's mom rocks back and forth, loudly crying out his name. Bagpipes play Amazing Grace and I just wish the earth would open up and swallow me. Sam's sister hands me a white rose to place on the casket, which I do but then some moron throws dirt on top of my rose and then someone else does the same and it hits me: oh my God, they're BURYING my Sammy. Then his casket starts to *move* ever so slowly into the ground and Sam's mom breaks free of the hands holding her back and stumbles to his grave then tries to throw herself on top of his coffin. Thank God the media aren't present. But I know how she feels for, I, too, want to go where Sam is going.

Recognizing the pending disaster, someone pushes a button and Sam's casket stops moving. But then the police helicopter is overhead again and I start shivering uncontrollably. My teeth are chattering so loud I figure everyone must hear. The sense of wholeness I experienced in the church earlier dissipates and the hollow emptiness returns. I whip around, push my way past the crowd and half-run, half-stumble back through the slush towards the limousine.

I'm almost there when Harry catches up with me. "Are you OK?"

"What do you think?" I snap. "It's time to get the fuck off the property."

Inside the limo, we sit in silence. Just one more little party to attend, I tell myself, and then I can go home and . . . what? Stare at Sam's picture? Drink a case of beer? Build a funeral pyre to throw myself on?

A few minutes later, the door opens and Sam's family pours in. Nick takes one look at my face and taps the limo driver on the shoulder. "Could we please leave *now*?"

As the vehicle pulls away, I look out the window and see that dozens of people are still standing around Sam's grave.

"Thank you," I say to Nick.

Ah, the funeral reception: let's all eat, drink and share stories in memory of the dead guy who unfortunately can't attend his own party because he's six feet under. I'm grateful for the police service's generosity in hosting the event, but how am I to feel about *celebrating* Sam's life with him no longer around?

Since skipping this soiree isn't an option, my first stop is the bathroom to salvage what I can of my appearance. I splash water on my face, put on some lipstick, re-adjust my hat and head out into the world to try again. Inside the banquet hall, I'm directed to sit at a raised head table. I really *am* a bride without a groom. So I sit beside Sam's dad and he asks me if I'm going to get something to eat. At family dinners, he's always concerned that I get enough food – like that's ever an issue.

"Um . . . maybe in a bit," I say, looking out into the crowd of faces.

Here I am in a room full of family and friends and I have never felt so alone in my entire life. In every uniform, I see Sam. After five minutes, a lone police officer comes over to the head table and reaches his white-gloved hand up to shake mine.

This, I realize, is bullshit. So I excuse myself from the table and head out into the crowd to talk, listen, laugh, cry . . . and get hugs from some very good-looking cops.

There's an open mike for people to share stories. One of Sam's friends has put together a special tribute and begins reading it out to the crowd. "What I'll miss the most about Sam is his laugh. It was more like a giggle, which sounded so funny coming from such a big guy."

"I'll remember his conviction," he continues, "not to bring children into this world but rather make it a better place for ours."

And there's the truth, announced casually in front of a thousand people. I was married to the man, yet hadn't fully grasped this concept until his funeral reception.

"I'll also remember the deer I hit on a country road at the same time of his accident," his friend says. "As I sat in the ditch waiting for the deer to die, I had no idea that I was comforting an angel for Sam . . . someone to ride up the elevator with him."

Next up to the mike is Tom. He tells the story of how he and Sam flooded the bookshelf in my office last year while renovating the bathroom above it.

Then there's a break in speakers and I happen to be standing at the buffet when I feel a sort of push from behind. I turn around but the nearest person is two feet away. The next thing I know *I'm* standing at the podium without a clue as to what I'm going to say. Boy, does the room go quiet quickly.

"I'd like to thank everybody for all the love and support given us these past few days. I uh . . . I also want to say that I loved Sam very much and I'm determined to find some good in his death."

I just verbalized the contract I'd placed in his casket.

Then I step down from the podium and an officer I don't know comes up and hugs me. Then another one does, and then another. Soon there's a little lineup. But it's different from the receiving line at the prayer service last night. Or maybe *I'm* different.

"Adri?"

I recognize that purr. I turn around and look straight into the eyes of the officer Sam had dreamed I'd cheated on him with, five days before his death.

"You might not remember me," the officer says. "But you went on a ride-along with me years ago."

I smile politely and adjust my hat. "I remember."

"I'm very sorry about Sam," he says. "But you take care, OK?"

I nod dumbly as he walks away.

After the reception, we return home to find a birthday card for Sasha on the kitchen table. It's from the neighbours. Inside the fridge is a homemade hamburger with cream cheese frosting and three candles sticking out the top. I laugh. Two years ago, Sam and I had thrown Sasha a legendary first birthday party. Sam had flipped bone-shaped burgers on the barbeque – and a boxer guest had beaten up a beagle.

So, instead of a funeral pyre, I light Sasha's birthday cake and we all sing happy birthday, then watch as she devours it.

After dinner, several of Sam's buddies drop by for a visit. We're reminiscing when one guy suggests we make the Christmas movie tradition happen this year. During his twenties, Sam and his buddies always went to a movie on Christmas night. It'd only been in the last few years they'd stop doing this because everyone was busy with their own families now.

"And remember the pub-crawl sprawl?" Wayne, another friend, teases me.

"Oh man . . . "

"I haven't heard that one," someone says.

"Adri came home from a pub crawl one night," Wayne explains, "but she'd had a few too many drinks, so when Sam and I came home later, we found her face down in the hallway with her pajamas wrapped around her head."

"And the worst part," I admit, "was that I wasn't wearing any underwear. Sam was mortified!"

"Even the paramedics came and had to put her on oxygen for a bit," says Wayne.

We're all still laughing when the phone rings. I feel pretty good so I answer it.

"Is Sam there?" a man's voice asks.

"Pardon me?"

"Is Sam there?" he repeats, sounding irritated.

If the guy used Sam's last name, I could chalk it up to a telemarketer with lousy timing. But I can't fathom who else would be calling Sam by his first name and yet not know he'd passed away. I hand the phone to the nearest person and leave the room as the tears begin again. Sam's buddies leave shortly after.

Tonight, I take Sam's badge to bed with me and fall asleep clutching it against my chest. Maybe I *can* cuddle up with virtues.

PART II
Religion

One

I wake up Thursday morning with the familiar sickening sensation in my stomach and the lump of Sam's badge under my back. There won't be a knock on my door from Katrina, ready to put back together what the night has shattered. She's gone back to work. Life, as I've been told dozens of times over the past week, goes on. Well, it sure as hell doesn't feel like it to me.

In the kitchen, Ed hands me the newspaper. I see a close-up of a woman's face I scarcely recognize but the hat, coat and falling snow are familiar.

After breakfast, I get a call from Nick, asking me if I'd like to go with him to Sam's work today. It's Sam's team's first shift back and Nick, Angela and I have been invited to join parade – the meeting at the beginning of a shift. I figure I may as well go to Sam's work; I'm certainly not going to mine. Typing up break and enter reports doesn't seem overly conducive to my mental health.

Just after lunch, Nick picks me up. During the drive, I tell him about the phone call for Sam the night before.

"Are these weird things just coincidences?" I ask.

"I don't know," he says. "But I still think the letter in the clouds was a sign."

I think about this. "It was backwards, right?"

"Yeah."

"When Sam wrote his name upside down at the airport restaurant before we left for L.A., he'd gotten the first letter backwards, too."

Nick doesn't say anything.

What am I implying? That Sam is capable of writing his name in the clouds, from the OTHER side of the sky – the heaven side – and he'd got the damn letter backwards again? Or maybe we're in a movie like *The Truman Show* and Sam, remembering how I complained that Universal Studios didn't show any real behind the scenes action, found the director's workstation and thought he'd have some fun with the sky-set.

"How are your mom and dad?" I ask.

"Awful. The only thing giving them comfort is knowing Sam is in a better place."

I shift in my seat. "Do *you* believe that?"

He nods. "I have to, Adri."

Angela meets us at the police station and we're directed to the parade room. When Sam's team is all seated, Tom goes around the room and introduces each officer. Then he requests that each person share a story about Sam. This surprises me – I expected business as usual.

"He always liked the car so damn hot," jokes one guy. "It was like a sauna inside."

"His favorite phrase," says another, "was: *Let's go catch some bad guys!*"

Whoops – false alarm! No bad guy here: sorry for the mix-up.

"I called him the energizer bunny," Amanda says, breaking the tense silence, "because he always had so much damn energy."

I lean forward. I've never heard Sam described as *energetic* before. But I also notice, for the first time, that Amanda looks and sounds kinda like me.

"We were partners that night," she continues from across the table. "He had all the equipment signed out and the car ready to roll by the time I got here."

Sam had always been an hour early for his shift.

"He told me all about your vacation, Adri. He said you guys had a riot."

Since Sam couldn't be with me on the last night of his life, maybe he spent it with the nearest approximation: a female friend similar to me in age, personality, character and appearance? I share the contents of my thought balloon with the group. Sam's teammates shift uncomfortably in their seats. Some stare at the table. One person coughs. You'd think I'd have learned to keep my obscure observations to myself.

Tom then informs his team that the detective in charge of investigating Sam's death will now give another debriefing.

"And you're welcome to stay for that," he tells Nick, Angela and me.

"Sure," I reply, before thinking the decision through.

As the detective begins to explain the sequence of events, I am aware of my body posture. I'm leaning back in my chair, with my left arm folded across my ribs. With my right hand, I'm resting my chin on my thumb, my forefinger on my cheek and my middle finger beneath my nose. I listen carefully to a replay of the last few minutes of Sam's life, complete with diagrams on a flipchart.

It started with a funny sounding alarm when the first employee of the day entered the building. The employee got suspicious and called police. The K-9 officer and Sam went into the warehouse together. There was a ladder the police dog could not climb so Sam did. It was dark. Sam stepped over some wiring and through a false ceiling: one fatal step from a solid surface to an unsafe one because there was no railing in place to mark the difference. The nine-foot fall. The dent in the drywall caused by Sam's flashlight. The black marks left behind on the wall from his boots. Sam's legs hit the back of a chair, projecting his upper body towards the lunchroom floor. The force and angle at which the back of his head struck the concrete caused a massive brain injury. The K-9 officer found Sam and immediately began CPR. Chaos ensued.

"Any questions?" asks the detective.

Sitting around listening to anecdotes about Sam is one matter; hearing the factual details of his death is quite another. It takes every ounce of strength I have to not disintegrate.

My hand goes up.

All chairs swivel to face me.

"What was *funny* sounding about the alarm?" I ask.

"That's a good question," replies the detective, "although we don't yet have an answer. So far, we think that when the employee arrived that morning, he heard – or thought he heard – several slow beep, beep, beeps, followed by a series of rapid beeps."

I lean back and fold my arms across my chest.

"The alarm sound he heard was one you'd usually hear right after an alarm has been set," the detective says. "This confused him so he called 911. What we do know for sure is that there was no intruder in the building."

I hold my hands out, palms up, and shrug.

"We'll be re-interviewing the employee. We will do everything we can to get all the answers."

Since criminals don't tend to reset alarms after they've broken into a place, *somebody* had to have set it – or was it malfunctioning?

And what about Sam? Did he suffer as he lay dying on the lunchroom floor? Why don't I ask this?

Because I already know the answer.

"And now," the Detective says, "I have something special for all of you."

He pops a video into the VCR, explaining this is a clip from one of Sam's courses.

Surprise! A living, breathing, laughing Sam appears on the TV monitor and I nearly fall off my chair at the shock of seeing him. He and his buddy have stuffed their clothes to make themselves look ridiculously muscular and, between fits of laughter, are instructing the group on how to work out. Sam points at the camera – at *us*. "VE VANT TO PUMP," he yells in a lousy Austrian accent, "YOU UP!"

Thank Christ I remember Sam showing me this video a couple of years ago, otherwise I'd be in cardiac arrest by now. I just buried him yesterday, for God's sakes, and not five minutes ago, heard confirmation that he gave his life protecting a premise that didn't need protection. I don't want to be PUMPED UP. I want some fucking answers.

As the video drags on, I become increasingly impatient and irritated. All I can think of is Sam's catch-phrase: *let's go catch some bad guys*. I have an overwhelming urge to stand up and tell everyone to stop slacking off and get back to work – myself included.

Tom finally releases his team back to the street and I am returned home to find my living room has been transformed into a flower shop. The funeral home dropped off all the bouquets from Sam's funeral so several of my girlfriends are over, sprucing up arrangements and re-labeling the tags so that some bouquets can be redirected for others to enjoy. How many flowers can one girl smell?

After Sam's former partner, Matt, and Anthony leave to deliver the flowers to various locations around the city, I sit on the couch with a cup of tea and a brownie. I stare at Tom's basket of autumn flowers on the coffee table and think to myself how beautiful they are . . . the ones left behind.

After tea, I head into my bedroom to start some serious grieving. I'm curled up in the fetal position, with Sasha at the foot of my bed, when my mom comes in the room.

She sits beside Sasha and squeezes my foot. "Oh, Bigoo . . ."

This is the long-form version of my nickname.

"I just came up to tell you that I'm going home," she says. "But I don't have to."

"No mom, that's OK."

"I can stay overnight. Your brother is staying over – but I can too, if you like."

I still haven't uncurled myself from the ball I'm in. "Nah, I'm fine."

She gets up, walks over and touches my cheek with the back of her hand. "I love you very much, Adri. I'm so sorry you have to go through this."

My tears spill over my nose onto the pillow. "I know."

"I'll help you any way I can, OK?"

"I'm gonna be all right, mom . . . some day."

She leans over and kisses me then walks out, softly shutting the door behind her. The house is still. I stare at Sam's shrine and I ask myself: why did he die?

The police are conducting their investigation; perhaps I shall conduct my own.

Two

My dad joins me at the off-leash park the next morning.

"I'm proud of you," he says partway through the walk. "You've been through an awful lot in a very short timeframe."

"Thanks." I throw the ball for Sasha.

"And there certainly doesn't seem to be a shortage of people offering you their opinion or religious belief."

I turn to him. "You don't believe in any of that God and Christian stuff do you?"

"That's a very general question, Adri."

"Do you believe there was a person called Jesus?"

"Yes."

"Do you believe he was the Son of God?"

"No."

"Who was he then?"

My dad sighs. "I think Jesus was probably a very kind and compassionate man who profoundly touched many people's lives."

"What about the Bible? How do you explain all his miracles and prophecies?"

"The Bible is a religious document written over hundreds of years," he says, throwing the ball, "which means there were many different people altering the original story of Jesus, likely to suit their own personal or political agenda."

"But how do you know that for sure?"

He stops and looks at me. "Read your history. The birth of Jesus didn't happen in a vacuum. The Jews and Arabs had been at each other's throats for centuries – that's what most of the Old Testament is about."

"Oh."

"The crisis going on today in the Middle East stems back thousands of years . . . there's a real danger in not understanding history."

"Dad, I just lost my husband. I can only handle so much right now."

He nods. "You're right."

"I guess I just want to know why you don't believe in Christianity."

He's quiet a moment. "Well, there are parts I believe in."

"Such as?"

"The common sense teachings of Christ – like treating others as you'd like to be treated yourself. I believe in *that*."

"But the story of Jesus, as a whole, you do not believe?"

"Look," he says, facing me. "I'm sure there are elements of truth to the story. But the chances of the whole thing being a completely, *literally* true story are extremely slim."

"So how do you know which parts are true?"

"That's up to the individual reader to decide, although common sense is always a good rule of thumb. Unfortunately, people believe what they *want* to believe – whatever makes them feel better."

"That's a pretty shitty thing to tell me right now," I reply, thinking that feeling better was my main goal at this point.

"I don't mean to upset you, Adri."

"Then don't."

"On the other hand, I'm not going to lie to you about my beliefs."

"So I see."

"I'm just concerned about all the religious crap coming at you. You've suffered a huge loss and a significant shock. That puts you in a very vulnerable position, so I just want you to be careful about what you choose to believe at this point."

"I want to be happy again," I say.

"Then be prepared to do the work to get yourself there because religious beliefs won't do that for you."

"They can *help*."

My dad shrugs. "It just seems to me that reality itself is far more miraculous than anything *we* could ever dream up or imagine."

I sigh and throw the ball for Sasha.

"So what's on this afternoon?" he then asks.

"Ed and I are choosing Sam's headstone."

"Would you like me to go with you?"

"Yeah."

An hour later, I'm tombstone shopping with my dad and Ed, the geologist in the family.

"You'll want granite," my brother advises, "because it's the strongest rock."

I nod. "Strong is important."

"And the carved lettering," he adds, "will never fade on granite."

I point to a shiny black stone. "What about this one?"

"Very nice," says my dad.

Ed suggests we find out where it's from.

"I believe it's from India," is the headstone guy's response. "But I'll have to check . . . I mean, we don't usually get asked that question."

"I hope it's from India," I say when he leaves to check.

Ed, also the traveler in the family, turns to me. "You've always been pretty keen on India haven't you?"

"Uh huh. Maybe one day I'll make it there."

"You will."

"Uh guys," says my dad, "what significance does *India* have in choosing a headstone for Sam?"

Ed and I look at our dad, as if he's the weird one.

"It's important to me is all," I say, not knowing why myself.

The headstone guy returns and confirms the stone is from a quarry in India.

"See?" says Ed. "Now you have a reason to go to India."

My dad shakes his head. "Which is . . ."

"So she can see the earth where Sam's rock was created."

"As for the epitaph," says the headstone guy, perhaps thinking today is not the best time to go into details, "our graphic artist will be in touch."

Ed accompanies me to the dog-park the next morning. Since he's catching a flight home to northern Ontario this afternoon, this is our last chance to visit.

"I can't believe you spoke at Sam's funeral," he begins, "I mean, that was quite something."

I shrug. "Well, I *am* determined to find some good in Sam's death."

"I know you are."

I pick up Sasha's tennis ball and huck it as far as I can. "It's my job."

I can't help but notice the concern on Ed's face.

"Sam touched a lot of lives, Adri. He won't be forgotten."

"I know. But I'm just worried that now all the excitement's over, people are just gonna carry on like nothing happened."

Ed stops walking. "People are going to do what they're going to do."

"What did you whisper in Sam's ear?"

"At his funeral?"

"Yeah."

We resume walking.

"I said, 'Good game, Sam . . . you played a good game.'"

I smile. "He really did, didn't he?"

"Yep. He accomplished everything he set out to. Sam's a real inspiration to me."

As we near the parking lot, I ask Ed if he has any more advice before he leaves.

"Nope. You're doing just fine on your own."

"But what about my finances?" I say. "I'm kinda freaked about all that."

"You can handle it – and what you can't, you ask for help. But just remember that free advice is free for a reason . . . and you tend to get what you pay for in life."

"So I should get a financial advisor?"

"That'd probably be wise, yeah. I've spent the past ten years hammering financial advice into you and Sam but your situation has really changed now." He lets out a little laugh. "That you've got your wills, retirement fund, mortgage and life insurance in order tells me you guys were listening after all."

"Don't you think it's a bit odd that we had our act together so young?" I ask.

"I think," he says carefully, "it was just common sense planning."

But on our California vacation, Sam and I had experienced his ideal retirement. We'd always joked that there'd be no motor home for us – just an open road with the top down. We did the convertible thing, sipped tall fruity drinks by the pool in Vegas, and held hands watching the sunset over the Grand Canyon.

Our vacation was an encapsulation of all the fun stuff life has to offer: sex, food, beaches, laughter, childhood, retirement. Could Sam have been on some sort of accelerated life plan? He died young but he accomplished more in his four years on the job than many people do in twenty-five. Even his hair had turned prematurely gray in those four years.

I turn to Ed. "Could there be some sort of greater plan at work here?"

He pauses a moment before replying. "If I were you, Adri, I'd be very careful about reading too much into things."

Three

After lunch, Dad and I take Ed to the airport while Anthony holds down the fort. Though only gone an hour, when I get home Anthony hands me a substantial list of phone messages.

I scan the names and point to a hastily scribbled sentence. "What's this?"

He takes the piece of paper and squints to read his own writing. "Oh right . . . a friend of yours from Vancouver called and said she wants to talk to you because," he makes mock quotations marks in the air, "He told her to call."

"He?" I say.

"Uh huh. That's why I wrote 'he' with a capital 'h.'"

I peer at the piece of paper, frowning. "He . . . as in Jesus?"

"I guess," my agnostic half-brother replies with a shrug. "I'm just the scribe."

"Well, that's strange. She's a Christian but I wouldn't expect that kind of message from her. I mean, she's usually pretty low-key."

"Call her and find out."

"I will – later."

First I have to get through Thanksgiving, Sam's favorite holiday. He'd loved it partly because it was the one holiday where he didn't have worry about buying presents.

"You're a bodge," I'd reminded him.

"Well yeah, but you gotta admit, it's kinda nice to just hang out with family without all the commercial pressures. Plus," he'd added, "I like how you and I bundle up and take hot chocolate with us for a walk around the neighbourhood."

Whoever planned this nightmare is pulling out all the stops. Why not throw in Thanksgiving for me to agonize through ten days after his death? I obviously need a few more character-building experiences.

For this year's festivities, I've been invited to Sunday dinner with Katrina's parents' and Monday dinner with Sam's family. Sam and I had usually spent holiday dinners with both our families, so I accept both offers. Besides, I'm eating for two now: my body and his spirit.

After Sunday dinner, Katrina's mom slips an envelope into my pocket on my way out the door. Inside is a Christian sympathy card with a handwritten note: "I noticed Sam died at thirty-two, which is very close to the age the Lord our Saviour was taken home."

At Sam's parent's place, a large photograph of Sam rests where his plate would normally be. We pray for his soul, toast his spirit and eat his favourite meal, all the while staring at his photograph and empty chair.

Back home, I down two glasses of sherry, put on Sam's clothes and collapse into bed. As much as I'd like to bundle up and go for our traditional walk around the neighbourhood with Sasha then curl up and watch our favourite Thanksgiving movie, I'm too damn exhausted from doing what everyone else wants me to be doing.

Tuesday, it is back to dealing with the business side of death. After breakfast, Tom comes over with a pile of papers to sign. I'm about to join him at the dining room table when I see Cassie and Cam – close friends of ours– and their daughter in my garden. I open the front door.

"Don't mind us," Cassie calls out from where she's kneeling in the dirt. "We're getting your garden ready for winter. I want to make sure you have tulips next spring."

I force a smile and thank her. But I don't want to be here when the tulips come up.

"I'm not sure if you're aware of this," Tom says, once I've sat down, "but because Sam passed away on the job, you're entitled to continue receiving his salary."

"No. I didn't realize that."

He nods. "For the rest of your life, actually."

I am thirty-two years old.

"Adri?"

"Don't ya think that's just a bit odd?"

"It's in our contract."

Shit! That means I *will* still be here in the spring because Sam would freak if I only collected seven months worth of compensation from the City.

"Are you sure you're up to handling this today?" Tom asks.

"Tomorrow will be the same as today."

But then his cell phone rings and he has to take the call. So my mind, recognizing the window of opportunity, takes off. Maybe I'm being paid Sam's salary to work? If Sam's death is part of some greater plan, then could I be working for, you know, the Big Guy? Or what about the idea my Simple Abundance book touched upon? When you begin to do what you love, you get a new employer: Spirit.

Only in this case, I seem to have got the new employer – whoever it is – so that I can begin to do what I love. Many times, Sam had told me that he wished he could figure out a way for me to stay home and write. For a writer, today's news is a dream come true. Why is it being delivered to me on the same platter as Sam's life?

When he's off the phone, Tom then tells me that in addition to the supplemental compensation, which is Sam's salary, I'll also be receiving the life insurance from his policy through the City. Did I just get a raise?

"And the payout from your own policy with the City," he says.

A bonus?

"Then there will be the financial settlement from workers compensation."

Another bonus?

"And there will also be a payment from the police association," he finishes.

"Sam always said he'd be worth more dead than alive."

Tom stares at me. I stare back.

"When Sam phoned you on Wednesday," I say, "and told you he wasn't going to work that night, did he give you a reason?"

"No. He just said he needed another court day. Why?"

Because if Sam had worked Wednesday night as he was scheduled to, then our walk in the park on Thursday wouldn't have happened and therefore, nor our argument about my writing.

"Just trying to put the pieces together," I say, resting my head on the table.

Tom starts to gather up his papers. "I think we've done enough for today."

Four

At 9:00 Wednesday morning, Dale arrives, briefcase in hand. We have an 11:30 appointment with a lawyer – a friend of Sam's who specializes in tax law and accounting.

Over the past few days, my brothers have come up with a game plan. Dale will spend every Wednesday helping me sort out the financial, legal and estate matters. Harry's job will be to manage the home front.

"You're a bit early, aren't ya?" I say to Dale. I'm still in my pajamas.

"We don't want to be late."

"But it's only . . ."

"And I thought we could pick up burgers for lunch on the way."

This expedites my getting ready.

At the lawyer's office, all three of us dig into burgers, fries and milkshakes. "It's kinda weird," the lawyer remarks, "but everything in regards to Sam's estate is working out perfectly."

"How so?" Dale asks.

"Well, most of the assets are in Adri's name while the debts are mainly in Sam's name. This means that very little money will be transferred into Sam's estate."

Dale nods. I eat a fry.

"And since Adri is the sole executor, disbursing these funds should be very straightforward."

"Will Sam's will need to be probated?" Dale asks.

"Probably not. From a legal and tax perspective, this is an ideal situation."

Two chairs swivel in my direction.

"Ya got me," I say then take a sip of my milkshake.

In the evening, I return the call to my Vancouver friend who'd left me the Jesus-message last week.

"I got a bit of a strange message to call you," I say, not mentioning the 'He with a capital h' detail.

There's a pause. "Adri, I know how swamped you are with phone calls these days, so to be honest I only called because YOU told me to. At Sam's funeral, you asked me to phone you, so I did."

"Oh."

"You don't remember?"

"No."

"Well, you were talking to a lot of people . . ."

But off to the races trots my mind. Anthony had clearly written down the message as 'He told her to call.' Anthony hadn't written she, which would have been me. Unless He is ME since I was the one who told her to call. But then wouldn't that mean that . . . OH SHIT, MAYBE I'M JESUS! What if I'm the long-awaited Second Coming of Christ, who just happens to have returned in female form? Wouldn't that piss off the Christian fundamentalists? 'We want a man!' they'll cry, pounding spikes into my pedicured feet. 'But I'm the Daughter of God,' I'll whisper, my life ebbing away as some kind soul gently dabs vinegar, preferably balsamic, on my parched lips. But then the work involved in being the Saviour . . . saving the planet and rescuing humankind from its suicidal path. Mind you, I will be receiving a regular paycheque for the rest of my life – I suppose I should do *something* useful. And I don't have a husband or kids. Still, that's an awful lot of responsibility placed on one gal's shoulders . . .

"Adri?"

"Huh?"

"Are you all right?" my friend on the phone asks. "It's awfully quiet."

"Oh sure," I say, giving my don't-you-worry-about-me wave to the nearest plant.

But lying in bed, I must confess to being a tad overwhelmed by my newfound fate – never mind the crushing weight of a massive ego.

When I wake the next morning, I laugh out loud at my ridiculous thought.

"You OK in there?" Harry asks from the hallway.

"Yup."

"Well, coffee's on and breakfast will be ready in a sec."

"Thanks!"

In the kitchen, I ask him what's on for today.

"The registry office," he replies.

I scrunch up my nose. "Ummm . . . what for again?"

"Sam's death certificate."

I snap my fingers. "Right."

An hour later, we're at the registry, waiting to pick up the documentation. I turn to Harry. "Do you remember how terrified of bears Sam was?"

"Yeah."

"Well, I've been thinking about that – his fear of bears, I mean. And you know how the markets are pretty wonky right now?"

He nods. "They've certainly been in better shape."

"So would you say we're probably headed into a bear market?"

"I think it's inevitable. What goes up must come down."

"And did you know Sam was a Taurus?" I ask.

"Er . . . no."

"And what is a Taurus," I say, "but a bull."

Harry shifts in his seat, clearly uncomfortable. "So?"

"So? So what if Sam's death marks the end of the bull market and the beginning of the bear one?"

Harry breathes in sharply, which I suspect is more a response to my state of mind than the state of the market. He's about to reply when the registry lady calls my number.

"I'd just be VERY careful with your investing these days," I say, wagging my finger at him as we walk up to the counter.

When 9:00 a.m. on Wednesday rolls around again, Dale's at my backdoor.

Our first stop today is the bank where our three-year old mortgage is held.

The banker offers me her condolences then opens up our file. "I just have a few papers for you to sign then we can discharge your mortgage."

At thirty-two, my home is paid for.

During the drive to buy burgers, I ask Dale if he's ever heard of Virginia Woolf.

"Vaguely."

"She wrote *A Room of One's Own*," I explain. "It's one of my favourite books. It's about the importance of women having a secure income and a room of their own in order to write."

He stops at a red light and turns to me. "What are you saying?"

"That Sam's death has not only given me a guaranteed paycheque for the rest of my life, I just received a whole friggin' house in which to write."

The light turns green and he resumes driving.

"Sam and I used to fight about that damn book," I continue.

"You guys fought over a *book*?"

"Yeah. Sam figured the motivation to write had to come from within, whereas Virginia Woolf figured outside factors – like a secure income and a quiet place to work – were also necessary."

"And what do you think?" Dale asks.

"That they're probably both right."

When we pull up to the drive-in, he turns to me. "Then I guess you know what you'd best be doing in that room of yours."

After lunch, we tackle most of the remaining debts. I write out a cheque to pay off our visa bill. Paying off our car loan and my student loan follows. When Dale takes me home at the end of the day, I ask him why he's so adamant that I deal with all the financial matters so quickly.

"Because they need to be dealt with and the sooner you do it the better," he replies, tapping the side of his head with his index finger. "You're gonna have a heck of a lot of other stuff to deal with."

The I-am-Jesus thought pops into my head again. I nod, blushing.

"The only remaining debt now," Dale continues, "is Sam's federal student loan and I've already written the government for you. If I can get them to forgive that loan, that'd be my parting gift to Sam."

I open the car door. "Oh, he'd be pretty pleased if you could pull that off."

Five

We're at the dog-park the next day when I ask Harry what the term soul mate means to him.

"Geez Googie . . . I don't know anything about that kinda stuff."

"That's why I'm asking you."

He sighs. "Let me think about it."

Home again, we're barely in the back door when the front

doorbell rings. I open it to find a police officer, wearing tall black boots and holding a large cooler.

I open up the lid; it's full of personal-sized lasagnes. "Thank you!"

He smiles. "My wife made them for you."

I invite him in for a coffee and we sit at the kitchen table.

"I hear you've traveled quite a bit," he begins.

"I guess."

"So where's next?"

"I dunno."

"Somewhere interesting, I'm sure."

But traveling is the last thing on my mind right now. I ask him which area of the police service he works in.

The officer sticks out one boot. "Traffic."

For dinner, Harry makes Caesar salad and garlic toast to accompany our lasagne.

"I have an answer for you," he says, passing me a piece of toast.

"To?"

"Your soul mate question."

"Cool."

"Soul mates," he says carefully, "are opposite sides of the same coin."

I nod slowly, recalling a long lost truth. "You're absolutely right."

This evening, there is a meeting about Sam's memorial fund. But just as I'm about to leave the house to go to the meeting, Charlie phones to tell me that the men attending tonight aren't actually involved with the fund.

"Well then who are they?" I ask.

"Senior officers and one of Sam's old college instructors – there's talk of using the money for a scholarship. But I don't think we should move so fast."

Judging by what I feel inside at the moment, neither do I. For in a matter of seconds, my anxiety has become unbearable. I hang up, creep over to my big chair and curl up into a quivering ball, which is how Harry finds me moments later.

"I can't go to the meeting!" I hiss.

"OK."

"This isn't how Sam's fund is supposed to play out."

"Should I call and tell them you can't make it?" he asks.

"Yes. And remind them NO decisions are to be made without us!"

"Holy shit, Goo. Relax."

"I can't relax," I say through gritted teeth, "because I can't lose any more fucking control than I already have."

Harry stares at me. I glare back. Then he goes into the kitchen and makes the call. When he returns, I'm curled up into an even tighter ball, shaking my head – sending a resounding 'no' out into the universe.

"I think it's time I talk to you know who," I say. "His card's on my desk."

"I was wondering when I'd hear from you, Adri," says the police psychologist a few minutes later.

"Here I am."

"What's up?"

"Everything."

"OK . . . what are you thinking about right now?"

"That I can't handle this."

There is a pause. Then: "I'm going to have to ask you a question now – more for ethical reasons than anything else, OK?"

"Uh huh."

"Are you having thoughts about taking your own life?"

Surprised, I sit up. "No. I mean, as much as I'd like to throw in the towel, I know I can't take the chance of screwing anything up."

"Such as?"

"Seeing Sam again. Suicide isn't part of the deal – I know that."

"Good. So what made you call me tonight?"

His question is akin to pulling the plug out of a bathtub; all the words rush out. "I'm just so incredibly anxious because too much has happened too fast -- and I miss him so much -- I can't stop thinking about stuff -- and everybody wants something . . ."

"What do you mean?"

In a wave of half-finished sentences, I tell him about to-night's meeting.

"You have to say no, Adri. You can only handle so much and right now, you're likely not in any shape to be dealing with Sam's memorial fund."

"I just want to make sure everything gets done right."

"I don't blame you. What's the rush anyway?"

"I don't know."

"Relax," he says. "Take it slowly – one hurdle at a time. As for all the other things on your mind, I think you better come in and see me."

"That's probably a good idea," I reply, thinking the Jesus-thought is a bit much for a phone conversation.

After hanging up, Harry and I go downstairs to watch TV to try this relaxation-concept. But instead, we come across a nature show and watch in horror as an entire pod of whales lie dying on the beach. Great. As the commentator gently strokes their massive backs, trying to comfort them as they pass away, I burst into tears on Sam's Perch.

"It's both a mystery and a tragedy," the commentator explains, "why these whales have chosen to die."

Oh ho! I can relate to that there pod of dying whales. Would they be going straight to Whale Hell? Wildlife purgatory? Would their suicide negate the possibility of them seeing their whale friends again?

"You OK?" Harry asks.

"Not really."

He changes the channel, pausing long enough on the latest images of violence in the Middle East for us to discern that the fighting between Israel and Palestine has really heated up again over the past few days.

"Maybe," I say, "those whales made their grand exit from here because they were disgusted with their living conditions.

Perhaps they perceived their oceans full of oil and garbage to be too hostile an environment into which to bring their off-spring."

Harry eyes me cautiously and resumes flipping channels.

"Stop!" I cry.

He pauses at an update of the US Presidential election fiasco and the voting recount taking place in Florida.

"Sam really liked Gore," I say. "He'd be very interested in all this."

Harry turns the TV off.

"Did you know he's very pro-environment?" I ask.

"Who?"

"Al Gore!"

"Goo?"

"Yeah?"

"Tomorrow you're going to see your doctor, right?"

"Uh huh."

"And you've booked an appointment with the psychologist for early next week?"

I nod but Harry seems to be waiting for me to say something else.

"I just can't seem to get my thoughts under control," I say. "It's as if everything that's happening in the world is somehow related to me."

"You're gonna drive yourself crazy."

"I know but it's kinda hard to stop."

"Well, you're going have to learn how. You're the only one who can control your thought patterns."

"I'm gonna have to do something," I say, "because this anxiety is brutal."

"Maybe your doctor can give you something for that."

Sure enough, the following afternoon my family doctor writes out a prescription then hands it to me.

"It's for a book," I say.

"And a good one," is his reply. "It's about relaxation."

"Thanks." I shove the paper in my purse. "So no drugs, huh?"

"Nope."

"What about those little blue pills I have for my migraines? Can I take those to help me sleep at night?"

He flips through my chart, finds the medication I'm referring to and gives me a stern over-the-top-of-his-reading-glasses look. "That might not be a bad idea for awhile."

From his office, I go straight to the pharmacy then hit the bookstore.

Back home, I start reading. Basic meditation, advise the authors, is a practical method that humans have used for thousands of years to cope with stress. Buddhism utilizes meditation in order to quiet the mind. Drooling at the prospect of this, I flip to the chapter that explains how I am to achieve the miracle. The technique suggests repeating a word or simple phrase and passively disregarding the recurring thoughts.

"God is Love," I say, sitting cross-legged and cradling a steaming cup of tea.

Sam is dead!

God is love, I whisper back.

You're on your own.

God is love! I hiss.

He's gone, honey.

God is love?

It's over.

The phone rings. It's Nick, asking me if I'd heard about their cousin's dream.

"No."

"He saw Sam in his dream and said he looked really happy."

"That's good," I say. At least one of us is.

"Then Sam said something to the effect of 'I love having all my debts paid off.'"

I look around my living room and smile. Then I go upstairs, swallow two little blue pills, climb into bed and pass out for nine hours.

Six

The next morning, Harry comes downstairs to find me at my computer. It's exactly two weeks since Sam died. I remove the earphones I wear when I'm writing – the same kind the airline workers wear on the tarmac.

"Hi!" I say.

"Hi."

"How did you sleep?" I ask.

"Fine thanks. You?"

"Fabulous."

Harry folds his arms over his chest. "Are you OK?"

"Uh huh."

"Googie . . . have you been writing?"

Have you been smoking? Drinking? Sneaking out the bedroom window again?

"You betcha."

"How long have you been down here?"

"Fifteen minutes."

Harry sighs. "I'll be upstairs if you need me."

I last ten more minutes. After typing several rambling pages of chaotic thoughts and feelings, the grand total of words I'm satisfied with is two: "Sam fell."

That much is clear.

As Harry is serving us homemade hashbrowns and sunny-side up eggs on toast, he asks how the writing went.

"It isn't going to be easy," I reply, stuffing in a spoonful of potatoes. "But at least I know what I have to do."

Standing in the kitchen, with a tea towel in one hand and a frypan in the other, my brother – the chief worrier in a family full of worriers – is clearly concerned.

"I'm going to write our story," I say.

"Sam died two weeks ago."

"Yes. I realize that. But I have to do this."

He opens the cupboard and places the frypan inside. "Why?"

"Because it's my job."

I put my dirty dishes in the sink and am on my way back downstairs when Harry says, "Remember that the police want to meet with you today."

I turn around. "Ummm . . . what for again?"

"Sam's investigation, Adri."

"Right."

Harry takes me to the police station, where we're directed again to the parade room. Tom and the two detectives are waiting for us. The main detective starts off by saying they've further investigated the alarm question.

"Uh huh," I say, suspiciously eyeing a storage box on the table.

"There's still confusion," he explains, "as to what sound the employee heard that caused him to call 911."

I lean back in my chair, assuming Sam's best thinking position.

"The alarm," adds the other detective, "actually went off twice earlier that night."

I blink. Surely I didn't hear correctly. "Pardon me?"

The first detective clears his throat. "The alarm went off two other times that night and both times, it was false. Apparently, a hole in one of the overhead doors was triggering the alarm."

"A worker had driven a forklift into the door the day before," adds Detective Two, "leaving a large hole – and the wind going through it likely set the alarm off."

"You're fu . . . kidding me, right?" is my response.

"They're not yet through investigating," Tom says.

"But the company was ordered to put up a safety railing," says the first detective, "and they immediately complied with that order."

A hell of a lot of good that's gonna do Sam now.

"The final police report will be completed in January," continues the first detective, "and the Occupational Health and Safety report sometime after that."

The second detective stands up. "We also have a few more of Sam's personal effects for you."

Ah, the contents of the box. I, too, stand up for this portion of the program. But out come Sam's running shoes, worn at Disneyland as well as to work on the last night of his life. Next is his fuzzy gray jacket. Not feeling so good, I sit down again. His security clearance card and identification tag follow, then his keys. Then the twenty-dollar bill and loose change, last seen in the plastic bag at the hospital, appear.

Detective One hands Sam's holster to me. "That held his gun. But we obviously can't give you the weapon."

I smile. "Probably not a good idea, no."

As I watch the second detective place the items back inside the box, I do a mental recap. On the day Sam died, I received his watch and chain; the next day, his cross and medal were returned to me. At his funeral, I was given his hat and badge. Is all this evidence for my investigation into Sam's death?

Tom lifts a black duffle bag from the floor and, with a pained expression, hands it to me. "Here's Sam's duty-bag. I thought you might want it."

After leaving the police station with what remains of Sam's career neatly divided between a box and a bag, Harry drives me to the cemetery. The two of us stand on the freshly packed dirt, staring at the white wooden cross temporarily marking Sam's grave.

"I still don't believe this," Harry says.

"Oh, it's pretty real to me now," I reply, dropping to my knees.

Harry returns to the car to give me some time alone with Sam.

"You are my sunshine," I sob, rocking back and forth. "My only sunshine . . ."

"You must be his wife."

I look up to see a middle-aged woman standing beside me. "Yeah."

"I'm sorry for your loss, dear."

"Oh. Well, thank you. I . . ."

"But your husband is facing the wrong way," she says.

"Excuse me?"

"Jesus is coming back from the East – and your husband is facing West."

Before I can formulate a response, she turns and walks away.

Back at the car, I tell Harry what the crazy lady said.

"That's why you've got your bullshit filters," he says.

"My what?"

"Your bullshit filters. Just like those big-ass headphones you wear when you're writing, bullshit filters are your best line of defense against all the crap that's coming at you. Remember that you *choose* what you let into your mind."

Then he drives what's left of me home.

On the kitchen table is another box, with an attached note, on the table. I place Sam's box and duty-bag on the floor then pick up the note and read my dad's handwriting: "The funeral home dropped these off for you."

I lift up the lid and a waft of formaldehyde hits me. I grab a handful of the leftover memorial service pamphlets and am frantically sniffing them when Harry walks in the back door.

"Sam's here!" I cry. "Oh my God, I can smell him!"

Harry's face crumples. "Seeing you go through all this," he says, "is the toughest thing I've ever had to do."

"Well, it's no picnic experiencing it either!" I snap.

Then I grab my precious cargo and stomp up to my room.

I place Sam's duty-bag on the bed and unzip it. Resting right on top of the other items is a city-map folded open. I pick it up: it's open to the location of Sam's fall. This is one of the last things Sam would've touched.

But I know I've had enough for today, so I carefully place the map back in the bag, zip it up and put it on the chair.

Meanwhile, Harry does what he can to redeem this incredibly shitty day among many by making me an onion casserole for dinner. He dishes me up a huge plateful, saying, "This'll give ya some fantastic farts tomorrow."

Seven

Unfortunately, the next day is my first non-death-related social engagement. The Hope Chaplain's wife asked me if I'd like to attend a weekend retreat for spouses of police officers. That my husband isn't a living officer doesn't seem to pose a problem – at least not in terms of my qualifications as a participant.

"I don't know about this," I say from the backseat, cranking down the window and hoping no one notices. "I feel like I have 'worst case scenario' stamped on my forehead. Who's gonna wanna talk to the widow of a cop who just died on duty? I mean, they're obviously going to this retreat thing to get *away* from the stresses of being married to a police officer."

"You don't have to go," Harry says. "I can still turn around."

"It might be really good for her," adds Katrina.

Harry turns off the highway onto a side road and drives through a wooded area, until pulling up alongside a beautiful log cabin.

"Are you sure you want to do this?" he asks me.

"She'll be fine," Katrina assures us all.

After I receive my information package, I take a seat and am waiting for the festivities to begin when a woman sits besides me.

"I just want to say how sorry I am about Sam," she says.

"Thank you."

"How are you doing?"

I shrug. "OK I guess."

"I won't pretend to know what you're going through, Adri. But I do want to tell you about my own experience."

I smile, inwardly groaning. Please not another goddamn story about losing your ninety-year-old grandmother back when you were twelve.

"I lost my first husband when I was twenty-two," she says.

I don't like the adjective 'first' one bit.

"I was very angry at God," the woman continues. "I really lost my faith in Him."

"Uh huh."

"And then a few years later, I met the most incredible guy . . ."

My stomach tightens.

"And he became my second husband."

Traitor!

"And now," she finishes, "we have two wonderful kids."

I want to smack her across the face.

"I'm glad it worked out for you," is what I say.

"Please take care," she says then sashays off to her happy little life.

I *wish* I'd farted.

The first speaker of the day is a policewoman, the partner of a city police officer who'd been violently killed in the line of duty eight years earlier. As far as my mental health is concerned, things are not looking up. I've come here to retreat from my new reality – hearing about another cop's death doesn't seem overly conducive to that.

"I'm going to talk about the actual incident," she says, looking directly at me, "so I hope this won't offend anyone."

I give her the nod. I've come this far, haven't I?

"I remember one moment seeing my partner laying down the spikebelt – that's the belt with spikes on it which is used to stop vehicles – and then watching his body being torn into two pieces the next."

OK, I really ought to have stayed in bed this morning.

"And the car that hit him just kept on going . . ."

I swallow rapidly, trying not to throw-up. What a fun retreat!

"I went on the radio," she continues, "and thought I was speaking normally but when they played me the tape later, all you could hear was this horrible high pitched wail."

The room is silent.

She looks at me. "It didn't even sound human. They say shock does funny things to people."

The I-am-Jesus-thought springs to mind. I sink lower in my chair. The woman goes on to describe how the deceased officer's sister worked diligently to raise public awareness about the need for a police helicopter.

My ears perk up. Helicopter?

"His sister realized that similar incidents might be prevented in the future because the necessity for car chases, and the use of spikebelts, would be reduced if there was a helicopter to do those chases instead."

Up till now, I hadn't known the history of our police helicopter.

"Sufficient money was eventually raised to purchase the helicopter," she finishes, "but it took my partner's death to get this done."

As I'm scarfing down my third donut during the coffee break, I decide that my attendance at this retreat is no coincidence. Clearly, not only is there a greater plan at work, it's one I'm meant to be figuring out. Maybe the helicopter story is supposed to teach me what to do in the wake of Sam's death? But if so, what would I raise awareness *about*?

After the break is the main speaker.

"My goal today," she says, waving her arms as her cape – yes, that's right, cape – swings behind her, "is to get each of you to come up with a personal mission statement. I want you to ask yourself: what is YOUR life purpose?"

Who the hell wears a cape nowadays?

"So let us start today's journey with . . ."

The police chief did at Sam's funeral!

". . . the world around us."

And that certainly marked the end of his career. Is the cape-clad chick at the front of the room signifying the start of mine? For the meaning of my life seems a logical place to begin unraveling the mystery of Sam's death.

"For it is in the natural elements," says the speaker, "that we're often able to see our own selves."

I nod. What harm can a little more self-analysis do?

"So what are you?" she asks. "Earth, wind, fire or water?"

Sam would be rolling his eyes about now. I, in contrast, eat this stuff up.

"Take a few minutes to think about your personal qualities – and which element those most represent."

That's easy. I'm water – constantly moving and full of chaotic energy.

Sam is earth – solid and dependable.

Next?

"Now write down the qualities of your element and then draw from the list of action verbs to come up with your one-line personal mission statement."

To grow, change and fertilize happiness.

Hmmm . . .

To fish, float and cleanse thought.

Oh dear.

To live, act and give love.

Perfect! It sounds lovely – even though living, acting and loving don't have much to do with water. However, it is a start.

Armed with my newfound purpose in life, neatly wrapped in a single sentence yet, I then proceed to spend the next hour belly dancing as that just happens to be the only afternoon activity that interests me. I tell myself Sam is smiling down at me from heaven, watching everything. Well, maybe not the *whole* retreat . . . he sure as heck isn't paying any attention to the craft room where a bunch of ladies are sticking buttons on jars.

On the way home, Katrina asks me how it went. I tell her about the exercise in discovering one's life purpose.

"You've been busy," says Harry.

"Yeah but then some lady told me how she'd lost her husband at a young age and then remarried a couple of years later and popped out a coupla kids."

All's quiet in the front seat.

"I will NEVER remarry," I say.

Katrina turns to face me. "Well, you never know what could happen ten years from now . . ."

I feel the panic rising. "Oh, but I DO know! You can't have two soul mates!"

"Calm down, Adri," says Harry. "Nobody says you have to remarry."

"Damn rights."

Then I fold my arms tightly across my chest and stare out the window in silence all the way back to the city. We stop at a restaurant for fish and chips, which temporarily cheers me up. But halfway through the meal, it suddenly seems wrong for me to be doing something as normal as eating in a restaurant – without Sam.

"I need to go home," I announce as the anxiety builds again.

Harry requests our meals be packed in doggie bags and we leave.

At home, I head straight to my room, sit on the edge of the bed and close my eyes. "God is Love," I whisper.

God's an idiot.

I open my eyes and see Sam's duty-bag on the chair. I walk over, unzip the bag and pick up the folded-open map. I flip to the front but its Amanda's name on the cover. So this *wouldn't* have been one of the last things Sam touched because he would've been driving. Amanda would've been co-pilot, so it makes sense this is her map.

Eight

Harry has to return to work tomorrow so Dawson, a gay friend of mine, takes over Adri-sitting. Figuring s'mores might be good comfort food, we roast marshmallows on forks over the stove after dinner.

"If Sam could see us," I say, "I bet he'd be howling."

"Oh, I'm pretty sure he can," Dawson replies, turning his fork over to brown the other side of the marshmallow.

"But where do you think he is?"

"Heaven – for lack of a better term."

"I didn't think you believed in heaven," I say.

"Before Sam died, I didn't."

"So what made you change your mind?"

"It just doesn't make sense that someone as decent as Sam would die without there being a reason for it."

"But what's heaven got to do with that?"

He thinks about this. "Well, heaven may be a better place than here but I highly doubt it's perfect."

I put my toasted marshmallow between two graham crackers and pull the fork out. "Don't forget the chocolate," he says.

I laugh. "Like that's gonna happen."

"I mean, Sam was one of the people actually doing some good here on earth so why would he get taken unless he was needed for something else?"

"So you think Sam is somehow working in heaven?" I ask.

"It's possible. But who really knows? I mean, aside from . . ."

I hold up my hand, like a cop stopping traffic.

"What?"

"Don't say God."

"Why?"

"Because if I hear one more time how Sam's death is part of God's plan and therefore I ought to accept his death and move on, I'm gonna snap. The existence of some grand plan is ludicrous if nobody on earth knows what it *is*."

"But . . ."

"It's like a CEO," I interrupt, waving my s'more, "who creates a brilliant business plan for her corporation and then buggers off, leaving her employees to try and run the company without actually letting anyone *read* it."

Dawson, a business student, smiles. "That's not a bad analogy."

On the second of November, Tom calls to let me know his team has something for me, and could I drop by the station later this afternoon to pick it up?

But I'm developing a bit of an aversion to the old parade room. If I'm not hearing about the angle and force at which Sam's head hit the concrete or being told that he died searching for a non-existent bad guy because the *wind* set the alarm off, then I'm being given personal articles of clothing he'll never wear again.

"Is this a good surprise?" I ask Tom. "Or a bad one?"

"Good. I promise."

Sam's team has just finished dayshift so the parade room is full when I walk in.

"We had this made for you," Tom says, handing me a beautiful framed picture of a wolf. "It's in memory of Sam."

"Thanks!" I reply, genuinely excited. "Wolves are very significant to us."

His face brightens. "Really?"

"Yeah. We even sponsor a wolf in the wild. Her name is Nakoda."

"Well, I'm glad you like it," he says.

"I love it!"

Tom smiles. "We're heading to the pub now for a drink, if you'd like to join us."

In the pub, I sit beside him. One of Sam's teammates sits on the other side of me. I'm halfway through my beer when the teammate asks me how I'm doing.

"Hanging in there."

"Adri?"

I turn to him. "Yeah?"

"I, uh . . . I was with Sam in the ambulance."

I place my beer bottle on the table as the air in this room gets sucked out.

"What was he like?" I ask, terrified of the answer.

"Unconscious."

"The whole time?"

"Yes. He was completely out of it."

"Oh."

The officer clears his throat. "I was also in the emergency room when they first brought you in to see Sam."

My most horrific moment comes crashing back.

"And for what it's worth," he says, "seeing you that day was the worst experience of my career. I've never seen a human being look so . . . vulnerable."

I force a smile. "That's a good word for it."

Except that it's now been five weeks since Sam's death and I'm feeling *more* vulnerable with each passing day.

The next afternoon, I visit Sam's parents as per his mom's request.

"What the heck is all *this*?" I ask, walking into the kitchen.

The kitchen table and the top of the two beds in the spare bedrooms are covered with bags of supplies and containers filled with what appears to be grains of wheat mixed with red seeds.

"It's for Sam's forty-day ceremony tomorrow," his mom says.

"Oh."

"When a loved one passes away, Adri, this is what we must do."

I scrunch up my nose. "But *what* do you do with all this stuff?"

"That's what I'm going to show you."

I watch as she sprinkles icing sugar on top of one of the mixtures. Then, tears flowing, she places a piece of waxed paper on top and uses both hands to gently smooth out the icing sugar beneath.

"But what," I ask from the peanut gallery, "does this *mean*?"

"Well, the wheat symbolizes what's left behind when the seed goes on to new life – just as the human body is the shell left behind when a person passes away."

"OK . . ."

"And the seed represents the soul that has gone on to eternal life with God."

I point to the mixture. "The wheat seed? Or the red one?"

"That's a pomegranate seed."

"So which one represents the . . ."

"*Your* job," she says, reaching into a plastic bag, "is to decorate this mixture."

So, under her watchful gaze, I place candied almonds and silver decorations around the edges of the icing sugar. Then I stick a silver-studded cross in the middle.

The next day, at Sam's Greek Orthodox forty-day service – November 4th – I find myself in the front row again, this time with the chief of police beside me.

"Adri," she whispers, "what exactly is the significance of today?"

Having been well briefed myself by this point, I reply: "Apparently these past forty days have been a time of reflection for Sam's soul. From the ninth day to the fortieth day, the Archangel – St. Michael – took Sam back to review all the good and bad deeds he's done over his lifetime. And today is the day St. Michael takes Sam to God, where he is told what work he'll do in heaven."

"I see," she says, then resumes staring straight ahead.

The ceremony itself is sadly reminiscent of Sam's prayer and funeral services. In case we weren't paying attention the first two times, we listen again to an hour of chants in ancient Greek accompanied by the powerful smell of incense. Instead of Sam's dead body, however, now there is a large photo of him at the front of the church.

After the service, the congregation is directed to the hall, where each person is given a small white bag containing the wheat mixture. Most of our non-Greek family and friends suspiciously sniff their packets. Out of courtesy to Sam's parents, I devour mine. Crunch goes the pomegranate seed. Am I symbolically eating Sam's soul, his body, or both? Finding none of these possibilities remotely comforting, I toss back a shot of throat-burning brandy and continue my own spiritual quest.

"So let me get this straight," I say to the nearest Greek lady, "today is not only Sam's forty-day ceremony, it's also St. Michael's day – according to the Greeks?"

"That's right."

I gulp another glass of brandy and approach the Tall Chaplain. "So lemme get this right: according to you Catholics, *September 29th* is St. Michael's day?"

He nods. "And since St. Michael is also the patron saint for peace officers, that's why we hold a Mass on that date every year."

"Huh?"

"*That's* why we just happened to be having a Mass for police officers on September 29th."

"You were?"

"I thought you knew that, Adri."

"Are you telling me that Sam died on the same day as a Mass planned specifically for police officers?"

"All peace officers, yes."

"And you don't think that's just a bit of a coincidence?"

"There are no coincidences."

I throw up my hands. "Then why am I the only person trying to make sense of what's going on?"

He opens his mouth but I hold up my hand. "Don't say God's plan."

"OK," he replies, smiling.

I pull out Sam's medal. "What about St. Jude? I thought he was the Patron Saint of police officers?"

"It depends on what you read. St. Jude is mainly known as the patron saint of desperate or hopeless causes – and hospitals, too, if I remember correctly."

Geez . . . maybe Sam really *was* with Jesus and Jude the day he died – AND St Michael the Archangel! I toss back another shot of brandy and resume wandering, half-cut, around the room full of family and friends – most of whom have no clue as to the religious meaning of the day but have simply come to support me. Regardless of what may or may not be going on in the spiritual realm, I'm certainly getting the sense that both Sam and I are in good hands. We just aren't together.

"Adri?"

I recognize that voice. I whip around.

Tom asks how I'm doing. Funny, I've never noticed before how blue his eyes are.

"Not bad," I reply, smiling. "Thanks for coming today."

"You're welcome. Would it be all right if I drop by your place tomorrow?"

"Sure!"

"I have another insurance cheque for you."

"Oh."

Nine

The following afternoon, Tom is standing in front of my fireplace, where the wolf picture from Sam's team rests on one chair and the blue 'mean streets' picture from his recruit class sits on another. In front of the blue picture is a small branch, which Tom asks me about.

"It's from an olive tree," I explain. "Sam's family sent it from Greece. It's for when a hero dies."

"Oh man . . ."

I nod. "I know. I haven't let my heart go there yet."

I walk over and sit in my big chair. Tom sits on the couch.

"Can I ask you a question?" I say.

"Sure."

"Do you pray?"

"Yes."

"What do you pray *for*?"

He tilts his head to one side. "It's strange you'd ask me that because ever since Sam died, I find that I'm praying differently. I don't ask for specific things from God anymore. My prayers are less selfish . . . now I pray for other people not myself."

I nod. "That's how Sam prayed."

"Really?"

"Yup. He said the exact same prayer every night before going to bed. He just asked God to look after me, his family and friends – and that was it."

"You and Sam talked about everything, didn't you?"

"Uh huh," I reply. "That's what's getting me through this."

Tom looks to the floor then back at me. "Adri, I know how close you and Sam were, so don't take this the wrong way. But I don't think your shared past is the only thing that's going to help you."

Thinking he's referring to my support system, I say: "Well, I know all my friends and family and you guys are helping, too . . ."

He shakes his head. "That's not what I meant."

"Oh."

"I just think that you're going to have to find your *own* path."

"But it's Sam's path," I hear myself say, as if finally remembering my lines to a script memorized long ago, "that will lead me to that."

Soon after Tom leaves, my doorbell rings, sending Sasha into a barking frenzy. Standing on my front porch, with a suitcase in one hand and container of peanut butter cookies in the other, is this week's Adri-sitter: Kristy, a friend of mine since Junior High.

Over lasagne, I ask for her help getting my photos in order.

"Of course," she says.

"Tonight."

Up go both brows. "Are you *sure* you're ready to do that?"

"I think so." Because with me gone, who else will do it?

"What's the rush?"

I shrug. "I just want stuff organized."

So, over hot chocolate and cookies, Kristy and I devise a plan. I'll sort the photos into chronological order and she'll place them into albums.

I soon come across a picture taken of Sam at a New Year's Eve party back when we were twenty-one. He's wearing a shower cap, grinning and waving at the camera.

"Geez, do you remember this night?" I ask Kristy.

"Yeah."

"He got a straighter nose out of the deal, you know."

Sam had ended up in hospital after getting into a fight in the hotel elevator. Actually, it wasn't much of a scrap; two guys had sucker-punched him in the face, breaking his nose and shattering his cheekbone. The cosmetic surgeon had asked Sam if, while he was wiring up his cheekbone would he also like the bump filed off his nose.

"Well why not, eh, Adri?" Sam had snorted at me through the bandages.

Killing two birds with one stone was reflective of his life philosophy. The wiring of his cheekbone was a necessary repair;

improving the shape of his nose was an added bonus. Maybe grief works like that too. While coming to terms with Sam's death, perhaps I ought to deal with a few other issues, such as us not having a child . . .

"Adri?"

I look up.

"Are you all right?" Kristy asks. "You look pretty pale."

"Did I ever tell you about the oil Sam's mom rubbed on his face after that surgery?"

She shakes her head. "I don't think so."

"Well, she put some sort of holy oil on Sam's face and when the doctor removed the bandages the next day, the bruising had disappeared – but only where the oil had touched his skin."

"Oh."

"You could see a really clear line between the bruised area where the bandage had covered his skin," I say, "and the healed area where the oil had done its thing."

Kristy looks rather concerned. "Are you sure you're OK?"

"Mmm . . . hmmm . . ." I reply and resume sorting pictures.

I come to a lakeside photo I'd taken of Sam during a camping trip years ago. I recall the source behind his flushed face wasn't just a tan but another afternoon spent with me in our tent. Then I whip past a cute shot of him cleaning the oven in our first apartment, then a picture of him lying on our old futon in his pajamas, wearing glasses and reading a textbook. I flip faster.

"Let's take a break," Kristy suggests.

"Soon."

I come to a photo of me and Sam at my farewell party prior to my seven-month backpacking trip. There are only six months left till I see him again – and I won't even be picky about the reunion details: eternity, heaven, the afterlife, reincarnation, hell, purgatory or a combination there-of . . .

Kristy reaches over and removes the photographs from my hands. "That's enough for today, my friend."

The next day, I return to a task somewhat higher on the list of priorities – and less emotionally onerous. The graphic artist wants to discuss with me the wording and artwork for Sam's headstone. I take Angela along, partly because I value her opinion but also because I no longer trust my own.

"How about a photograph of Sam?" the artist suggests.

I shake my head. "What if some kid draws a mustache on him or something?"

"Uhhh . . . you don't see that very often," is her reply. As an alternative, she suggests a laser etching of his badge.

I think of Sam doing similar work in heaven that he did here on earth. "That's not a bad idea," I say.

She then asks if I have any ideas for his epitaph. I shrug and look to Angela.

"Let's check with my mom to find out what other Greeks have on their headstones."

"The closest English translation," Sam's mom says an hour later, over lunch at her kitchen table, "is *Until We Meet Again*."

"Done," I say.

Then I resume eating enough meatballs, spanikopita, tirama, bread and olives to sink a battleship. I'm reaching for yet another meatball when Sam's dad gets up from the table and leaves the kitchen. We hear him crying softly in the living room.

Sam's mom looks at me. "He is *so* worried about you, Adri."

I give her the wave. "I'll be fine."

On November 10th, Stan and his wife, Megan – now eight months pregnant – fly in from Vancouver to visit me. They wake up on Remembrance Day morning to find me sobbing in front of the TV. The two of them squish together on the loveseat while I remain sprawled out on Sam's Perch and we all watch the wreath ceremony at the Parliament Buildings in Ottawa.

How many people will bother to take a moment out of their crazily busy lives to *stop* for two lousy minutes of silence? Just like the soldiers who had died to secure our freedom, so, too, had Sam given his life protecting the peace we take for granted.

Who remembers the dead soldiers and surviving veterans? Who will remember Sam?

Stan asks me what I'm thinking.

"That people don't appreciate that Sam gave his life serving this goddamn city."

He and Megan stare at me, mouths open.

"Sam will never be forgotten," says Megan.

"In the ways that matter," I reply, "he already is."

"Adri!" she cries.

Although I know our family and friends and the officers close to Sam won't forget him, is simply *remembering* enough? What about asking a few questions? Like why do we need to alarm our homes and workplaces in the first place? Why are there so many break and enters? Why is our legal system more concerned with protecting the rights of the bad guys than the rights of the victims, or those of the peace officers trying to enforce the law? Why do we accept crime and violence in society with a shrug of the shoulders and a flip of the channel? Why does the responsibility for maintaining peace and order fall on the shoulders of police officers, but the real power and money goes to big business? What about the circumstances that led to Sam's fall – doesn't anyone else find them unacceptable? Why does everyone else get to go on with their precious little lives, baking and having babies while I'm stuck asking the questions that no one else, it seems, can be bothered to?

"It's like people have written off Sam's death as a freak accident," I say.

"I don't know what to think," is Stan's reply.

"Well for God's sakes," I snap, "think *something*."

All three of us resume staring at the TV until Megan breaks the silence by suggesting we visit Sam.

When we arrive at the cemetery, we find his candles lit and fresh footprints in the snow.

"Sam's mom and dad have already been here," I explain. "They come every day."

We toast Sam with brandy snifters full of sherry then Stan empties Sam's glass out onto his grave. I watch as the liquid soaks into the snow and think back to the three of us standing beside Sam in his ICU room. How solid is Sam now?

Stan looks at me. "If you need *anything*, let me know. Sam made me promise that if something ever happened to him, I'd take care of you."

"He said that?" I ask.

"A few times, actually."

I drink the rest of my sherry. "Everybody wants to help me by phoning or sending a card or dropping off food. But as grateful as I am for all the support, what I really want is assurance that Sam's death wasn't in vain."

"People help you in ways they know how," Megan says.

"But I can only eat so many cookies! What I *need* is help solving the problem."

"Is Sam's death a problem to be solved?" Stan asks.

I nod towards the white cross marking his grave. "You're goddamn right it is."

Megan places a hand on my shoulder. "Adri . . ."

I turn to Stan. "You're an investment banker – do you know of anyone who could handle my finances?"

Ten

By mid November, the weather has shifted again and the snow from Remembrance Day melted away. It's now been six weeks since Sam's death and I've been deemed sane enough to stay at home alone. With the constantly ringing phone, drop-in visitors, requests for coffee, appointments, writing and relentless thinking, I figure when bedtime rolls around, I'll be too tired to notice no one's in the spare room. That Sam isn't in bed beside me, however, is still a significant source of concern.

I meet up with Mark and Charlie for lunch to discuss the funds being raised in Sam's memory.

"I appreciate all you've done," I tell them. "But I'm really concerned we do the right thing with the money."

"Then let's take our time," Charlie says.

"Pin sales are going well," adds Mark. "Ten thousand bucks so far."

"That's a lot of cash," I say, taking a mammoth bite of my chicken sandwich.

Charlie nods. "And a lot of court time."

Sam had cashed in most of his court time to pay for our California vacation. So, since officers were donating their court time to Sam's fund that meant their hard-earned money wasn't going to family holidays or buying braces for their kid's teeth. Maybe that's why the earlier meeting had upset me so much. The money donated by police officers should go back to the police community – not college students.

I devour a fork full of fries, followed by a swig of beer. "This is weird, isn't it? Me having lunch with you guys, instead of Sam?"

"You eat as much as he did," Charlie teases.

Mark smiles. "Or more."

"Hah hah. By the way," I say to Mark, "I did tell Sam you wanted to meet him for lunch."

He nods. Charlie looks at him.

"Adri took a report from me right before they went on vacation," says Mark.

I nod. "It ended up being my very last one."

"There are more than a thousand cops in this city," Charlie says, flipping his thumb towards Mark. "What are the chances your last report would be from this clown?"

Pretty slim, I'd say . . . signpost-slim.

Back home, I'm sorting through the mail for sympathy cards when I see a large envelope from the wolf conservation organization Sam and I belong to. Thinking that reading about Nakoda, the radio-collared wolf we've sponsored for the past three years, might cheer me up, I open the envelope.

Nope. A hunter had shot her on September 22nd – the day Sam and I had been at Disneyland. Through my tears, I read how the nine-year old alpha female had been sighted outside the small, protected area allotted to wolves. Since the hunter hadn't noticed the collar around her neck, identifying her off limits for hunting, he'd shot her. For several weeks, her pups and pack-mates had repeatedly returned to the den site, either searching for her or grieving her death. Oh, how I can relate.

I phone the Hope Chaplain. "This," I sob, "*hurts*."

"I bet. I noticed you have a lot of pictures of wolves in your home."

"Yeah . . . we both liked them."

Then he says, "Maybe Nakoda is now Sam's companion, just as Sasha is yours."

It's OK for *me* to say weird shit like this but when other people do, it really does sound ridiculous. "Maybe. But let me guess: this, too, is part of God's plan and therefore none of my business to figure out?"

"Not necessarily," is his reply.

I decide it might not be a bad idea to have Sasha blessed after all. Sam is dead; Nakoda is dead; I'll be dead in six months. The least I can do is save our dog.

The following Tuesday, I march my mother and Sasha downtown to church. My Anglican reverend – the man who married me and Sam – has agreed to bless her, even though we're now two months past the 'blessing of the animals' ceremony. But when he leans over to touch Sasha's head, she snaps and snarls at him. I struggle to hold her back, apologizing profusely. Then I take my seat in the pew and Sasha climbs up beside me. I can almost hear Sam laughing.

After the service, I ask the reverend to explain the difference between the soul and the spirit.

He thinks about this. "I would say that the spirit is the life force of the soul."

"Ah, yes . . ." I reply, nodding as another long lost truth clicks into place.

Then he asks me how I'm doing.

I flash him a big smile. "Not bad."

"Honestly?"

I blush. "Well, it's up and down."

As we're leaving the church, my mom tells me she's glad we came today. "And I put in a prayer for the polar bears, too," she adds.

I stop walking. "Why?"

"Because they're not in very good shape, Adri."

My stomach tightens. "What are you talking about?"

"I don't want to upset you."

"Too late."

"Well, some are starving," she says, "because the ice isn't frozen long enough for them to hunt seals."

"Why isn't it?"

"Because of global warming."

"Like I need to hear this," I snap, as another issue gets added to my to-do list.

We walk in silence until we come to a small gift store where, in the window, I spot drink coasters made of slate – each with a different Chinese character and corresponding element written in English.

"Hey!" I cry, "It's the earth, wind, fire, water thing again."

"Oh?"

"From the retreat I went to last month," I explain. "I'm water and Sam is earth."

She goes inside the store and buys me the coasters.

At home, I put the water coaster beside my big chair and the earth coaster where Sam used to place his cup, on the coffee table in front of the couch.

"There," I say to my mom, "that's better."

"Ummm . . . are you sure you're OK staying here on your own?"

"Uh huh."

"I think you're doing marvelous, Adri. It's just that –"

"Mom, do you believe in Jesus?"

"That's a very personal question."

I shrug. "Then don't answer it."

"I will," she says. "I think of Jesus as my friend."

"So you do believe in Him then?"

"Of course."

After she leaves, my next visitors arrive: two co-workers lugging a cooler full of frozen food and a large gift-wrapped box, which I immediately unwrap. It's a table-top water fountain. They help me set it up on the fireplace hearth.

After they leave, I settle into my chair and revel in the wide selection of coping mechanisms from which I can now choose. I can chant *God is Love*; drink sherry; pop sleeping pills; eat cookies; kiss Sam's earth coaster and photos; fantasize about seeing him again in heaven, Nakoda by his side; or watch water trickling over my new fountain.

Eleven

"YOU were my rock, Sammy!" I wail at the fountain over coffee the next morning. "My granite container! For what am I without you, but water running all over the place? You were (sob) the quiet strength behind my chaotic energy. Now *I* must be the solid one!"

Off to a great start, I stand up and am about to go into the kitchen when I notice a pile of old newspapers beside the couch. Shit! The recycling gets picked up today. I'm cramming the papers into a bag when a Halloween article catches my eye. In the pagan tradition, October 31st marks the end of the six months of summer and the beginning of the six winter months.

Six months will take me to . . . the end of April! Just as Sam was earth and I'm water, so too was he summer and I winter. He loved the heat; I love the cold. Is this the stuff of true soul mates?

"Oh yes," I say to the fountain, as the recycling truck rumbles past, "things are starting to make sense."

Two days later, I meet Amanda for lunch.

"You have such a positive attitude," she remarks between bites of spinach salad.

"I guess that's how I come across, eh?"

"But?"

"On the inside," I admit, "things aren't so rosy."

"I bet."

I dip a fry in ketchup. "Right from the beginning it was as if two of me existed: strong on the outside, terrified on the inside."

"And now?" she asks.

"And now my two selves are even *more* separate. But showing people the Adri *I* want them to see is the only way I know how to cope."

She frowns. "And who is the person you want them to see?"

"The same one *they* want to see! The merry widow."

"Maybe you underestimate those around you."

I take a drink of water. "*I* can't handle what's going on inside me. How could anyone else?"

"Or maybe you're afraid that by being your true self, you'll drive people away?"

I shrug. "Maybe."

The waitress pours more water in my glass. I take a sip. "I'm ready to hear about the night Sam died."

"Are you sure?" asks Amanda.

"Yes."

She places a file folder on the table but doesn't open it. "At the beginning of our shift, Sam told us all about your holiday. He said you guys had an awesome time. And then later in the shift, he told me about the convertible and how friggin' hot it was with the top down. He said he'd look over at you in the passenger seat and you were roasting."

"I was *so* uncomfortable! And there he was, soaking up the sun like a cat."

We both laugh. Then I point to the folder. "So what's that?"

"It's a printout of the calls we went to during our shift."

"Oh."

"I thought you might want me to go through it with you."

"I do."

"Are you sure?"

I take another drink of water. "Absolutely."

So Amanda goes through the calls, thereby giving me a play-by-play of the last night of Sam's life. They'd interviewed a sexual assault victim at the hospital, checked out a suspicious vehicle, then attended a house party complaint. They'd then met Tom for coffee, done a traffic stop, checked out two false alarms and were on the way home when another call came in.

I lean forward. "Home?"

"Yeah. Sam knew you were working dayshift and wanted to stop in and say hi."

I crunch a piece of ice, my water gone. "What time?"

"Well, let's see . . ." she says, running her finger down the printout.

"OK, yeah, it'd be here – sometime between 5:20 and 5:30 a.m., which I thought was kinda early for a visit."

I wouldn't normally be up that early for a dayshift. I hadn't told Sam that I'd planned on waking up at 5:00 a.m. to write. Nor had I followed through on my promise to myself. Knowing me better than I know my own self, had Sam been coming home to make sure I was awake?

"We were only about four blocks from your place," she says, "when another call came in."

So his death woke me up instead.

The waitress fills my water glass and I take a big drink.

"Are you OK?" Amanda asks.

"Not really. But I do need to hear this, so keep going."

"Well, something else happened earlier in the night," she says, "that I think you should know about."

"OK."

"We were doing a traffic stop and this huge truck had barreled past us, so I made a comment about how dangerous it is working on the side of the road. Then Sam told me about the time he was sitting in his police car, with the lights activated, and had glanced in his rearview mirror to see this semi flying up behind him. He said it was the weirdest sensation thinking he was going to die."

"Sam said *that* a few hours before he actually did die?"

"Yeah! Adri, I honestly think Sam chose me to work with that night for a reason."

"Which is?"

"Maybe he knew we'd have this conversation."

Thus I add traffic safety to my to-do list of issues to tackle.

Amanda then slides the printout towards me. "You can keep that."

"Thanks," I say, glancing down at it. The 5:47 line catches my eye. "Hole through drywall in main entrance," I say.

"Sam said that."

Then I read the 5:49 line: "With K-9."

"That too," she says. "In fact, that was the last thing we heard Sam say."

I take a deep breath. "He's a good guy, right? The K-9 officer."

"The best."

"So Sam was in good hands?"

She nods. "He was with people who loved him. Tom and all the guys were awesome. Everybody did their best for Sam."

It's not until we're in the parking lot afterwards that I remember about the city map. I retrieve it from my car and hand it to her. "This was in Sam's duty-bag."

"It was?"

I nod. "Yeah."

"Oh. I wondered where that ended up."

"So it *was* you reading the map?"

Amanda shakes her head. "No. Sam was. I was driving."

"But Sam ALWAYS drove."

"Not that night he didn't. He asked me to drive." Amanda hands the map back to me. "You can keep that, too."

On the way to my next appointment, I realize that this means the map *had* been one of the last things Sam had touched after all – which also means he'd been the one who'd left it folded open to the location of his fall.

Twelve

"How goes the battle?" the police psychologist asks me, as he's my next appointment.

"I don't think I'm winning."

"How so?"

"I'm having some pretty bizarre thoughts."

"Such as . . ."

"I think Sam knew he was gonna die that night."

He nods. "OK. Why do you think that?"

I take a deep breath then let loose. "Well, I just had lunch with Amanda and she told me that Sam asked her to drive that night, which was totally uncharacteristic of him because he always drove – but that meant that *he* was the one reading the map that I found, open to the location of his fall, in his duty bag and now I'm wondering if that's some sort of clue as to what we're supposed to be doing with his memorial fund, and then Amanda *also* said that during their shift, Sam told her a story about the time he was nearly rear-ended by a semi and how he had some idea of what it must feel like right before you're gonna die – and then he *did* die a coupla hours later! So not only was Sam possibly aware of his pending death, he'd specifically chosen to work with someone who would FOR SURE pass on all the relevant information to me, so I'd know what to do."

"That's the most you've ever said to me, Adri."

Though this is our third visit, I guess I haven't shared much – and certainly not the I-am-the-Second-Coming-of-Christ possibility.

I feel my cheeks flush. "That's not my only wacky idea."

"It's perfectly normal to have strange thoughts," he says, "especially after the shock you've experienced."

I haven't come across *that* one in the grief pamphlets.

"Although," he continues, "it is important to remember that any thought you continue thinking can become a belief."

I scrunch up my face, struggling to wrap my muddled mind around this concept.

The psychologist clears his throat. "So I just need to ensure that what we're referring to here doesn't have anything to do with you harming yourself?"

Again with the suicide-stuff. I'll be dead by spring but it won't be by my own hand. "I told you before," I say, "that'd be cheating. There are no short-cuts."

"Good. Now do you have a close friend to talk to?"

"There doesn't seem to be a shortage of people in my life."

"But is there *one* person you share everything with, Adri?"

"That would be Sam."

He tries a different approach. "Would you consider attending a grief group?"

I picture myself sitting in a circle of widows, revealing that I am the female incarnation of Christ. "No."

"Why not?"

"Because I don't want to sit around listening to other people's sad stories."

"Grief groups are about sharing," he says. "Some people find that valuable."

But hearing about other people's losses might lessen the significance of my own. This is about Sam and me. At this point, I don't give a shit about what others are going through and I certainly don't have the time or energy to listen to *their* crap.

The psychologist then asks me how I'm feeling about next month.

I shrug. "What about it?"

"Christmas . . ."

"Oh. I hadn't got that far."

"Well, you might find the season really tough without Sam," he says. "After the death of a spouse, most people have a difficult time receiving Christmas cards addressed to both husband and wife."

I stare at him.

"That's just an example . . ."

Oh how I *wish* I were worrying about Sam's name on a goddamn envelope. I stand up. "Thanks for the tip."

"Adri . . ."

I pick up my purse. "What?"

"Promise me," he says, "you'll talk to *someone*."

When I get home, I call Jodie to test the waters. "Have you read Revelations?"

Pause. "Uh . . . no."

"It's loaded with crazy symbolism and is totally dark and gloomy. I think it was written to scare us into smartening up."

"Maybe. But who reads that stuff these days?"

"Actually, I'm reading a book about a group of people who are trying to interpret Revelations so they can figure out when Armageddon will be and who'll be involved. They're using numerology to interpret historical events."

"Why are you reading *that*?" she asks.

"I dunno. But for the record, I think the end of the world is a self-fulfilling prophecy. If we believe it's all gonna end in a fiery mess anyway, then wouldn't our actions lead us to that very ending?"

"I guess . . ."

"I also read in Revelations about a war breaking out in heaven, where Michael and his angels fight the bad guys. And there's a white horse and its rider, called Faithful and True, who apparently save the day."

Silence.

"What if Sam really *is* working in heaven?" I ask.

"Huh?"

"St. Michael is the archangel! Sam died on the Catholic celebration of St. Michael's Day and his forty-day ceremony fell on the Greek Orthodox celebration of St Michael. What if Michael *needed* Sam to help fight the bad guys?"

"Uh . . ."

I laugh nervously. "I'm losing it, aren't I?"

"Not necessarily. I mean, I suppose anything is possible."

I give the water fountain a wave. "Nah . . . I'm just making all this up because I can't accept Sam's death."

"But you *have* accepted his death," she says. "And now you're just trying to figure out why."

"I got my pictures back from our vacation."

"Oh man, that must've been tough . . ."

"Yeah. But there's a great shot of Sam on the merry-go-round at Disneyland – and he's on a white horse."

No reply.

"What if Sam is the rider on the white horse who's gonna save the day?" I ask.

Pause. "What day?"

"Judgement Day!"

"I honestly don't know," Jodie replies carefully, "what I'm supposed to say."

In bed, numerology on my mind, I do an Adri-style calculation by adding up the digits in Sam's regimental number. With his badge clutched against my chest, I turn out the light and whisper "eleven" into the darkness.

Thirteen

Sam's buddy, Wayne, visits the next afternoon and we sit at the kitchen table, reminiscing about his and Sam's college days. We get on the subject of Noam Chomsky and Wayne asks me if I remember how fascinated Sam had been with his work.

"Yeah," I reply. "But now I can't remember why."

"Because Noam exposed the shitty track record of U.S. foreign policy," he says. "Sam couldn't believe what was going on behind the scenes all around the world."

"Right . . ."

"It was as if Noam Chomsky opened Sam's eyes to reality."

I nod, recalling Sam's passion for learning and justice, so similar to mine. How had we both got so off track in terms of believing we could make a difference?

Wayne leans towards me. "I think differently since Sam died."

"How so?"

"Well, you know how he was always so damn righteous about things being good or bad, right or wrong?"

I laugh. "It was either black or white for him. There was no gray area."

"I know. So, now when I'm faced with a moral dilemma, I find myself thinking about how Sam would behave. It's almost like he's become my conscience."

Sasha gets up from where she's snoozing under the kitchen table and walks to the fridge. Wayne had given Sasha to Sam and me as a belated wedding gift.

I look at Wayne. "What do you think is going on?" I ask.

"Whaddya mean?"

I wave my arms in a circle. "You know, like in the bigger picture."

Sasha whines, pawing at the fridge. Wayne watches her.

"Her treats are up there," I say, standing up. "I mean, don't you think the way Sam died was pretty fluky? He only fell *nine* feet."

"I know."

I give Sasha a cookie. "So?"

Wayne shifts in his seat. "This is gonna sound kinda weird . . ."

I laugh. "Oh, I wouldn't worry about that."

"Well, it's almost like on the day Sam died, there was a funny . . . blip in the universe – like a bright light went streaking across the sky."

I raise my eyebrows and smile. "That is kinda weird."

Sasha finishes her cookie then stands up on her back legs so that her two front paws are touching the upper part of the fridge.

"She's acting strange, Adri."

Sasha whimpers and scratches at the fridge. So I gently lift her down, which is when Wayne and I see that where her paws were is a photograph of Sam.

Tonight is the annual Christmas party for Sam's team and Tom invited Nick, Angela and me. I said yes, thinking it might be nice to carry on the tradition – and because I *should* go. For I am The Cheerful Widow whose job it is to make everyone else feel better by pretending I'm A-OK. In public, I'm the smiling little trooper who asks lots of cute questions. Back home, I'm weaving the answers into a dangerous rope into which my own neck might fit quite nicely.

Half an hour before Nick and Angela are to pick me up, I find myself in front of the bookshelf, staring at the box of love letters Sam and I had written to each other when I was travelling for seven months. So I open the box and read a couple of letters and what strikes me most is what a spoiled princess I'd been, traveling on an inheritance while bitching about atrocious living conditions that were the everyday reality for the locals. Back then, I could have hopped on a plane and gone home to Canada – and Sam. This is no longer an option. There are no return flights to visit the dead; it's a one-way ticket and there's no guarantee you'll see your loved one.

The doorbell rings so I stuff the letters back in the box and am placing it on the bookshelf when a title catches my eye: *A Widow For One Year* by John Irving.

I shake my head. "The deal is seven months."

At the Christmas party, I soon realize that being the widow of a fallen officer watching her dead husband's teammates trying to party is a like a drug addict in rehab, watching other addicts shoot up. I'm not emotionally equipped to observe the reality that life *is* going on without Sam. So off to the buffet I waddle.

With a heaping plate of food in one hand and a beer in the other, I find a seat in the living room and a woman I've never seen before sits beside me.

"And who are you?" she asks.

"Ummm . . . my husband was the police officer who just passed away."

"Oh now, which one was that?" she says loudly, waving her wineglass. "There's been so many lately, I get them all mixed up!"

Her callous reference is to another other young police officer who died three months before Sam. He'd been struck and killed by a drunk driver on his way home from work, leaving a young widow and two-month old daughter behind. Both Sam and I had been working the night that officer died. I'd taken a report from the officer over the phone a few hours before his death; Sam had attended the scene of his crash.

"When they pulled him from the car," Sam had said to me the next day, "and I saw his uniform, it was brutal. I was *so* angry."

When Sam had first arrived at the collision scene, it was believed there had been two people in the vehicle that hit the officer. So Sam and several other officers had searched for that possible second person. As it turned out, there was only the one person in the vehicle: the drunk driver who died at the scene.

"So you thought there might have been *two* bad guys?" I'd confirmed with Sam. "Yeah," he'd said, "and I totally wanted to catch whoever had done that to him."

Recalling this conversation now makes me realize that the 'bad guy' isn't always a person. Just because the drunk driver died didn't mean there wasn't a bigger issue to be addressed. One less drunk on the road isn't the end of impaired driving. I think about the map in Sam's duty-bag, folded open to the location of his death. Maybe it *is* a clue pointing me in the direction of the 'bad guy issue,' whatever that might be.

After the party, Nick, Angela and I trundle clear across the city to yet another one. I still haven't mastered the use of the word 'no.' Friends and family are obviously concerned about me, judging from the number of social invitations coming my way. But the busier I allow myself to be, the more anxious and upset I am when alone again.

The following afternoon, I'm walking up the stairs from the basement to the family room when each step takes exponentially more effort than the last. I can scarcely make it up five stairs – the weight of sorrow I've been carrying has become a physical entity. In the family room, I stumble over to Sam's couch and fall into it, face first. I scream into the pillows, pound my fists and kick my feet in the air. For just a moment, instead of thinking about how best to avoid the hurt, I allow myself to actually *feel* it.

However, considering this sensation is similar to a stake being driven through my heart, it's no wonder I've been avoiding the experience. At least with a stake, death comes quickly. I hear Sasha whining and open my eyes. She's up on her hind legs again, this time scratching at a shelf directly below a photo of Sam and Stan as teenagers. She's never before shown any interest in this shelf nor are there any cookies or pig-ears around.

"Sam?" I say quietly.

Sasha looks at me then lets out a groan as her paws slowly slide down the wall.

Maybe Sam really *does* exist outside my imagination . . .

"BUT THAT'S NOT GOOD ENOUGH!" I scream at the photo. "I WANT MORE! I don't wanna be married to a spirit. I want my husband back."

"At least, I think I do," I add. "I mean, you might not be looking so good right about now . . ."

I shake my head. "But that's OK. Of course I want you here, Sam – in ANY condition."

How Adri?

"Jesus rose up from the dead," I say to the shelf. "Why can't you?"

Because he's not the Son of God, you idiot.

"Or maybe you are!" I cry.

Don't do this.

I nod. "You're right . . . that'd be a public relations nightmare."

In bed, I fall asleep with Sasha curled up beside me. My subconscious mind goes to work and I dream of Sam. He's lying on the operating table in the OR, just as he was in real life when I last saw him alive. But in my dream, I don't leave the operating room before his surgery begins. Instead, I watch the surgeon make incisions in his body, except that wherever he cuts, tiny red particles of light float up – like the magic dust from Tinkerbell's wand.

Fourteen

My dad joins Sasha and me at the off-leash park the next morning. A walking encyclopedia, my father has become a handy reference for my historical, religious, philosophical and scientific questions. But his honesty and skepticism are really starting to piss me off.

"I can't get it out of my mind," I say, "that there has to be a reason for Sam's tragic death."

My dad doesn't reply immediately. "Please don't take this the wrong way – but I don't think Sam's death was a tragedy. I think it was an accident."

I stop walking. "Pardon me?"

"What *you* do with your life from here on in, Adri, is what will determine whether Sam's death was a tragedy or not."

The gentle truth smashes against my forehead like a two by four.

"Fine," I snip. "You *might* be right about that."

"And at some point, you're going to have to move . . ."

"But what you're *not* right about," I say, surprised at the clarity of my thoughts considering the psychological quagmire I've been in, "is using the term 'accident' to describe Sam's death."

"Oh?"

I make mock quotation marks in the air. "An accident is something that could *not* have been prevented – like getting hit by a meteor. Sam's death was a case of cause and effect: no safety railing, no husband. So I would appreciate you not using the word accident because it's not only a misnomer, it's a copout."

"I'm sorry, I . . ."

"Calling his death an accident just gives people an excuse for their apathy."

My dad doesn't say anything, which is fine by me because I'm not ready to go down this road yet.

"You seem very interested in physics these days," I say, redirecting the conversation. "Why is that?"

"I find it a fascinating subject."

"So what are you reading about now?" I ask.

"Well, I don't think this is up your alley, Adri, but . . ."

"How do *you* know?"

The poor guy scratches his head. "I just assumed . . ."

I stop walking again. "I'm not an idiot, Dad. I'm an emotional and mental basket case but I don't ride the short bus."

"I know," he says softly. "I'm sorry."

Then I listen as he rambles on for twenty more minutes about time, space, energy, matter and light.

"Uh dad?" I finally interrupt.

"Yes?"

"In light of the circumstances, moderation might be prudent."

He laughs. "You're right."

"So why are you telling me all this?"

"I don't know. I just get off on these tangents . . ."

But I no longer believe in random conversations: if one is happening, there must be a reason for it. Although Christianity is currently blooming in the garden of my mind, I suspect the seeds of science are dormant, not dead.

On the last Sunday of November, I again find myself in the front pew of Sam's church. His parents wanted me to come today because members of the Greek community are concerned about me. I bring Harry along for back-up.

I'm reading the English pamphlet that explains the service and I can't help but notice that the content of the Orthodox service is basically the same as the Anglican one – it's simply the means of delivery that differs. I have another moment of fury recalling the fuss made over our wedding. We'd wasted our engagement bickering over Orthodox regulations, particularly about baptizing children. The attitude of Sam's church had infuriated me: *nobody* was going to tell us which religion to raise our kids by. Likewise with the ridiculous notion that if we didn't get married in the Greek Church, Sam couldn't have an Orthodox funeral.

I lift my head and stare at the panel with Jesus hanging from the cross. We'd not produced any offspring and Sam had been handed an Orthodox funeral on a public silver platter, thereby making the stress of our engagement and subsequent strain on our marriage a complete waste of time and energy. Is all this water under the bridge – or am I *supposed* to be noticing that when religious beliefs take precedence over common sense, good people get hurt?

I look at the pamphlet again. The phrase "Pay Attention" jumps out at me.

I lift my head and meet the martyred gaze of Jesus. I AM paying attention – but I seem to be the only one who is! Like a terrified kid on the first night at summer camp, wide-awake in the middle of the night and longing to be home in my own bed, all the other kids around me are sleeping soundly. But it's been nearly two months: is everybody else really sleeping or just pretending?

After the service, Harry and I are in the foyer greeting Greeks when a voice rasps in my ear, "You're going to *hell* if you haven't been baptized!"

I whip around to see the speaker is an old lady, dressed all in black with a black kerchief on her head. I stare at her, dumbfounded, and she disappears into the crowd.

Then another woman kisses me on both cheeks. "God bless you, Adri."

"And God bless you," I say.

"You're so strong," another lady comments.

"We love you," says the next. "Thank you for coming today."

On the drive to Sam's parent's place, I tell Harry what the nasty lady said.

"Remember to use your bullshit filters," he advises.

"I'm trying. But it's getting kinda confusing. On the one side, I've got an atheist father telling me about the dual nature of light, and on the other, there's a shitload of Christians who seem pretty damn sure of their beliefs."

"And the truth," Harry says, "is probably somewhere in between. Just because a person speaks with conviction doesn't mean they speak the truth. Most of the time we say things because we *want* to believe them, not because we really do."

"You sound like Dad."

"Just be very careful about believing what you're told because I highly doubt *anybody* knows what's going on." He glances over at me. "And your guess at this spiritual stuff is just as good as anyone else's."

I laugh. "Thanks for the vote of confidence."

For lunch, we have fried chicken at Sam's parent's place. Sam loved the stuff so I eat a couple extra pieces for him, in addition to my own three, potato salad, plate full of fries and two slices of chocolate cake. Being strong is requiring a great deal of fuel.

Cassie, Cam and their daughter sleep over in my spare bedroom tonight. Just after midnight, I wake up to see the reddish-orange light again. But this time, it's hovering to the left of my bed, above the miniature shrine to Sam. I blink to make sure I'm really awake and the light begins drifting towards me. This scares me so I shake my head and the light slowly dissipates.

At breakfast, I tell Cam and Cassie about the light.

"Do you think it was the same one you saw right after Sam died?" Cassie asks.

I butter my toast. "Yup."

Cassie nods expertly. Cam's eyes expand.

"What light?" he asks.

"Adri saw a red light in her window on the morning of Sam's surgery," she says. "Right around the time his heart was removed."

I nod. "And I had a dream the other night that I saw Sam in the operating room. It was just like in real life except that I stayed for his surgery and when the doctor made the incisions in his body, tiny particles of red light came floating up."

"Wow!" is Cassie's response as Cam gives us his rendition of the goldfish.

After they leave, I call the Hope Chaplain to brainstorm about the red light.

"What often matters most about our dreams," he says, "is the feeling we have when we wake up from them."

"First of all," I say, "I *was* awake and secondly, it scared the crap outta me."

"So what did you do?"

"I shook my head."

"And?"

"It went away."

"Well what do *you* think the red light was, Adri?"

"Sam. But he knew it might scare me, so he chose a night when I wasn't alone."

Then the chaplain asks me what the colour red means to me.

"Anger."

"What about passion?" he suggests. "Or love?"

"Or sacrifice."

After our conversation, I look around the living room. If the red light was Sam, then why was I afraid? Was it because a light in lieu of a husband is rather disconcerting – or was it because I really don't want Sam to come back to me in any form? As in our marriage, I figure honesty is the best policy.

"If that was you, Sam," I say to his nearest photo, "then you better find a new way of communicating with me because you damn near gave me a heart attack."

"Or maybe," I add, "just don't come so *close*."

Fifteen

For American Thanksgiving, I order Chinese food from our favourite restaurant and watch our favourite Thanksgiving movie, *Planes, Trains and Automobiles*. Since I didn't watch it at Canadian Thanksgiving, I figure watching it now would be acceptable to Sam – in our new relationship as red light and wife.

What I don't remember about the film is that the main character is a widower who carts around a photo of his dead wife. At one point, he's sitting in his car during a snowstorm chatting away to her. Sitting on Sam's perch, surrounded by pictures of him, I can certainly relate. The dead *are* often better companions than the living. I'm far happier staying at home alone, talk-ing to the walls than I am venturing out into the world and hearing what the mortals have to tell me. For as the two-month marker of Sam's death approaches, I'm noticing a definite shift in the clichés coming my way.

'You're young, dear,' is a popular one from the over-fifty crowd.

'I'm so sorry,' is being replaced by an oddly enthusiastic, 'Well, at least you didn't have children!'

That's right, you fucking morons: now I don't have a hus-band OR a child.

And my all-time favorite, occurring with alarming frequen-cy and frightening conviction, is: 'Losing a spouse isn't as bad as losing a child.'

'GRIEF IS NOT A PISSING MATCH!' I scream at the water fountain when I get back home again.

Then there are the dozens of people who take my hand and softly confide, "Adri, I just want you to know that your loss has really made me appreciate what *I* have."

I'm so pleased my nightmare could be of assistance to you. Not.

After *Planes, Trains and Automobiles*, I head to bed with my cheery Armageddon book. According to it, nothing is pre-de-termined. Rather, all St. John does in his Book of Revelations is warn humanity of what *could* happen. Since God made us free to choose our destiny, the choice to live or die is ours – not God's.

Perhaps there is a God, but not a plan.

"But that," I remark to Sasha as I reach over and turn out the light, "would be a rather ineffective way to run the universe. No wonder we're in such a pickle."

The next day is November 29th. Two months down, five to go. At 9:00 a.m. sharp, Dale picks me up and drives me downtown to meet my potential financial advisor, recommended by Stan. But *how* is one to invest one's money when one will soon be dead or Judgement Day upon us? Throw in the possibility that

the investor is the Second Coming of Christ – or His widow
– and another dilemma arises: surely Jesus the sequel wouldn't
invest in environmentally unfriendly multinational corporations
whose extreme wealth is made on the backs of the poor?

". . . the federal government."

I turn to Dale. "Huh?"

"I said I heard back from the federal government about
Sam's student loan."

"Oh yeah?"

"And in light of the circumstances, they've forgiven it. So
this means all your and Sam's debts are now paid off."

I nod. "I know."

He frowns. "Did the federal government write you, too?"

"Not exactly."

When we meet the financial advisor, Dale asks him a bar-
rage of questions.

Seemingly satisfied with the answers, he then turns to me.
"Were there any other questions you had?"

"Well," I say, shifting in my seat. "Because of all that's happened, I'm a little . . ."

Both men lean forward as I pause to think of the best words
to use, without coming across as a complete lunatic.

". . . freaked. So it's really important to me that the money
is wisely invested."

"Of course," replies the financial advisor.

"I don't want anything risky," I say. "It has to be *very* safe
– as in able to withstand something really bad happening."

The advisor looks perplexed. "What, like if the world markets collapsed?"

My face reddens. "Something like that."

He leans back again. "I guess anything is possible. And I do
agree with you: this money ought to be very wisely invested. It's
your future."

"Well," I say snottily, "I'll certainly be earning my *own* income down the road."

"Of that," he replies, "I have no doubt."

"My financial picture is looking pretty good, isn't it?" I remark to Dale as we're leaving the parkade.

"I'll say. It seems that Sam has put you in a very unique situation."

I turn and look at him.

"You have a real opportunity to do some good in the world, Adri."

Billions of souls, some reading magazines in heaven's waiting room, climb upon my shoulders.

"I mean," he adds, perhaps noticing I look a tad overwhelmed, "when you're ready."

After Dale drops me at home, I reflect upon my situation over hot chocolate and Bailey's. Female incarnation of Christ or not, I *do* want to achieve some good in the world. I'm just hoping my youthful death – gruesome and spectacular as it will undoubtedly be – will accomplish this for me.

On my way upstairs to fold laundry, I check the mail and find an envelope from a woman whose name I don't recognize. Inside is a sympathy card from the twenty-four year old widow of the police officer who was killed by the drunk driver three months before Sam died.

"I sort of have some idea of what you're going through," reads the handwritten note, "so please call me if you want to talk."

In my bedroom, I'm reaching over to pick up my little gray t-shirt when I see Sam, in my memory but clear as day, standing on the other side of the bed.

"This is cute," he'd said in the summer, standing in that same spot, folding this same shirt, "and it looks great on you but I wish I could afford to buy you more expensive clothes."

I fall onto the pile of laundry, sobbing. I can afford any shirt I want now but I don't want new clothes; I want Sam.

But I can't have Sam. And judging by the collapsing sensation going on inside me, I know I need to talk to someone. But I don't want to talk to a person who understands what I'm going through because then I'll have to accept that what Sam and I had, though wonderful, other people have also had. And lost. Sam and I were special; we were different.

I phone Jodie.

"It's me," I say.

"Hi."

"No, I mean it's *me*."

"Huh?"

"Remember how I was nattering on about Revelations and the Second Coming?"

"Yeah."

"It's me."

Silence.

"I think I'm Jesus," I clarify.

A pause, then: "Oh dear."

"I know that's totally crazy and it can't be true but I can't get this stupid thought out of my mind, ever since that phone call . . ."

"What phone call?"

So, starting with the phone message relayed to me by Anthony, I explain to Jodie what had triggered my original Jesus-thought.

"Have you told Anthony?" she asks.

"God, no! My family already knows I'm going off the deep-end. They'd for sure send in the men in white suits with butterfly nets."

"No they wouldn't."

"I know I'm creating this delusion," I continue, "to avoid the reality that Sam's body is now rotting in a grave downtown."

"Listen, I'm not saying you *are* the Second Coming of Christ because that's . . . pretty weird. But if you were truly delusional and mentally unstable, then you probably wouldn't be so aware of it. And besides, you're a woman. Jesus was a *guy*."

I laugh. "Yes. I do realize that. But since the past two thousand years have been so shitty in terms of the treatment of women, it makes sense that God – or whoever's calling the shots

– would send a daughter to follow up when society is more willing to accept women as equals."

"I don't think the bible mentions anything about sending back a daughter."

"So? For one thing, Christianity isn't the only game in town. And even if it were, it was a bunch of patriarchal men who wrote the bible. I betcha most of what Jesus actually said and did was totally distorted to fit other agendas. It makes sense that Jesus would come back as a woman because a female perspective is *totally* what's needed to get us back on track. The world is way too male-oriented – we place far more value on fighting wars than on actually solving problems. And don't get me started on how we treat the environment! Dominating nature is a predominantly male perspective, whereas women are more interested in working *with* the natural world . . . conserving what we have instead of destroying it."

"So hypothetically," she says, after another significant pause, "why do you think it took you until the age of thirty-two for you to come to this realization?"

"Because nothing else but Sam's death would have woken me up!"

"C'mon, Adri – do you *really* believe you're the Second Coming?"

"Geez, when you say it out loud like that, it really does sound wacky."

"That's because it is."

"You're right," I say. "Of course, there's also the possibility that *Sam* is Jesus."

"WHAT?"

"Well, his death sure gave *me* new life – if I can ever get past the suffering and guilt to enjoy it. That's pretty much the idea behind Christianity, isn't it?"

No response.

I sigh. "Regardless of what's going on, no single person should be responsible for pulling humanity out of our own goddamn mess."

"So maybe your job as a writer is to help demonstrate that."

"How?"

"By sharing your experience of losing Sam. I mean, look at what you're learning."

"I suppose . . ."

"But for God's sakes," she adds, "do it in a way that you live to tell the tale."

Sixteen

"HE'S DEAD," I scream, "but he's NOT FORGOTTEN!"

Then I run out my cousin's front door, leaving behind a house full of family trying to celebrate my mother's seventy-fifth birthday. However, since there's a snowstorm on this particular evening in early December, I have to stop at the front door, *after* my embarrassing outburst, to put on my jacket, mittens and boots. Only then do I charge down the icy front walkway, stomping as angrily as possible in my new ridiculously high-heeled boots. I climb into my car, slam the door and slowly inch my way home on icy roads.

"They didn't toast Sam!" I blubber into the phone from my living room.

"Adri?" says Dawson, on the other end of the line. "What's wrong?"

"I was (sob) at my mom's birthday and my family didn't even include him (sob) in the toast before dinner. I just can't believe them!"

"Do you want me to come over?"

"Could you?"

A few minutes later the doorbell rings. But it's not Dawson; it's Dale's wife.

"So they sent you, huh?" I say.

"Yup."

"I'm pretty pissed off."

"Oh, we gathered that."

"I can't believe my own family. Not one person mentioned Sam the whole night —not even at a goddamn toast *to my mother.*"

My sister-in-law winces. "Everybody feels just terrible about that but I think we all figured we'd try and give you a break from the hurt."

"Hah!" I give a shrill laugh. "Well that certainly didn't work."

"You're right. We screwed up and I'm sorry."

"Mentioning Sam's name and talking about him is really important to me because if we don't, he'll be forgotten."

"You do know, Adri, that at that dinner table tonight, Sam was on every single one of our minds?"

I shrug. "If no one says anything, how would I?"

The doorbell rings. I let Dawson in.

"Well," she says to him. "We messed up."

"It happens," he replies. "It's hard to know what to say sometimes."

"Here's a tip then," I say. "Not mentioning Sam is gonna bury him a hell of a lot faster than the dirt they threw on his grave."

I get the double-goldfish. Is the nice-widow façade finally crumbling?

Recognizing that a change of scenery might be wise, I plan a farewell tour to Vancouver to visit our friends and old stomping grounds, then on to Kingston to see my grandpa. It seems wisest to keep moving; stopping means vulnerability.

An hour before I'm leaving for the airport, I get a call from the Hope Chaplain's wife. "I have some bad news," she says.

"Oh?" I sit down in my chair.

"Another officer died today. He was in a head-on collision on his way to work."

"Shit," is my first response. "Who?" is my second.

She tells me the name of the city police officer, adding: "He was a recruit classmate of the officer who was killed by the drunk driver last June."

I process this as I process everything else these days.

"Adri?"

"So let me get this straight," I say. "One cop was killed driving home *from* work. Three months later, Sam died *at* work. Three months after that, a recruit classmate of the first officer dies on his way *to* work."

"Yes."

It would appear God is plucking cops like daisies. "So when's the funeral?"

"You'll be out of town for it," she replies. "Which I think is a blessing."

Since the blessings being handed out these days are few and far between, I shall take this one and run.

Stan picks me up at the Vancouver airport.

"You look great!" he lies, giving me a bear hug.

Although dangerous on slippery surfaces and uncomfortable to walk in, my new boots do give me an extra three inches of height, an attempt to draw attention away from the twenty pounds I've put on from all the damn cookies and comfort food.

"We haven't planned much for your visit," he says, "because you need a break."

The problem, however, is that I don't know *how* to take a break. Nor do I deserve one. Sam's death was wrong and it's my job to figure out how to make everything right again. If I'm not thinking about Sam, the circumstances surrounding his death, societal issues or higher spiritual questions, then I'm not being a responsible widow.

I borrow their car and head to Abbotsford the next day. Sitting outside the apartment where Sam and I lived four years ago, I stare up at our old balcony, bawling. Then I hook up with Sam's college buddies for a beer. Several of them work at a prison so I ask one girl how that's going.

"Very frustrating," is her reply.

"How so?"

"Well, most of the inmates are repeat offenders and the

main reason they re-offend is because life in prison is easier than working for a living."

That's absurd!" I cry.

"It's easier to get their drugs in prison than on the street," another girl explains.

"So let me get this straight," I say, "once a bad guy gets released from jail, he goes out and promptly commits another crime . . . say a break and enter, just so he can go back to prison again and buy drugs?"

And yet another room goes quiet.

The following morning, I continue on to Chilliwack to visit a friend.

"I think I'm going to die violently," I confess to her over tea. I don't add 'in the spring.' No sense in alarming anyone.

She puts down her teacup. "Most of us are going to die violently."

"Huh?"

"Think about it. How many people actually pass away peacefully in their sleep, simply of old age?"

I shrug.

"Not many. Car crashes, cancer, heart attacks . . . that's the usual stuff and it all seems pretty violent to me."

"I guess."

"So where are you at these days – in terms of accepting Sam's death?" she asks.

"That's the million dollar question."

"It just seems that you're pretty OK with everything. Am I right?"

I sigh. "Yes and no."

She gets up from the couch, leaves the room and returns with a book. "You might find this interesting."

I flip through it and a sentence catches my eye: "Love is the energy of the soul."

"Thanks," I say, "I seem to be on quite the spiritual journey."

"We all are, Adri."

Seventeen

I return to Stan's place in Vancouver and sit on the floor with Megan – now days away from giving birth – gluing beads to Christmas decorations.

"It's a bit odd," she remarks, "that both Sam's best friend *and* his brother are going to be having their first child right around the same time."

I nod but don't look up. Its two fucking slaps in the face, is what it is.

"Adri?"

I lift my head. "Yeah?"

"Do you wish you and Sam had a baby?"

"I think I'll go for a walk," I reply, placing the half-beaded Styrofoam decoration on the table. I want to smash the goddamn ball and throw the stupid beads out the window.

"Are you OK?" Megan asks.

"I'm fine . . . just need a little break is all."

I try to zip up my jacket but my hands are shaking too much.

Megan struggles to stand up. "I'm so sorry. I didn't mean to upset you."

I look her in the eye. "Yes. I *do* wish we'd had a child. Not having a baby with Sam is my greatest regret."

"Adri, I . . ."

"If we'd had a boy," I continue, "Sam wanted to name him James. If we'd had a girl, I'd chosen the name Alexandra Grace. But of course that had been back in the old days, when we'd both actually *wanted* children – before we perceived this fucked-up hellhole to be an unsuitable environment in which to bring offspring."

Her bottom jaw drops.

"I'll be back in a bit," I say.

Then I put on my runners, walk out the door and down the hill to the boardwalk where I last walked with Sam five months ago.

Deciding whether or not to have a child had been an evolving process for us. When we were in our mid-twenties – before we were married – we just assumed we'd one day have a family. "You'd be an awesome mom," Sam would say, "although I'd have to be the disciplinarian in the family." A year into our marriage, when we were back in our hometown and Sam was a police officer, our conversations were more like this:

Sam: You wouldn't believe the brats I have to deal with every day. Kids have no respect for adults, let alone cops.

Me: *We'd* be good parents, though.

Sam: I'm not convinced that's enough anymore. When I take the really rotten kids home, sometimes they're from good families too.

Me: Oh.

Two years into our marriage, when I was working part time as a receptionist and trying to write a novel, our conversations resembled:

Me: Maybe we shouldn't have a child.

Sam smiles.

Me: At least, not until I'm happier with myself.

Sam appears puzzled.

Me: I'm terrified of having a kid before I've written a book.

Sam: How so?

Me: I don't want to live vicariously through my child.

Sam: Not a good idea, no.

Three years into the marriage, when I was still working on the novel – my main character, Liz, droning on and on about what's wrong with the world and the wisdom of bringing another human into it -- our conversations had shifted:

Sam: When are you gonna finish that damn book?

Me: It's coming.

One month before Sam's death:

Me: I'm getting closer to wanting to become a mother.

Sam: You haven't finished writing your book.

Me: Maybe that's not a realistic dream.

Sam: Well sweetheart, you may be a good mom, but you're gonna have to look elsewhere for a father. I'm *not* bringing a kid into this world.

I follow the boardwalk to the end and continue walking along the beach in front of the beautiful homes. I stop in front of a white mansion and close my eyes. I imagine Sam and me on the verandah, watching our kids laughing and playing on the beach. Is this what heaven will be like?

This evening, I'd planned to drive across town to visit a friend but the Lion's Gate Bridge is too icy to cross. I call to cancel and end up talking to his wife, a psychologist.

"You must get this question an awful lot," she says, "but how are you doing?"

"I'm all right." I sit down on the guest bed where Sam and I used to sleep. "I'm writing about it and that seems to help."

"Like putting together the pieces of a puzzle, eh?"

"Pretty much – except now there's no picture on the box to go by."

"And there was before Sam died?"

"Yeah."

"May I ask what the picture was?"

I tell her I always wanted to be a writer who lived by the sea.

"You live in the prairies, Adri."

"That's where Sam's dream was."

"But not yours?"

"No. I was there for Sam." I clear my throat. "I've been thinking a lot about heaven and hell."

"And?"

"Do *you* think good will ultimately triumph over evil?"

She chuckles. "Oh, I don't believe in hell, Satan or Evil."

"Seriously?"

"Yeah. I think evil is simply pain manifested," she states matter-of-factly. "If you love and are loved, you experience joy. If you don't love and are not loved, you experience pain. And pain leads to fear and that leads to anger."

"Oh."

"Although I don't agree with all aspects of Judaism," she continues, "I do believe our bottom line – and that's to heal the world. I think every person has a part to play in healing this planet, be that through leading a nation, writing a book or cleaning a toilet."

"Are you saying that it's up to *us* to save ourselves?" I ask.

"You could put it that way, yeah."

"So you don't believe in heaven, huh?"

"Sure I do. I just don't believe it's an external place. I think it's a state of mind."

Before falling asleep, I finish reading *Tuesday's With Morrie* and come across the part where Morrie, dying of Lou Gehrig's disease, says that given the choice, he'd reincarnate as a gazelle. I smile. Me too.

Tonight I dream of Sam. I am again with him in the operating room prior to his organ removal surgery. Everything is exactly as it had been in real life except that when I go to kiss him goodbye, his eyes open and he says, "I love you."

I awake damn near ecstatic.

Eighteen

I check in for my flight to Kingston and am told I'll be changing planes in Toronto. Then, perhaps inspired by my father's lecture on physics, I buy the book, *E=mc²; A Biography of the World's Most Famous Equation*, by David Bodanis, in the airport bookstore.

So, during the flight, I read all about energy, mass and light and am reminded that energy is neither created nor destroyed, it just changes form. A sprout of science breaks through the thin layer of Christian topsoil. I come to the part that explains how the 18th century scientific work of Emilie du Chatelet – the love of Voltaire's life – contributed to the squared component of Einstein's equation two centuries later, and how she loved to work at her desk with a pile of books and a pad of paper, enthusiastically sorting out ideas. This sounds like me! Then I read how, in contrast, Voltaire's *Candide*, written near the end of his life, reflected a strangely passive view of the world that suggested no fundamental improvement could be made. This was Sam at the end of his life!

Unexpectedly pregnant at forty-three, du Chatelet had been writing furiously to get her ideas down on paper because she knew she was going to die in childbirth. Here on the plane, I can feel *her* fear of wanting so passionately to write but knowing there wouldn't be enough time.

Why not?

Because I'll be dead by spring.

Do you really believe that?

Yes.

Or does it just make you FEEL better believing that?

I know a child will mean the end of my writing.

I thought your greatest regret was not having a child with me?

"Whatever you're reading must be pretty interesting."

I look up. The flight attendant is standing in the aisle, holding a thermos of coffee. "Top-up?"

Smiling, I hold out my coffee cup. "Sure."

I resume reading and come to Voltaire's comment upon Emilie's death, three days after she gave birth: "I have lost the half of myself – a soul for which mine was made."

Clunk goes the coin. Was I Emilie du Chatelet in a past life and Sam Voltaire? Emilie had died young, leaving Voltaire behind to pick up the pieces. Maybe now it's *my* turn to experience the death of a soul mate?

I reach into my knapsack, pull out the book given me by my friend in Chilliwack and flip to the line, "Love is the energy of the soul."

Energy can be neither created nor destroyed, it simply changes form.

"A severe snowstorm has hit Toronto," announces the pilot over the intercom. "All flights from Pearson airport have been cancelled."

Love can be neither created nor destroyed, it just changes form.

"So if you were planning to catch a connecting flight," the

pilot continues, "please go to the airline check-in counter and you'll be assigned a hotel."

I stand outside Pearson airport for three hours waiting for the shuttle bus to take me to my hotel. When I finally get to my room, I race into the bathroom then go downstairs to the pub for a beer and a burger. Monday night football is on TV.

Back in my room, I'm brushing my teeth when I glance over and see pee in the toilet. But I distinctly remember flushing the toilet before going downstairs. So if it's not mine, whose is it?

OH MY GOD! What if Sam *did* come back from the dead?

I stumble out of the bathroom and search the room, unsuccessfully, for the non-flushing intruder. Then I sit on the edge of the bed and watch as the snowflakes whip against the window. I think back to the funeral director's suggestion about placing Sam's casket within a concrete vault. Was that to ensure the body decayed as slowly as possible so that when Jesus came back, the raising of the dead wouldn't be such a technical challenge? Or was that to protect *against* the body coming back from the dead?

Sam isn't in a vault.

The wind picks up and the snow gathers in chaotic swirls. And I admit to myself that even if Sam could come back, *I'm* not ready for him to. I burst into tears. It is so wrong for me to think this. I'm supposed to want him back – at any time, in any place and in any form. But if he came back, then I wouldn't have the financial freedom to write.

Sobbing, I crawl into bed and listen to the storm raging outside and in. I don't take a sleeping pill because I don't deserve to escape one moment of guilt.

Throughout the night, flashes of lightning illuminate the room and I half-expect to see someone or something at the foot of my bed. Around 3:00 a.m., I awake to a car alarm and listen to it for a few minutes before calling reception.

"Uh, that alarm is kinda annoying," I say to the girl who answers the phone.

"What alarm?"

"That car alarm that's going off."

"I haven't heard it. And no one else has called about it either."

I hang up and go to the window but I can't tell which vehicle is making the noise. However, I do see a red car, similar to my own, pull into the parking lot. While trying to park, the driver goes back and forth several times before finally stopping. Then he gets out, opens the rear door on the driver's side, takes his knapsack out of the back seat then puts it back in. Then he takes it out and puts it back in again. He takes the knapsack out one last time then wanders off into the snowstorm, *away* from the hotel. The alarm stops.

I shake my head. Why am I stranded in a Toronto hotel room, wondering if my dead husband peed in the toilet then hearing a car alarm that nobody else does while watching a drunk driver trying to park in the middle of a snowstorm?

The next morning, I return to Pearson airport to find my flight to Kingston has been even further delayed. So I sit in the departure lounge, across from the shoeshine booth, and continue reading my $E=mc^2$ book.

Around hour three, I decide to take a break and get my boots shined – the poor guy hasn't had a single customer since I got here.

I climb up onto his raised platform, sit down and stick one foot out.

"How are you?" I ask.

"Fine thank you," he replies, carefully wiping away the salt and dirt.

"I've got a question for ya."

He nods.

"Do you believe in God?"

The man blinks in surprise.

"Is that too personal?"

"No. It's just not a question I get asked very much."

"And?"

"Yes, I believe in God. But to me, He is Allah."

I watch him polishing my boot. "Why did you come to Canada?"

"Because my wife and I wanted a better life."

"Do you have children?"

"One."

"That's nice," I say.

He looks up at me. "For many years, my wife couldn't have a baby and some people back home told me to find a new wife. But I knew that wasn't right, even though it's acceptable where I come from – to some. I'm glad I didn't listen because my wife and I finally did have a child. I'm a very lucky man."

When I arrive in Kingston in the late afternoon, my uncle picks me up at the airport and takes me straight to the nursing home to see my grandpa, who's ninety-three and has severe dementia. He's asleep when I first walk in, so I sit by his bed and rest my cheek on his arm.

"I've lost so much," I whisper.

My grandpa opens his eyes and turns to me. "But you've also gained so much."

He's right. I've learned more about love, life and death in the past two months than I did in thirty-two years.

Nineteen

Back in Alberta, I return home to a cold house. I check the thermostat and find it's stuck at thirteen degrees. I punch the 'up' arrow to get the heat going again. An hour later, the house is still cold so I re-check the thermostat – it's still at thirteen. I push the 'up' arrow again. Another hour passes but the temperature doesn't increase.

I call Dawson and half an hour later he's in my basement.

"You better call someone right away," he says. "The controls must be stuck."

I roll my eyes. "Great."

"Wasn't thirteen Sam's lucky number?"

"Yeah."

"Then just be thankful he's still looking out for you."

Since I'll be celebrating Christmas this year with a mischievous spirit instead of a husband, I forego the traditional tree. Instead, I loop two strands of small white lights through the plants, plaques, pictures and fountain accumulated on our fireplace. The overall effect at night is lovely, though rather shrine-like.

Christmas morning is spent with my mom, Ed – home from Northern Ontario – and his new girlfriend. After opening up our stockings, including one for Sam (in which I put a chocolate orange), I unwrap my presents. My mom gives me a suitcase. A bolt of anger shoots through me; I don't need a suitcase where I'm going.

But I thought you were enjoying your newfound financial freedom?

No! That's not what I meant.

What did you mean then?

That in my own haphazard way I'm learning to live without you.

So if you could have me back, you would choose me over the money?

After brunch, I load up a bottle of sherry, two brandy snifters and his chocolate orange then head to the cemetery, where I pour us both a drink.

"Cheers, big ears," I say to his cross.

Christmas dinner is spent with his family, photo, and empty chair.

Back home again, I down two sleeping pills with more sherry and pass out.

"I had an interesting dream last night," Ed's girlfriend says to me on Boxing Day morning. "There was a dark-haired man in it. I couldn't make out exactly what he looked like but I knew I'd never met him before. And he *really* wanted me to go to a movie with him . . . he was very insistent about it."

This takes a second to sink in. I look at Ed.

"I figured you'd want to hear that," he says.

How could a woman, who had never met Sam and certainly hadn't known about his tradition of going to a movie with his buddies on Christmas night, dream about it – in his house – on Christmas night?

In the afternoon, we host an open house for family and friends, during which Tom presents me with a plaque in Sam's memory. He explains to the group that Sam posthumously received his District's Leadership award for the Most Valuable Officer for 2000 – and that the award has now been renamed in his memory.

After the presentation, I toss back a shot of left-over Greek brandy and am on my way upstairs when I pass Dale's wife and Katrina closely examining our main wedding photograph of Sam helping me out of the car.

"Have you noticed anything strange about this picture?" Dale's wife asks me.

"No."

"Look behind Sam's head," she says, "in the background."

I lean in to examine a mural painted on a building. Because of the angle of the photograph, Sam's upper body appears to be in the middle of two hands that represent God in the mural.

"Sam," says Katrina, "is literally in God's hands."

The white dove of peace, just released from God's hands, is above my head.

The next day, my family drags me to a local ski resort – another attempt to, as my mother puts it, 'get me away from the sadness.'

But it just comes along with me. Thus I am a grieving butterball, rolling along the cross-country ski trail, huffing and puffing, dreadfully out of shape.

At the lodge afterwards, a group of us are hanging out by the fireplace when my eldest niece, perhaps catching a rare moment of honesty in my expression, leans over and gently whispers, "You miss him, don't you?"

My tears begin instantly. I nod and allow myself, for just a moment, to ignore the conflicting thoughts and simply *feel* the sorrow and agonizing sense of loss.

By New Year's Eve, however, my mind is in charge again. My friends join me at the cemetery for a drink; five concerned faces watch as I pour beer on Sam's grave.

"I don't know how you do it," Kristy says.

I look at her. "Do what?"

"Be so . . . accepting of all this."

"Because she *has* to," Jodie replies. "Adri doesn't have a choice."

Oh, but I do. And I just hope that when the time comes – as I suspect it will – I'll have the courage to make the right one.

Smiling, I raise my beer bottle towards the white wooden cross. "To Sam," I say.

New Year's Day, 2001

"What are you doing?" I'd asked Sam a year ago today, after walking into our bedroom and finding him packing his suitcase.

"I'm leaving you."

I'd laughed. Sasha had tried to stick her nose in the suitcase but Sam had pushed her away.

"I've had it with you, Adri."

"Why?"

"You know damn well what I'm angry at."

I'd giggled nervously as he shoved in t-shirts and boxer shorts, socks and ties.

"You think I'm kidding?"

"Oh for God's sake, Sam, chill out."

He'd stopped packing and turned to me, his eyes black.

"It's a day trip to the mountains," I say.

"That's not the issue and you know it. Why *do* you think I'm so pissed off?"

"Because I have to take my mother with me."

He'd clapped his hands. "Bingo."

I'd started crying.

"Today was supposed to be a special day for you to spend *alone* with Ed. You get to see him once a year, if that."

"But . . ."

"And your mother just *has* to go along."

"She loves that sort of thing," I'd said, "and I don't want to hurt her."

"Then you know what?" He'd snapped the suitcase shut. "If you want to keep your mother so damn happy then go fucking live with her."

Then he'd picked up the suitcase and walked out the door. "I married you, Adri, not your mother."

Sasha and I had followed him down the stairs. "Sam, don't do this."

He'd stood by the front door, his jacket in one hand, suitcase in the other. "I fell in love with an independent, free-spirited woman who dreamed of becoming a great writer."

I'd slumped onto the stairs. Sasha crept up beside me.

"And what you've turned into is a thirty-one year old puppet who has given up on her dreams."

"All this because I'm taking my mother to the mountains?"

"No. All this because you can't say no."

Sam didn't leave me that day. He'd saved his grand exit until nine months later.

Twenty

On January 10th, Nick's wife is scheduled for a 9:00 a.m. C-section. Why I, the nuttier-than-a-fruitcake recently widowed *childless* auntie, has been asked to attend the birth, I'm not sure. Perhaps it has something to do with my refusal to tell people how I'm really feeling. And still not having grasped the concept of saying no, off I go.

At 9:30, a baby girl with the middle name of Hope arrives. When she's shown to me, I shiver.

"You're being held by Sam," the baby's maternal grandmother says to me.

"Huh?"

"The way your body just reacted," she explains, "it looked like someone was standing behind you, wrapping their arms around you."

I'm handed the infant to hold while her mother sleeps off the anesthesia. But as I look down at the baby, I realize with absolute certainty that all living creatures follow a cycle of life and death. Such a small and simple truth, yet finally accepting it dislodges the first pebble of a landslide. A human being is born and then, one day, he or she dies. There are no exceptions to this rule. Another pebble slips away. It's impossible that *anyone* can physically come back from the dead. A stone breaks free.

"She's cute, isn't she?" Nick says to me.

I force a smile. "She sure is!"

"Sam would have loved her, eh?"

I nod, grinning like an idiot as he snaps a photo of Hope and me. Then I hand the child back to her father.

"Are you gonna stick around for awhile, Adri?"

"No. I uh . . . I gotta get going."

Then I watch as he leans in and kisses his wife, who, though still groggy from the medication, smiles up at him.

Sam and I will never experience parenthood. A boulder joins the slide.

I excuse myself, drive home, make a cup of tea, give Sasha a pig's ear, sit in my big blue chair, stare out the living room window and promptly have a mental breakdown.

Jesus is no more the Son of God than I am His Daughter.

There will be no Second Coming of Christ.

There is no perfect place called heaven where Sam is waiting for me.

Sam is not coming back.

I will never see him again.

I am alone. I am a widow.

To try and stop the slide, I drag myself downstairs to Sam's Perch to watch TV. I can hear his sister leave a message on my answering machine. Then a couple of friends leave messages. My mom does as well. People are obviously concerned about the impact of the baby's birth on me. But I'm now past the point of wanting to be consoled. I just want to be out of the fucking pain, so eloquently labeled grief. I've had it with the mental anguish, the heartache, the loneliness, the guilt, the lies to my self and those around me, the confusion, and the self-pity associated with the realization that while other people are allowed to be in love and have babies, I am not.

Then I hear Tom begin leaving a message on my machine and it hits me: I *do* want to talk to him.

I pick up partway through his message. "Hi."

"I just called to see how it went today," he says.

"Brutal."

"I bet."

I start crying. "I can't take this much longer."

"I don't know what to say, Adri."

"There's nothing left to say."

I remain on Sam's Perch for another hour, staring into the fire. Then I go up to my bedroom, turn on the light, walk into the middle of the room and stand there.

Why am I still here?

I don't have to stay.

There's a bottle of Tylenol 3's in the bathroom.

Sasha jumps on the bed and rests her snout on her paws, watching me carefully.

I stare at the bathroom door.

Don't go so close to the edge!

"I'm nowhere near it," I snap at the periwinkle walls.

Yes you are. Don't be stupid!

"Fine." I sit down on the bed, still a few feet from the bathroom. "Then give me a good reason to stay."

I already did.

So I take two sleeping pills, curl up in bed with Sam's badge and fantasize about a romance with Tom. Sam's not coming back on his white horse to save me. But it's not just saviours who ride white horses. Knights do too.

Plan G.

PART III
Reality

One

January 11th, 2001

The doorbell wakes me in the morning. Wearing Sam's boxer shorts and hawaiian shirt, I stumble downstairs to answer the door. Standing on my front porch is the detective in charge of Sam's investigation, final police report in hand.

He takes one look at me. "We don't have to do this today."

"I'm OK."

"Honestly, Adri, I can come back another time."

I give him the wave. "I can handle it."

He frowns. "I'm going to stay here with you while you read the report."

I go into the kitchen to start coffee then join him in the living room.

"Now, I've covered up all the photographs of . . ." He coughs and hands me the document. "Well, that I don't think you need to see."

"Thank you."

As I begin reading the report, it occurs to me that typing up incident reports had been my job; understanding and questioning the investigative findings from Sam's death seems to be my *work*. Plus it's the least I can do, considering the transgression of the heart committed last night. Only, what's the first thing I notice reading through the list of officers who were at the scene? That the digits of Tom's regimental number also add up to eleven. What are the odds of this?

After reading through the witness statements given by police officers, paramedics, firefighters and hospital staff, I look at the detective. "It was over very quickly for Sam, wasn't it?"

"Yes."

Then I read through the scene exam and investigative details. "Do you think Sam thought he was stepping from one safe surface to another safe surface?" I ask.

"Sam is the only person who could answer that question."

"I'm only asking for your opinion."

He nods. "Sam stepped to the side of the ceiling, where there was a beam but unfortunately it wasn't wide enough for his boot."

I think about this. "Are you saying that maybe he *knew* it was a false ceiling – and was stepping to the side for better footing?"

"We'll never know that either. It was dark, Sam had his flashlight out, he was looking for an intruder and had every reason to believe there was one in the building."

"In other words," I say, "he was just trying to do his goddamn job."

"That's right. And both you and I know that Sam was very good at what he did."

"Would a safety railing have saved his life?"

"Again, I can't answer that question with absolute certainty."

I fold my arms across my chest. "How about with some certainty then?"

"Yes. It would have."

"And the alarm – what happened with the follow-up on that?"

"The employee insisted he heard an unusual-sounding alarm when he came into work that morning. But the alarm company has checked the system thoroughly and it was *not* malfunctioning. The employee may have been mistaken about what he'd heard."

I throw up my hands.

"Adri, quite often during an investigation, there's one piece of the puzzle that just doesn't fit – so we have to focus on all the pieces that *do*."

Since I can't force the missing piece of the investigation to materialize, I instead direct my energies into putting back together the pieces of my own life. I spend my days crying, walking Sasha, reading, writing a little, crying, feeling guilty, kissing Sam's photos, daydreaming about Tom, returning the occasional phone call, and crying some more. I also begin to put some of Sam's things away. The last towel he'd touched still hangs in our bathroom. I hold it up against my face then gently place it in the laundry basket. I move his deodorant and cologne from the bathroom counter to under the sink. Each act is another little goodbye and I'm not even throwing or giving anything away; I'm just changing its location in our home. For some reason, however, I can't bring myself to move his calculator and copy of the police contract with the City from where they sit on the back of the toilet.

As the end of January approaches so too does my three-month leave from the police service. "When are you going back to work?" I am asked over and over again.

I want to reply that I AM working my ass off, thank you very much. Grieving, writing about it, and trying to figure out what to do about the circumstances surrounding Sam's death is the toughest work *I've* ever done – especially since I'm trying to do it inside a goldfish bowl with people constantly tapping on the glass.

Gawker 1: Look at the little widow swimming around in circles!

Gawker 2: Gee . . . do you think she needs more food?

Gawker 1: Actually, she's looking pretty chunky. Have you been feeding her?

Gawker 2: Yeah.

Gawker 1: Whoops! So have I.

"I'm writing a book," I tell the inquiring masses.

"Uh huh," is the usual response. "But when are you going back to *work*?"

I phone the head of Records to request a year off, explaining I need more time to sort everything out.

"Take as long as you want," she says.

"I appreciate that."

"I hear you're writing a book."

"I'm trying to."

"I think that's wonderful!"

"Thank you."

"Adri?"

"Yeah?"

"Go to your destiny."

But since I don't know where my destiny is, I go to Sam's – every few days. While hanging out at his grave, I've taken to smoking the wine-tipped cigars he used to like. Since I'm a dreadfully naughty widow, dreaming of a new lover when the old one hasn't been dead four months, smoking fits my new bad girl self-image.

In late January, I pay a visit to the psychologist to run the Tom-thought, occurring with increasing frequency, by him.

"I don't know what your future holds," he says, "but right now, I'd say you're still very much grieving the loss of Sam."

"So how do I control my thoughts?"

He suggests I think of a recurring thought as a tangible entity and when I find myself thinking about something I'm not ready to deal with, gently push it away.

"For good?" I ask.

"Not necessarily. Assign a timeframe if you want . . . say a few months."

I'm sure this is a very useful tool – but I don't *want* to use it. I enjoy the quasi-good feeling that accompanies romantic daydreaming. It sure as hell beats grieving. As I'm leaving the psychologist's office, the I-am-Jesus-thought pops into my head again.

"Let's say a thought comes back and I *am* ready to deal with it. Is it OK to use a baseball bat?"

He smiles. "If that's what's needed, sure."

Two

At the end of January, the K-9 officer comes by for a visit. "I remember you mentioning that you wanted to meet the dog that was working with me and Sam that night."

So I follow him out to his car and, after snapping and snarling at me through the glass, the police dog cheers up considerably once out of the vehicle. He gives me a quick sniff then proceeds to pee all over the front lawn.

"He's just marking his territory," the officer explains.

But inside the house, Sasha's going nuts at the window. That's *her* territory he's marking. The K-9 officer puts the dog back into the car then comes inside for a coffee. I ask him about the night Sam died.

"When I arrived at the warehouse," he begins, "Tom, Sam and his teammates were waiting outside for me. So I looked straight at Sam and said, 'You. Let's go!'"

"Seriously?"

"Yes."

"Why Sam?"

"Because he was the best person for the job. So we went in and Sam went up the ladder and a couple of minutes later, I saw him fall through the ceiling. So I yelled into the radio what had happened and then ran looking for him."

The K-9 officer pauses, running his hand through his hair. "I found him in the lunchroom and started CPR. It took a few minutes for Sam's team to find us and when they did my dog went berserk with all the chaos, so two of the teammates had to take over CPR. Then Tom took control of the scene and I remember watching him, directing everyone what to do . . . it was amazing to see a leader like that in action, especially when you consider how close he was to Sam."

Oh boy.

"Thank you for getting Sam's breathing going again," I finally say. "Not only did that mean his organs could be donated, which in turn saved other people's lives, it also meant that I was able to spend his last day with him."

The officer looks at the linoleum then back at me. "There's something else I have to tell you."

"OK."

"About a month before Sam fell, I was clearing a building with another K-9 officer and his dog, which meant *I* was the one searching the upstairs level. One minute I was walking along and the next, I was sitting on some guy's desk one floor down."

"Huh?"

"*I* fell through a false ceiling a month before Sam did."

I give him the goldfish.

"But I wasn't hurt," he continues, "so I just got up, kept going and didn't think anything more about it . . . until Sam fell."

"Didn't you have to file some sort of report?"

"Yeah but that was the end of it. There are *thousands* of unsafe buildings in this city. Until Sam died, I just accepted that was part of our job."

"And now?"

"I don't."

I think of the map in Sam's duty-bag. Are unsafe workplaces the 'bad guy' issue?

"I also wanted to tell you," he continues, "that I really appreciated the letter you wrote me last fall. I showed it to my wife and we both thought it was the nicest letter we've ever read."

He stands up. "In fact, I keep it with me whenever I'm working. If that's what you can do with a letter, Adri, then the book you're writing will move mountains."

So when the phone starts ringing at 9:00 the next morning, I don't answer it. I don't putter around the house, rearranging knick-knacks and kissing photos of Sam. I don't think about the calls I ought to be returning and the months' worth of unopened mail. I don't stare at the water fountain thinking about writing nor do I daydream about Tom. I sit down at the computer to do *my* job. Sam's breathing wasn't the only thing the K-9 officer kick-started – he just got me writing again.

In the first week of February, I go for lunch with Charlie and Mark.

"I think I've figured out a way we could give some of the money raised in Sam's memory back to the police community," I say.

Charlie nods. "Let's hear it."

"Well, they've renamed Sam's District's Leadership award in his name. So how about we give the annual recipient some sort of cash award along with the plaque?"

"Hmmm . . ." is the collective response from across the table.

"Since our holiday in Disneyland turned out to be so significant to me," I explain, "it might be kinda cool to give the recipient time away with his or her family. For as much as Sam loved his work, being a police officer hasn't provided *me* with the greatest memories. In fact, I've actually got a fairly shitty reminder of his dedication. What has given me comfort is our last vacation together."

Charlie leans back. "So like a weekend away or something like that?"

"Yeah."

"And the purpose," Mark clarifies, "is to encourage spending time together, as a couple or a family or whatever, away from the stresses of work?"

"Uh huh."

"Then we'd need to make it very clear what attributes are recognized," he says.

Charlie nods. "Since the award is in memory of Sam, then the recipient ought to reflect what *he* stood for."

"Which is?" I ask.

"Integrity," Mark replies. "And honour."

"And courage and dedication," adds Charlie.

Mark nods. "Sam always went beyond what was expected of him . . . he was committed to excellence."

So I jot down integrity, courage, honour, dedication and a commitment to excellence in my notebook.

Mark then suggests that we come up with some sort of symbol for the memorial fund that represents Sam. Charlie and I nod in agreement. But I have no idea what this symbol could be.

When I get home, I look up integrity in the dictionary for a reminder on the meaning. Mark was right. Sam had been an honest man – but not in the sense of always telling the truth. Rather, he'd been true to himself and because of that, he'd been *real.*

Sometimes, however, his determination to be true to himself had been a pain in the ass, especially when it came to being my husband. Case in point was Valentine's Day.

"I love giving you gifts," he'd say, "but not when you're expecting them."

He'd still usually end up giving in to the commercialism and spend a portion of Valentine's Day lined up behind all the other procrastinators, waiting to buy chocolates. On occasion, though, he surprised me. When he was still a student and we were living in British Columbia, I came home on Valentine's Day to find dozens of Hershey's kisses in the shape of a heart on the kitchen table with a bouquet of pink tulips in the middle.

This year, so that I won't be sitting at home alone on Valentine's Day, staring at the fire and reflecting on all that is not, I join Cassie and Cam in celebrating their daughter's first birthday. Once the festivities are underway, however, self-pity rears her ugly head yet again. How come *I* don't get a husband or a child?

Around 9:00 p.m. I leave their house and go to the cemetery to have a cigar with Sam. Sobbing, I stumble in my stupid high-heeled boots to his grave.

"I FUCKING HATE THIS!" I scream at his shiny, new headstone all the way from India.

I fall on my knees. "I miss you so much."

Shaking from the cold, I mimic, in a horrible high-pitched voice, another oft-repeated comment made to me over the past five months: 'Adri, I just can't *imagine* what it would be like to be in your shoes.'

"Well," I howl into the night, "come spend Valentine's Day with the old widow – that'll give you a pretty goddamn good idea."

My teeth are chattering, my hands freezing and I no longer feel my toes.

"And here's another suggestion," I continue, surprised at the cruelty in my voice, "stand here at his grave, only pretend that instead of Sam's name, it's the name of the person *you* love the most in the world."

My words disappear into the wind.

"Then let your imagination do the rest."

As I watch the snow swirl around his headstone, it occurs to

me that loving an unseen and possibly non-existent entity called
God is rather like me trying to love a cold slab of granite as if it
were a living, breathing husband.

I stomp back to my car, turn on the ignition and hear Bet-
te Midler on the radio, singing, *You Are the Wind Beneath My
Wings*. My head slumps onto the steering wheel and I let the
tears come.

On the slow, slippery drive home, I wonder if perhaps I
ought to be less concerned with how Sam's death has or hasn't
affected other people and more aware of how it's affecting me
– for I am downright wallowing in self-pity.

Home, I take two sleeping pills and escape for ten hours.

At the computer the next morning, I don't write about Sam.
For the first time, I find myself writing to him.

At 11:00 a.m., Tom calls. "I just wanted to see how you
made out yesterday."

My stomach flutters. "It was tough."

"I bet."

"I miss him."

"I know."

"Today is better, though," I add.

"Adri?"

"Yeah."

"It takes a great deal of energy to miss someone you know
you're never going to see again."

"I realize that."

Then I call Jodie to debrief, but her husband answers the
phone.

"I've got a question for ya," I say to him.

"Shoot."

"What do you think Sam would say about me . . . you know,
hooking up with another guy?"

Pause. "I know he wouldn't want you to be alone for the rest
of your life."

"But let's say that wherever Sam is, he *can* still see me. How
would that work? I mean, he wouldn't want to . . . you know,
watch."

"He won't."

"But how do you know?"

"Because when the time comes, Sam will just . . . I dunno, pull the shower curtain across."

I laugh. "*What?*"

"Geez," he says, "I have no idea why I just said that."

Three

Since my birthday is two weeks after Valentine's Day, Sam used to tease me about the double whammy on his pocketbook.

This year, a few days before my thirty-third birthday, I'm in bed reading the paper and have just lit two candles on the bedside table, which still holds a photographic shrine to Sam. I glance over and see that one of the candles – the friendship kind with a small present hidden in the wax – has gone out.

I go downstairs to have breakfast and when I walk back into my bedroom, both candles are burning brightly. So I walk over to the friendship candle, look down and see a gold heart pendant floating in the melted wax.

I sit down on the bed to rationalize this. I must have been mistaken when I thought the friendship candle had gone out, as I probably just couldn't see the flame from my bed. However, just in case this *is* a sign from Sam, I fish the heart out of the wax, wipe it off and place it on his chain alongside his ring, cross and medal.

Then, since it was Angela who gave me the friendship candle as a gift, I phone to tell her what happened.

She gasps. "Oh my God!"

"What?"

"The candle in *my* room is still burning."

"So?"

"I know I blew it out before bed last night. And even if I hadn't, it's impossible for it to still be burning – it's a *tealight*."

When Katrina takes me out the next day for an early birthday lunch, I tell her about the candle incident. "Do you think it was a sign from Sam?" I ask.

"That wouldn't surprise me in the least."

"There's something else I have to tell you."

"This sounds serious."

I blush. "I, ummm, I think I kinda like someone."

"Thank goodness!"

"*What?*"

"Now THAT surprises me."

"Thanks a lot."

"I'm sorry, Adri, but you have no idea how happy this makes me."

"Why?"

"Because it's healthy. I'm not saying you have to get married tomorrow. It's just really good to hear that you can have feelings for another guy."

"Do you know who it is?"

She smiles. "I've got a pretty good idea, yeah."

Over dinner at my place, I run the Tom possibility by my father. Not only is my dad the least romantic person I know, he'll be sure to give me a brutally honest and rational assessment of the situation.

"I see," he says, after I tell him the details.

"And?"

"First of all, it's logical why you would fall for him. Secondly, knowing his character, *if* he decided that he could pursue a relationship with you, and I'm not saying he will, but if he did, then I can tell you right now you'll be waiting quite awhile."

"Oh."

"He was Sam's friend *and* boss."

I sigh.

"Besides," the realist adds, "doesn't he have a girlfriend?"

I nod.

My dad laughs. "That might be a bit of a problem."

I shrug.

"Whatever you do," he advises, "don't fall in love with love.

On the other hand, you don't want to be on your own too long because then you'll get stuck in your ways."

"But thinking about Tom gives me hope," I say.

Then I walk over to the dining room wall, where I've hung the framed first stanza of an Emily Dickinson poem. I point it out to my dad.

> *Hope is the thing with feathers*
> *That perches in your soul,*
> *And sings the tune without the words,*
> *and never stops at all*

He reads it then looks at me. "But your tune *has* a word."

On my actual birthday, I find a chocolate orange and a card in my mailbox. I rip open the envelope and read the words: "From your friend, Tom."

I figure it's time to have a chat with Sam about the matter.

"Is it wrong for me to have feelings for another guy so soon?" I ask his headstone.

The wind picks up. I try lighting a cigar but the match keeps blowing out. "I'll be right back," I tell the granite then run to my car.

Back at his grave, lit cigar in mouth, I kick the snow with my boot. "I know you wouldn't want me to stay single forever but is it, you know, taboo for one cop to date another cop's wife?"

Silence.

My feet are frozen so I blow his headstone a kiss and head home to resume our discussion in the bathtub.

"I'm not a piece of property," I tell the flickering candles at the corner of the tub.

But Sam had never thought of me as a possession, nor had he been a jealous guy.

"So you wouldn't be like Sasha," I say, turning off the tap with my toe, "angry when the police dog peed all over the front lawn, marking *her* territory?"

I take a sip of sherry and think about the dream Sam had

in California, where I'd cheated on him with the cop with the sexy voice. Had Sam been upset because I'd betrayed him with another guy? Another police officer? Or had the dream symbolized an altogether different sort of betrayal?

I hear a helicopter flying over the house. A few minutes later, it flies over again. Is it the police helicopter, searching for a bad guy? Or am I the bad guy, fantasizing about Sam's boss? It flies over again.

"This isn't just about my love life, is it?" I ask the shower curtain.

I know I'm not holding up my end of the bargain. In the contract I'd written and placed in Sam's casket, I promised that I'd find some good in his death. Have I?

I sink lower into the water. Three years ago, I'd told Sam I was going to take a correspondence course to help me with writing my novel.

"Good," he'd said.

"It's gonna cost us two thousand bucks."

"Ouch! Are you sure it's worth it? I mean, will it actually help you become a better writer?"

"Oh absolutely, Sam."

"OK, then let's make it happen." He'd cashed in court time to pay for the course.

Six months passed and I told him I was quitting the program. It was way too stressful . . . all that actual writing, never mind the criticism.

His response: "You're kidding me right?"

"Nope."

"That little effort cost us TWO THOUSAND DOL-LARS."

I'd shrugged. "I just can't handle the pressure right now."

"I don't believe you," he'd said, shaking his head. "You're quitting *again*."

"Whatever."

"Whenever things get tough, you give up – just like that writing contract in British Columbia."

I'd rolled my eyes. "Oh God, here we go."

"That organization really pushed you, *challenged* you to become better. And you just walked away from . . . how much money was it again?"

"Don't be an asshole, Sam."

But he'd been on a roll. "Refresh my memory, exactly how much cash did you turn down by not renewing your contract?"

"You know how much."

"That's right. *Ten thousand dollars* for two or three months of writing work, which – if I remember correctly – was your dream career."

"Uh huh."

"I was a full-time student and working two part-time jobs, Adri. We really needed the money back then."

"I remember."

"But you know it wasn't the money I was angry about."

"Yes, Sam."

"It was because you gave up and now you're doing the same thing."

I'd still quit the course. The funny thing is, although I kept giving up on myself, Sam never did.

"Let's get you a laptop," he'd suggested a year ago, "so you can go to a coffee shop, or wherever, and write."

"We can't afford it," had been my excuse, "and besides I prefer to write at home."

Yet here I am, five months after his death, hanging out in my bathtub talking to a bunch of candles about another guy. I still haven't bought a laptop, even though I could afford twenty of them. And although I am writing *something* in my basement, however meandering, I'm finding the process excruciatingly painful. Writing about and learning from Sam's death hurts. Fantasizing about a fairytale future with another guy makes me feel all warm and fuzzy.

"I'm repeating my pattern, aren't I?" I ask the showerhead.

"I'm putting excuses in the way of my dream *again*. I did it with you, my mom, with every 'yes' I said when I wanted to say no. And now I'm trying to do it with a guy who isn't even interested in me."

Feeling light-headed, I climb out of the tub, wobble to my room and lie down until the dizziness passes. But the damn helicopter flies over again.

"Oh for God's sakes," I snap at the ceiling, "*now* what?"

Sasha and I go downstairs and from my back porch, I can make out the blue and red flashing lights of the retreating police helicopter.

Why *does* it exist? Because a dead police officer's sister cared enough to help ensure positive change came from her brother's on-duty death.

I look to the sky. "I'm getting to that, Sam."

Four

On a Friday morning in early March, Harry and his thirteen-year old daughter pay me a visit. My niece hands me a wrapped gift that stands three feet high by two feet wide.

"Oh my goodness," I say, tearing away the paper, "she's beautiful."

It's an oil painting of an angel with long dark hair, wearing a pink dress.

"Wowsa!" I say, hugging my niece. "Thank you."

"It was supposed to be your birthday present but the framing took a little longer."

"How long did this take you to paint?"

"Five months. My art teacher gave us the project a week after Sam died and I knew it would be for you."

"She spent every Friday night working on it," Harry says.

This kid hadn't been sitting around thinking about painting and daydreaming about becoming an artist one day. She'd just shown up and done the work – until completion. After they leave, I hang the painting in my dining room.

The next morning, under the angel's watchful gaze, I tackle Sam's career scrapbook. I'd started it after he'd graduated from recruit class in 1996 but had only got as far as his first year on the job.

Since order had been so important to Sam, I want all his papers neatly organized. So I carefully sort into chronological order the letters of commendation, job performance and course reviews, police-related photographs and newspaper clippings from the remaining three years.

I come across a summary of Sam's accomplishments and courses taken. I'd typed this up myself for his application to the Priority Crimes Unit last August. When I read it through again now, his first course ever taken has new significance: Officer Safety.

I look out the window. Because of an officer safety issue, all of Sam's career accomplishments are now completely irrelevant. It hits me that I'm not just grieving the loss of Sam, I'm mourning the death of his dream.

"Sam," I whisper, "I think you better send me an angel pretty quick."

Two minutes later, the phone rings for the first time today.

I pick it up. "Yeah?"

It's my new neighbour from across the alley. "I made a whole batch of celery soup this morning," she says, "and I was just wondering if I could pop some over?"

Homemade celery soup comes my way about as often as peach juice.

Later in the afternoon, as I'm placing the newspaper clippings in the scrapbook, I notice there aren't any media photos of Sam from his last year and a half on the job. This makes sense because that was when he began focusing on a career in undercover work. Whenever the media had showed up at a scene he was working at, he'd asked them not to take his picture. But something had always bothered me about Sam's undercover aspirations: his physical appearance. In Alberta, he didn't exactly blend in with the masses. For starters he was Greek. Plus he was tall and broad-shouldered, had jet-black hair going prematurely gray, and a very distinctive, handsome face. When Sam walked in a room, both men and women turned to look. I would have thought the best undercover operators would be forgettable in appearance, not memorable.

I find the ending to his career scrapbook on his desk. On September 13th, 2000, he'd printed a poem off the Internet entitled, "When God made Peace Officers." It's about the emotional, psychological and physical impact that police work has on officers.

As I'm climbing into bed, it occurs to me that, except for my neighbour's call, the phone didn't ring today. My phone always rings.

The next morning, I tackle Sam's death scrapbook. I sort through the newspaper articles and letters to the editor then organize e-mails of condolence sent from police services all across Canada and the States, letters from politicians, the eulogies read at Sam's funeral, the memorial pamphlet, and a few special cards and poems.

I hate doing this. Will anyone else give a shit? Or is this little sojourn into the past solely for my benefit?

And why isn't the stupid phone still not ringing?

In the living room, I face the next excruciating task. Kneeling in front of the chair by the fireplace, I re-read the poem that's on the framed picture of Sam, given me by his recruit class: *Down these mean streets the police must travel, and yet themselves not be mean, nor tarnished, nor afraid.*

"Were you becoming tarnished?" I ask the picture.

I know the answer. The man who died on September 29th wasn't the same person I fell in love with eleven and a half years earlier. At the end of his life, Sam was tougher, jaded and disillusioned about his ability to make a difference as a police officer. He had begun to tarnish. But so had I. Maybe that's what happens with soul mates: when one side of the coin loses its shine, so too does the other.

"As for you being mean to me at times," I admit to the fireplace, "tough love was the best gift you ever gave me."

As for being afraid, clearly he hadn't been. But would fear have saved his life?

I gently touch the dried leaves of the olive branch resting in front of the picture. "You . . . were . . . my . . . hero," I sob.

Sasha snuggles up and licks my face. I hug her and we sit quietly on the floor together. Then I look to the blue picture again. Fear might have saved Sam's life – but what kind of existence is living in fear?

I wrap the olive branch in tissue paper and carefully place it in a box. Then I take the box, pictures and plaques from the fireplace downstairs to my office, where I set up an achievement corner for Sam.

Tonight, I dream of him again. I'm sitting at a table, selling magazines to cops when I glance up and see him standing in front of me. He's in uniform, looking very sexy, and his head is tilted down as he talks into the radio to someone at the police association – the union to which the officers belong.

"Hi!" I call out, excited to see him again.

But he just winks at me and smiles. "Get back to work, ya slacker."

The dream's potential meanings don't hit me until I'm at the dog park later in the day: 1) I need to focus on my writing; enough time spent on his scrapbooks; 2) Sam is still working. Perhaps he'd got his promotion to the Priority Crimes Unit after all . . . in a metaphysical kind of way? He'd wanted to work U/C – well, dead is about as undercover as a guy can get.

So instead of running errands that can easily wait until to-morrow, I drive straight home, turn on my computer and get back to working on my manuscript.

Two hours in, an unfamiliar female voice begins leaving a message on the answering machine: "This is the chief's office calling and . . ."

I pick up the phone. The woman tells me that the new police chief would like to talk to me.

I hang up and sing to the wall, "I get to go out with the big cheese!"

"Oh Sam," I reassure the nearest photograph, "of *course*, I'll behave myself."

Five

When I meet the chief for breakfast the following week, he asks how I'm doing.

"Not bad," I reply. "I'm getting there, thanks."

Good thing he doesn't ask me to clarify *where*, exactly.

"You seem strong," he says, "but we're here for you if you need us."

I nod, cutting into my sunny-side up egg. "I have a comment for you."

"Oh?"

"I'm concerned about the impact the job has on officers and their families."

He looks surprised. "Well, it's not an easy career. It takes a pretty special person to be an officer."

"I realize that. But Sam had changed an awful lot in four years."

"That's fairly normal, Adri. Police officers see a great deal of sadness very soon into their careers. They have to develop a 'crust' of sorts, so they can do their job."

"But isn't there a danger in that crust becoming too hard?"

He nods. "There is. But if an officer were to internalize all the pain, violence and hurt that he or she came across in a shift, they wouldn't last very long."

"So it's finding a balance that's the trick, huh?"

"That's right."

The chief tilts his head. "So what about *you?*"

"What about me?"

"Are you finding a balance?"

I stir my coffee. "Between . . ."

He leans in. "Remembering Sam and moving forward with your own life."

As I spread raspberry jam on my fourth piece of toast, I consider mentioning that, strange as it must sound, I dare say I *observed* said struggle for balance in the form of a drunk driver trying to park his red car during a snowstorm in Toronto. The indecision over whether or not to take his knapsack with him symbolizes *my* challenge of continuing Sam's dream while honouring my own. I also suspect that Sam, dead for two and a half months by that point, still managed to pee in the toilet earlier in the evening just to make sure I was paying attention. Then he set off a car alarm to ensure I was at the window to observe the aforementioned struggle.

"Adri?"

I smile at the chief. "It's pretty back and forth."

I ask Tom for coffee the next afternoon.

"It's hard to know all the right decisions to make," I say.

"What do you mean?"

"Well, since Sam died, I have so many choices. I can do what I want, live where I want and be whoever I want."

He thinks about this. "I bet choosing your new life is kinda like being in a car lot. You just have to keep opening different vehicle doors until you find the right one."

I take a sip of hot chocolate. "How long have you been a cop?"

"Twenty-one years."

"You don't seem jaded or bitter to me."

"That's a good thing, isn't it?"

I nod. "But why is that?"

"Well, we're sitting here in this coffee shop, right?"

"Yeah."

"But nothing bad is happening. The store across the way isn't getting robbed, neither is the bar next door. You don't see police cars going down the street with lights and sirens at the moment. So sure, bad stuff happens out there – but it's not the norm."

"But you see way more crap than the rest of us."

"True. So I just remind myself that although I deal with bad people on a daily basis, there are still far more good people in the world."

"Sam," I say, "was beginning to lose that perspective."

Six

"How would you like to do me a favour?" a friend of mine asks me at the off-leash park the next morning, pointing to the dog beside her.

I look down. Staring up at me is the fuzzy black face of a fatter, fluffier version of Sasha.

"I'm just temporarily looking after him," she explains, "but he needs a home with a lot of love."

Maybe Sasha would like a buddy to hang out with. God knows that's what *I* want more than anything else . . . my dog may as well be happy. I tell her I'll think about it while I'm out of town, as I'm heading to B.C. tomorrow for my post-farewell tour.

In Victoria, Cassie, her daughter and I hit the usual haunts: the teashop, chocolate store, Italian restaurant and favourite bookstore, where I pick up Jane Goodall's *A Reason for Hope* and *The Sacred Balance* by David Suzuki. The latter catches my eye with its earth, wind, fire and water theme; the former because if *I* can find hope for the future, so can the planet.

"You've got a bit of an environmental theme going on there," Cassie remarks when we're on the street again.

"Well, there are some very serious problems that need to be addressed."

"Oh I agree," she says. "It's just that the big issues like climate change seem so overwhelming that I think a lot of people have given up trying to solve them."

I look at her daughter in the stroller. "That's a pretty scary attitude."

"I know."

"Do you think it's also a lack of awareness," I ask, "or just plain apathy?"

"A bit of both," Cassie replies, zipping up her daughter's jacket. "But I bet most people feel that changing their actions won't make a difference, so why bother?"

"That stinks!" says the small voice from the stroller.

"What does?" I ask.

"That car," says the little girl, pointing to the vehicle beside us. "The farting one."

Though a warm day, the parked car she's referring to has been left idling.

"You're right," I say. "That *does* stink."

After Victoria, the three of us head to Vancouver to spend an evening with Stan, Megan and their new baby son. The girls go for a hot tub but since I don't have my swimsuit with me, I go in with just my bra and panties on. Stan ends up joining us but I don't want him seeing me in my wet underwear, so I figure I'll stay in the tub until he leaves. But he doesn't get out so I stay in the hot water for over an hour, drinking a beer yet. When I do finally emerge, I'm downright woozy.

"You better lie down," suggests Cassie.

"Or are you supposed to stay upright?" Megan asks.

I can't remember either so, like a homing pigeon, I wander towards the kitchen. Cassie follows close behind. Then, it's as if someone changes the channel on me. One moment I'm standing in the kitchen and the next, I'm sitting on the verandah of a house in the country, looking out into a yard where there's a big tree with an old-fashioned wooden swing and children are laughing and playing.

"I THINK I'M GONNA NEED SOME HELP IN HERE!"

I open my eyes to see who's hollering, which is when I realize that I'm flat on my back on the ceramic tile floor. Cassie is behind me, her hands cupped under my head.

"What are you yelling for?" I ask.

"You passed out!"

"But what are you doing back there?"

"I caught your head before it hit the ground. You scared the crap outta me."

Stan and Megan come running in.

"Adri!" cries Stan, arms waving. "What are you doing on the floor?"

"Just thought I'd have a little rest!" I snarl, struggling to sit up.

"You better stay still a minute," says Megan.

"Yeah well, I'd love to but unfortunately I have to go to the bathroom."

Three puzzled expressions watch me as I stumble towards the nearest toilet and slam the door behind me. Two minutes later, I hear a knock and Cassie asks how I'm doing.

"Not very good."

"Do you want me to come in?"

"Uh huh."

The door opens and she finds me on the throne, underwear around my ankles.

"Oh *man*," I hear from the hallway. "Somethin' musta died in there."

"Stanley!" Megan hisses.

"I can't help it!" I cry, lifting my head, which is when I catch sight of my whiteish-gray face in the mirror.

"OH MY GOD!" I howl. "I'M GONNA DIE ON THE TOILET!"

In rush Stan and Megan.

"You're *not* going to die," Stan reassures me.

"YES I AM!" I cry then faint into Cassie's arms.

As I'm coming to, I hear mention of 911 being called.

"No, no, no. I'm OK," I mumble then lose consciousness again.

"Hang in there," Megan says, "the ambulance is on the way."

Minutes later, two paramedics appear in the bathroom doorway. I give them the wave; not a shred of ego left. The male medic asks me if I've been drinking.

"I had a beer in the hot tub."

"How long were you in there?"

"An hour."

He shakes his head and takes hold of my wrist as I faint again.

"That's strange," I hear him say. "I can't find her pulse."

I open my eyes and look at him. I *am* dying.

He smiles. "Don't worry, you'll be fine. Some people just can't handle hot tubs."

Sure enough, he finds my pulse and then I'm relocated to another room, where the female medic places an oxygen mask on me for good measure.

"I'm a bit of a mess," I explain, "because my husband died."

"When?"

"September 29th."

"That's only been . . ." She glances at her watch. "Almost seven months."

"It's rather ironic," I say to Cassie in the car the next day, "because for so long, I couldn't wait to die. But then yesterday I realized I don't *want* to go yet."

"Good!"

"And sure as heck not on the toilet of all places."

She smiles. "Your performance reminded me of the pub-crawl sprawl."

"Hah hah."

"What's the pub-crawl sprawl?" pipes the little voice from the backseat.

Cassie glances in the rear-view mirror. "Auntie Adri once showed some boys her bare bum by mistake."

All three of us laugh.

"This is totally embarrassing," I say, "but you know when I was in the bathroom yesterday and Stan said that something musta died in there?"

"Yeah?"

"I think something *did* die."

She glances over at me. "As in . . .?"

"Mommy?"

Cassie looks in the rearview mirror. "Yes?"

"When's the Easter Bunny coming?"

"Well," replies Cassie, "tomorrow is Good Friday – so three more sleeps."

"What's Good Friday?" the girl asks.

Cassie looks to me. "Care to field that one?"

I turn to face the back seat. "That's the day Jesus died so that we could live. I mean, *really* live . . . you know, freely."

The little girl nods her head expertly. "Like a butterfly."

On Good Friday, I'm home again, curled up in my big blue chair reading the Jane Goodall book. I come to the part where, six months after her husband's death, Goodall confessed: "I knew it was time for him to move on and I did not try to call him back."

Clunk goes the coin. I drop the book into my lap.

"I have to let you go too, don't I?" I ask the living room.

I know the answer even though I don't like it.

"Sam," I whisper, "I let your spirit go."

Then I go upstairs, take two pills and crawl into bed. Sasha climbs up beside me but snaps angrily at Sven when he tries to jump up. With a sigh of resignation, Sven flops on the floor and we all fall asleep.

Seven

Not liking one bit the prospect of having released Sam's spirit without a replacement lined up, I phone Tom Saturday morning and ask him to come by.

Slight hesitation, then: "I'm working. But I can swing by, sure."

An hour later he's at my door. Now two dogs bark ferociously.

"Where did you find Sasha's clone?" he asks.

"The dog-park."

Tom sits on the couch; I take the blue chair.

"I have something to tell you," I say.

"OK."

"I like you . . . I mean, as more than a friend."

His eyes widen but he smiles slightly. "Uh well, um, gee, Adri, I had no idea."

"Yeah right."

"You *do* know I have a girlfriend?"

"I know. But I don't think it's serious."

"Well *I* think it is."

"Oh, I realize that," I say, reaching for my coffee cup. "I'm just telling you how I feel because I thought you should know."

"Thanks . . . I think."

"So is there *any* chance we might end up together in the future?"

He puts his coffee cup on the earth coaster. "I don't know what the future holds."

"I think it holds what you want it to hold."

"Perhaps. But timing is everything. Do you know what I think?"

"What?"

"That you loved Sam so much that now you're looking for someone to give all that love to."

"Is that wrong?"

He smiles gently. "No. But I just wonder if . . . well, I don't want to hurt you but maybe you need to learn how to love *yourself* again first."

I recognize the two by four of truth as it meets my forehead.

On April 29th, the seven-month anniversary of Sam's death arrives and along with it, Matt – Sam's former partner – on my front door step. He holds out to me a beautiful bouquet of pink tulips.

When the barking subsides, he points to Sasha's cohort. "Who's this?"

"Sven. He needed a home. Cute, huh?"

"Well yeah . . . but it's kinda weird how perfectly he matches Sasha."

Over coffee, he asks me how my writing is going.

"Slow. I'm finding it really difficult to stay focused because there's always so much going on around here."

"Then go someplace else."

The phone rings and I let the answering machine pick up. I ask Mark if he knows the significance of today.

He shakes his head. "No. I just thought you'd like flowers."

I tell him today is the seven month anniversary. "I promised Sam I'd make it this far without him."

"So what happens tomorrow?" he asks.

"I dunno."

"Are you going to be all right?"

"Yup. But I guess its time to come up with a new ops plan."

The phone rings again. I glare at it.

"Starting with a quiet place to write," says Matt.

"There's a lot going on right now . . ."

"There always will be, Adri. That's life."

"I know."

"Have you set a deadline for completing your manuscript?"

"No."

"Well, I've been working on a novel for years and trust me, there's a real danger in not having a goal to aim for."

The twenty-ninth of June will be the nine-month anniversary of Sam's death and since we didn't have a have a child together, maybe this book is the next best thing?

"June twenty-ninth," I say.

"That's only two months away – are you sure that's reasonable?"

"No. But at least it's something to work towards."

The phone rings again.

Mark looks at me. "How do you *stand* it?"

"Not very well."

Then the doorbell rings, sending Sasha and Sven into another tizzy.

"Getting a novel written in this zoo," Mark says, standing up, "would be nothing short of a miracle."

I open the door to let him out – and the detective, here to discuss with me the final report from Occupational Health and Safety, in.

In the kitchen, I pour a cup of coffee and hand it to him,

nodding towards the document in his hand. "So what's the bottom line?"

"That Sam's death," he replies, "sure is a case for fate."

"When you cops start saying stuff like that, it *really* freaks me out."

"It's just that Sam's case is very strange, Adri. I mean, the sequence of events that led up to his death are almost unbelievable."

Once we're in the living room, I ask him what the report says about the railing.

"As you know, according to legislation there should've been one. But as I found in the police investigation, the lack of railing was not a malicious act. It was an oversight. There was no intent to cause harm."

"Of course not. Safety simply wasn't a priority."

He puts his cup on the coffee table. "I'm not in a position to advise you of where you should go from here . . . if anywhere."

"I realize that."

"I just wanted to tell you that the entire investigation is now complete. The police are satisfied it was an accident . . ."

I shudder at the word.

". . . and Occupational Health and Safety are as well. The company where the accident took place . . ."

I clench my teeth.

". . . immediately made the necessary structural changes and, as I told you before, they felt very badly about what happened. So I guess I just wanted to remind you that there were several contributing factors that led to Sam's death, not just one."

"You mean the funny sounding alarm, the confusion of the employee, the forklift which made the hole in the drywall the day before, the wind setting off the alarm, the two *previous* false alarms, the poor lighting, the chair that gave that extra tilt to Sam's trajectory, the lack of railing, and the simple fact that Sam cared enough about catching the bad guy that he gave his life trying to do so?"

"You've certainly been thinking a lot about this," says the detective.

"I should certainly hope so. And ya wanna know what *I* think the bottom line is?"

"What?"

"That when Sam got to the landing at the top of that ladder, he saw what he *expected* to see on the other side of the wires: a safe surface on which to step. If there was no safety railing, why would it even cross his mind that there might be a false ceiling?"

"Adri . . ."

I hold up my hand. "Which begs the question: why would a company blatantly put its *own* employees at risk?"

"It wasn't an area that employees went on a regular basis."

"That area has been deemed a permanent workplace by Occupational Health and Safety, has it not?"

"Yes."

"Then I'd say Sam's death is a case of cause and effect: no railing, no husband – which tells me that workplace safety is obviously an issue that needs to be addressed."

But why do I have to do this on my own? After the detective leaves, I call Tom to debrief. He tells me he's off to Mexico tomorrow with his girlfriend.

"Oh," I say snottily. "And are you looking forward to your trip?"

"Of course."

"Well have fun."

"Thanks."

I don't say anything.

"Are you OK?" he asks.

"Not particularly."

"Adri . . ."

"Have a great vacation," I say, then hang up.

Then I walk into the dining room and re-read Emily Dickinson's poem. My dad's right: I'm hinging my hope for happiness on an expected outcome with a specific person. Not only do I want Tom to help me deal with the issue that led to Sam's death, I want him to drop his girlfriend and rescue me from widowhood.

"Come on guys," I say to Sasha and Sven, "let's go for our walk."

At the dog-park, I sit down on a rock and look out over the river. "Well Sam, I promised you I'd stick it out for seven months. Now here we are."

I remove my wedding and engagement rings from my left hand and place them on my right. My marriage to Sam is over. As much as I don't want to let go of the past until I know what the future holds, I'm learning life just doesn't work that way.

"They say if you really love something," I sob to the water, "you must set it free. And only if it comes back to you, was it meant to be yours in the first place."

So, for the second time in two weeks, I let Sam's spirit go. Now, however, I not only risk losing it, I have no backup in place.

Eight

The next day, I return to the realm of business matters and tackle a long overdue task. Since October, I've been receiving Sam's salary from the City through what's called 'supplemental compensation.' The payments have seemed low but I haven't yet checked into the matter. So I phone the police association, figuring they'll be able to explain the discrepancy.

"You're right," the union president says to me over the phone, "those numbers don't sound correct. You better contact our lawyer."

I ring up their lawyer.

"Bring in your documentation," he says, "and I'll look it over for you."

I gather up all the relevant papers, including Sam's copy of the police contract with the City, where it's still on the back of the toilet beneath his calculator.

Two days later, I'm in the lawyer's office, my papers strewn across his desk.

"I see . . . all right," he mumbles, shuffling through documents and punching numbers into his calculator. "Uh huh, hmmm . . ."

While he's working, I happen to glance down at the paperwork in front of me and, for the first time, notice my husband's handwriting on the back of his police contract:

August 9, 2000

DEPOWUCDO
UCDOC
CUCDEO
CPUCDEUOS
Sammy Pucdeuos

Clunk. *This* is the undercover name he'd been creating for himself last August.

"Very interesting," says the lawyer.

I look up.

He peers at me over his reading glasses. "Are you all right?"

"Uh huh."

"You're a little pale."

"I'm OK."

So he tells me that from a financial perspective, a few items may need adjusting but nothing is too terribly out of whack. The City is responsible for paying me the *net* equivalent of what Sam would be receiving, if he was still alive, which means that the WCB lump sum and pension payout I received last fall are being deducted and will continue to be until they're paid off at the end of year five.

I nod and start gathering up my papers.

"Not so fast," he says. "There's a far bigger problem here that you need to be concerned with."

"What's that?"

He reaches over and picks up Sam's contract. "According to this, you're never allowed to remarry."

I let out a snort. "That doesn't seem to be an issue at the moment."

"Maybe not *today* – but in the future, it could be a damn big issue. Although Sam's salary seems low now, it will go up significantly in years four and five. Plus, you're entitled to receive a pay increase whenever the officers themselves do."

"I know . . ."

"All that ends if you marry again – which is a glaring violation of human rights. Your future marital status has no relevance as to whether or not you receive Sam's supplemental compensation. What matters is that you were married to him when he passed away in the line of duty. This is archaic."

"Then why is it still in the contract?"

"Because nobody else has been in your situation since 1977 – that was the last time an officer died on the job and left behind a spouse." He stands up. "This is something that seriously needs looking into."

Over afternoon tea and cookies with my dining room angel, I investigate another matter needing looking into. Based on what little I know of undercover terminology, I come up with this possible explanation for the U/C name on the back of the contract:

Police **U**nder**C**over **DE**tective **U**nder **O**peration **S**ting

Corny, yes – but oh so him. As for his first name, I'm sure he chose Sam simply because it's a common Greek name, although not quite as popular as say . . . John.

I call Jodie to fill her in on the day's events, finishing with, "And guess what the lawyer told me right after I found the undercover name?"

"What?"

"That if I ever remarried, I would no longer receive his . . . OH SHIT!"

"*What?*"

"The police association -- *that's* who Sam was talking to on the police radio in my dream a few weeks ago."

"Huh?"

"Right after I finished his scrapbooks, I had a dream that

I saw Sam talking on the radio with someone from the police association. Sam called me a slacker and told me to get back to work – but maybe he was also telling me to contact the police association because of the remarriage clause?"

"That," says Jodie, "is unbelievable."

A few days later, I meet up for morning coffee with a tanned Tom, back from Mexico. I ask him how the trip went.

"Not so good. I don't think we're gonna make it."

Hooray! "How come?"

"Because she doesn't love me the same way I love her."

"Oh."

"Despite what happened to Sam," he says, "you're very lucky to have had the relationship you did with him."

"Still have, actually."

Tom nods slowly. "Have you seen the movie, *Gladiator*?"

"No."

"You might want to."

"Why?"

"There's some stuff in there about the afterlife that I think might interest you."

"The afterlife? You were the one who told me it takes a lot of energy to miss someone I know I'm never gonna see again."

Tom frowns. "I did?"

In the afternoon, Amanda joins me and the pups at the off-leash park.

"Did I ever tell you about the dream Sam had a few days before he died?" I ask, throwing the ball for Sasha. "The one where I cheated on him with another cop?"

"No. Who was it?"

"The officer with the sexy voice."

She nods. "Hollywood."

"Huh?"

"His nickname is Hollywood because he's so damn good looking. And what did Sam have to say about the alleged incident?"

"He was pissed. So when I actually *saw* the guy at Sam's funeral the next week, it was pretty weird."

"I bet," she says, throwing the ball for Sasha as Sven trots along between us.

"It's Tom I like, though."

She turns to me. "Really?"

"Is that wrong?"

"Of course not."

"But he was Sam's friend and boss."

"So? That wouldn't make it wrong . . . just highly unlikely."

I throw a stick for Sven but he ignores it and stays close. "I've been trying to figure out if Sam was mad at me because I slept with another guy, or because it was a police officer or . . . something else?"

One eyebrow goes up. "Such as?"

"Well, the dream was obviously about betrayal, right?"

"Yeah."

"But maybe it wasn't a *guy* Sam was worried about."

Up goes the other brow. "You're gonna bat for the other team now?"

"No."

"Then who else would it be?"

"Me! The *only* way I could betray Sam would be to betray my own self."

"And how would you do that?"

"By not living up to my potential . . . not becoming a writer."

"You *are* a writer!" she says. "You write every day, for God's sakes."

"A *published* writer who makes a living from her work."

"It'll happen. Shit – you have the tenacity of a bulldog." She sneaks a sideways glance at me. "Kinda like someone else I knew."

"Thanks for the vote of confidence," I say, bending over to pick up Sasha's poop.

"So what did you and Sam do that day?"

I straighten up and tie a knot in the plastic bag. "What day?"

"The day he had the dream about you and Hollywood."

"Well, that was Sunday so that's the day . . ."

"What?"

"That's the day we went to Universal Studios – the epitome of Hollywood. We were on the tram tour and I was bitching to Sam about not being able to see any movies being made – and Sam's response was that Hollywood only shows you what *they* want you to see."

Amanda throws back her head and laughs. "That's you, all right."

Nine

In early May, I'm on The Perch watching TV when I see a close-up of a child's bike helmet bouncing across the street. It's a safety ad sponsored by a local injury prevention organization – and it gets me thinking. Most drivers don't deliberately run over children in the street; people just don't think about the consequences of speeding or not paying attention. Likewise, the people that ran the company where Sam fell obviously hadn't considered the consequences of an unsafe area – not for their own employees nor for anyone else who might attend the premises after hours and in unfamiliar conditions.

I bring Sam's cross and medal to my lips, the dried blood long gone. What if I'd been given these pendants for more than just comfort, coincidence, or as a clue to what Sam is doing in the afterlife? St. Jude is the patron saint of police officers as well as lost and hopeless causes; maybe the work the memorial fund needs to be doing is connected to workplace safety *for* police officers? That's a hopeless cause if ever there was one: cops have one of the riskiest jobs on the planet.

When I meet Charlie, Mark and a third officer – a cowboy – for lunch later in the week, I run the idea by them. The cowboy is another of Sam's recruit classmates and was involved with setting up the fund. He handles the finances but hadn't been able to attend any of our meetings yet. I tell the three of them about the bike safety ad and how maybe we could do something similar about workplace safety for police officers.

"It's called a PSA," I finish.

All three look at each other then back to me.

"A what?" asks the cowboy.

"A public service announcement," I say. "It airs on TV."

"Like a commercial, right?" says Charlie.

I nod. "Yeah but it airs for free."

Mark smiles. "Well, TV would certainly be *Sam's* medium of choice."

"And it might help get the public thinking differently about workplace safety for you guys," I say, "or anyone working in emergency services for that matter. Maybe we need to start shattering the myth that death is an acceptable part of your job description."

Charlie thinks about this. "Kind of like . . . protecting the protectors?"

I break into a grin. "Totally!"

Mark asks me what the commercial would look like.

I shrug. "I haven't got that far . . . but maybe we could somehow use Sam's death as an example of the importance of making one's workplace safe for *everyone*."

"We'll deal with this PSA thing," says Charlie, "but first, you need a break."

Mark suggests I go traveling.

"Yeah," says the cowboy, "take 'er easy for a bit."

Tonight, I have dinner at a friend's and during the meal I bring up the idea of traveling. Her husband, also a police officer, suggests Spain.

"You'd love it," says my friend. "Paella, sangria, sexy Spaniards . . ."

"And it's also a safe place for you to travel on your own," her husband adds.

I book my flight the next morning. It's strange to be able to call up my travel agent and tell her where I want to go, without worrying about how I'm going to pay for it.

Then I check my e-mail. Another friend, Tamara, also plans to be spending the month of June in Spain – and would I like to join her? What are the chances of her going to the same country that I've just spontaneously bought a plane ticket to visit?

In the third week of May, I fly to B.C. to meet up with another friend who's visiting her parents on Vancouver Island. On the plane, I'm thinking about Mark's suggestion that we find a symbol that represents what Sam stood for. I recall the qualities we'd come up with and again jot down the words integrity, courage and commitment. And Nakoda, the wolf Sam and I sponsored, comes to mind. What about wolves had intrigued us? I write down the word wolf and circle it.

"Why did you write that?" asks a voice beside me.

I turn to see a teenage girl with long dark hair.

"Pardon me?"

"I was just wondering why you wrote the word wolf?" she asks, holding up the wolf pendant on her necklace. "Because that's my favourite animal."

"Oh, well I was just thinking about the characteristics that wolves have."

She smiles.

"So what would *you* say?" I ask.

"Let's see . . . they're loyal, beautiful and courageous. And they're excellent leaders . . ."

Then from her other side, the girl's mom leans forward, adding: "And they're also very calm and wise . . . almost as if they have an inner spirit. Yet they're also very opportunistic."

"But very family oriented and devoted," replies the girl. Then she turns to me again. "They mate for life, you know."

Thinking I just may have found the symbol for Sam's memorial fund, I ask the girl if she'd mind sketching the wolf on her necklace in my notebook. She does so and when she's finished, she hands it back. But when I go to put the book in my knapsack, her necklace falls out.

I hand it back to her. "You forgot this."

She shakes her head. "Oh no . . . that's yours now. I want you to have it."

Was Sam's spirit just returned to me?

"Spain eh, Adri?" asks my friend's father, over a pre-dinner glass of Chardonnay.

"Yup."

"Then you'll have to go to Morocco as well."

I laugh. "Why?"

"For a camel trek in the Sahara, of course," he says, as if no trip to Spain is complete without a sojourn south.

"Dad's an armchair traveler," my friend explains. "He's kept hundreds of clippings from the travel section of the newspaper."

Sure enough, after dinner he pulls out the Morocco file and hands it to me. I read the articles in bed and drift off to sleep, envisioning myself draped in a flowing robe and matching headscarf while traipsing into the Sahara desert on a camel.

Home again, I run the Morocco idea by Tamara. She e-mails me back in the affirmative but asks me to bring a Moroccan guide-book with me when we meet in Spain.

Then I call Charlie and run the wolf idea by him as a possible symbol for the memorial fund.

"I like it," he says.

"Don't you want to know why?"

"Sure."

I tell him about my encounter with the teenager and her mom on the plane. "And they totally described *Sam* while talking about the characteristics of a wolf."

"Cool."

"You don't think I'm a total nutbar?"

"No. I just think you're more open to that kinda stuff than most people."

The next call is from Dawson, telling me about a dream he'd had about Sam. "I was in the den at your place and I could hear Sam talking, so I turned my head and there he was, on TV."

"What – like on a show, you mean?"

"Kinda. I mean, he was *on* TV but he was talking directly to me."

"And what did he say?"

"That it's really important I look out for his best interests."

"Which is?" I ask.

"You, Adri."

At the end of May, my mom takes me to the airport for me to catch my flight to Spain via London. We have dinner at the same airport restaurant that she, Sam and I ate at before our California vacation.

"Hi," our waitress says, writing her name upside down on the paper tablecloth.

"That's an unusual name," I say. "Is that short for Adrienne?"

"Nope, just Adri. My mom liked the name."

So do I. Although rather unique for an undercover name, it's not as traditional as say . . . Maryanne.

At security, my mother hugs me. "I wish you weren't heading off alone."

"Mom, I'm gonna be on my own for *maybe* twenty-four hours."

"Just be careful, OK?" She hugs me again. "And please call."

On the plane, I find my seat, sit down, lean back and close my eyes.

"Adri?"

I open my eyes. One of Sam's cousins and her husband are standing in the aisle.

"Hi," I say, giving them the wave.

"You're going to Spain, right?" she asks.

"How did ya know?"

"Sam's mom told us. I'd say you're being watched pretty carefully these days."

So I ask them if *they're* going Spain, too.

"No, no . . . we're going to Greece," replies her husband. "We just happen to be on the same flight as you to London."

Is it my imagination or are the powers that be making *damn* sure I'm not alone?

Ten

It is in the resort town of Nerja, Spain where I meet up with Tamara. It's also where I make a genuine attempt to finally stop running. But all the hurt, sorrow, confusion, anxiety and guilt that have been following behind for the past eight months come crashing into me. So I start drinking.

Tamara finds me at the beach bar in the late afternoon, staring out to sea.

"I think I figured out how the spirit world works," I say.

She smiles and pours herself a glass of sangria from my pitcher. "Let's hear it."

"Maybe there was no God that made all this. Maybe it all just started with the Big Bang, then evolution kicked in and somewhere in there, we developed souls and now *they're* evolving, as well."

"How much sangria have you had?"

"Coupla pitchers. So as our souls become stronger, see, we're able to survive after the death of our bodies and can therefore communicate with the living."

"How?"

"Two ways," I say, waving my wineglass. "Directly and indirectly. Indirectly is through conduits, operators, mediums, hosts . . . whatever you want to call it when a departed soul temporarily exists in a living person to communicate a message."

"And directly?"

"That's when the departed soul actually does something on its own – like move a picture, light a candle, push a button on the computer or whatever."

Tamara pours the remaining sangria into her glass. "But why would they bother?"

"To help guide us," I reply, spearing a wine-soaked bit of apple with my straw.

"And how would *they* know how best to do that?"

"Because they can see the bigger picture . . . the future. I don't think they experience time the same way we do. We move chronologically from one moment to the next but I think they jump all over the place, from the present to the past to the future to the present again. And if that's the case, then they can see where we're headed. I feel like I'm in *The Truman Show*, with every move being watched."

She puts her glass down on the table. "Shit, you think a lot."

"It's a family curse," I say, pushing my chair back. "Ya ready for dinner?"

Tamara laughs. "What, am I busy?"

After *paella* and more sangria, Tamara and I return to our hotel where I promptly pass out on my side of the bed.

A few minutes later, I awaken to: "WE GOT IT!"

I turn to Tamara. "We got what?"

She sits up and stares at me, as if *I'm* the strange one. "What happened?"

"You tell me," I say. "You're the one who yelled."

She brings the palm of her hand up to her nose. "There was a man's face, right up close to mine."

"Were you dreaming?"

"No! I was just dozing off."

"Are you hassling me because of our conversation today?"

She shakes her head. "I wouldn't do that, Adri. Not about Sam."

"So what are we supposed to get?" I ask.

"I dunno. But it sure seemed important."

With a sigh, I get out of bed and walk towards the bathroom.

"I invited him."

I stop and turn to face her. "What?"

"I asked Sam if there was a message he wanted me to give to you."

I throw up my hands. "And yet you *forgot* the message."

"He came too close! It freaked me out."

I sigh and continue towards the bathroom.

"Maybe if the poor guy was invited to visit a little more often," she says, "he wouldn't get so fired up and come so damn close."

"I can't believe we're arguing about this," I say, shutting the door behind me.

"And I saw a little red light, too."

I open the door.

"Up there," Tamara says, squinting as she points to the ceiling above my head. "But I guess it was just the smoke detector . . ."

I look to where she's pointing. "There's no smoke detector."

The next two days are spent drinking, swimming, staring at the ocean and, unfortunately, writing towards my June 29th deadline. Many pitchers of sangria and twenty very disoriented pages later, we head to the port town of Algeciras to catch a ferry to Morocco. First, however, is a pub dinner in Gibraltar.

"I still don't know why you didn't bring a Moroccan guidebook with you," Tamara says, sipping her Chardonnay.

"It was forty-five bucks! Besides, it'll be more adventurous just to wing it."

"Suit yourself." Then she nods towards the TV above my head. "Hey, check it out – it's *The Truman Show.*"

On the ferry to Morocco, we don our headscarves – she in a giraffe motif; I in the leopard-print last worn in the convertible with Sam. We arrive in Tangiers in the late afternoon and, after purchasing *jelabahs*, the long, loose-fitting robe worn by Muslims, catch the night train south to Marrakech.

Prancing through the streets in our new outfits, we hear, "Bonjour gazelles!" repeatedly called out to us. Over mint tea in our fifth carpet showroom, we get the scoop. The carpet salesman, wearing an off-white *jelabah* remarkably similar to ours, explains that gazelle is a term of endearment for western women.

"But I'm curious," he says, "as to why you two are you wearing men's *jelabahs*?"

"There's a difference?" I ask, which is akin to a Moroccan asking a Canadian if men's suits and women's dresses are the same.

"Oui. Women tend to wear brighter *jelabah's* – more cheerful colors."

"A *man*," Tamara says, "sold us these."

He laughs. "A little Moroccan humour for our western visitors."

Waiting for the bus on day four, I'm drenched in sweat by 9:00 a.m.

"Gazelle," I say, as we've now taken to calling each other this as well, "is it my imagination or is it getting a tad warm?"

"Adri, are you *sure* you want to go to the Sahara?"

"Yeah."

"But you hate the heat."

"I realize that."

"Then why are we going?" she asks.

"Because I want to ride a fucking camel into the sunset."

"Bullshit."

"What the hell's that supposed to mean?"

She shrugs. "Nothing."

I pour half a bottle of water over my head then look at my watch. "Where's the goddamn bus?"

"We can still go to Casablanca instead – you're way nicer by the ocean."

"That's because I was drunk. I'll be fine once I'm on the bus."

Up goes one eyebrow.

"It'll be air-conditioned," I say as a decrepit old clunker of a bus, windows open, chugs up in a cloud of smoke.

Tamara smiles. "Last chance to go to the sea . . ."

I walk to the door and the bus driver asks me where we're going.

"Ourzazate."

"And then?"

"Tinerhir."

"Then?"

"The Sahara."

He shakes his head. "June is too hot to visit the desert."

I haul myself up the two steps. "So I'm gathering."

Tamara takes the seat across from me. "The guidebook would've mentioned that."

"Why aren't *you* broiling?" I ask.

"Because I don't have a thyroid. I don't feel the heat like you do."

"You're fucking kidding me, right?"

During the excruciatingly hot and winding ten-hour drive through the Atlas Mountains with a traveling companion who does not share my pain, I repeatedly pour water over my head in an attempt to keep from overheating. When we're finally on flat ground again, I see a cluster of red sandstone buildings in suspiciously good condition. I point them out to Tamara.

"Looks like an old film set," she says.

Half an hour later, we pull into dusty Ourzazate. I'm first off the bus.

"Bonjour gazelle," says a man in a military uniform, standing on the platform.

"Bonjour," I reply.

"Are you from Canada?"

"Uh huh."

Tamara joins us.

"I'm reading a book by a Canadian author," the man continues, in perfect English, "by the name of Northrop Frye."

I've heard of Northrop Frye but have never read anything by him. And if I'm thinking of the correct writer, he's not exactly light reading.

"The book is called *The Anatomy of Criticism*," the man says.

I smile politely. "That's nice."

"It's about earth, fire, water and hmmm . . ." He snaps his fingers. "What's the fourth element?"

"Wind," I say.

He breaks into a grin. "Right! Well, you'll have to read the book."

Tamara suggests I show him the Suzuki book so I reach into my backpack, pull out *The Sacred Balance* and hand it to him.

"David Suzuki is another Canadian author," she explains, "and a well-respected environmentalist. That book's all about earth, wind, fire and water too."

The man flips through it then hands it back. "You need to read Northrop Frye."

Then he turns and walks away.

"That was strange," says Tamara.

We find a hotel down the street from the bus station. No one is at reception so we take off our packs and are waiting in the lobby when I notice, on the wall, a framed photo of a familiar-looking group of sandstone buildings. I lean in closer.

"Gladiator," says a male voice over my shoulder.

I turn around to see a young guy, wearing jeans and a T-shirt, standing behind me.

"Pardon me?"

"The movie *Gladiator* was filmed here," he says proudly. "That's the set."

In our room, I grab my notebook and scribble madly about the military man, Northrup Frye and the *Gladiator* film set. I add in a Suzuki comment about western thought leading us to our alienation from nature, then resume writing about Sam's funeral – all in the same paragraph. I am creating a literary stew. I don't know *how* to write a book any more than I know how to grieve. But since Sam is clearly watching, I'd best be writing something.

Eleven

On the road to Tinerhir the next morning, we pass through the town of Boumaine.

"We have to come back here," says Tamara.

I look out the window at an even drier, dustier town than Ourzazate. "Here?"

"Yes."

"Why?"

"I don't know. We just do."

In Tinerhir, we meet up with a guide who takes us on a sunset tour. The following day, we're on a bus back to Boumaine.

"Now what?" I ask Tamara on the empty main street, watching our bus pull away.

"Let's see what there is to see . . . that's kinda the point of traveling."

We wander into the nearest café and order mint tea. Two white-robed Muslim men in their mid-twenties are seated at an adjacent table.

"Bonjour gazelles," says one as I'm putting my knapsack on the floor.

"Bonjour," I reply.

"You are from Canada?" asks the other.

"Oui."

"May we join you?" asks the first as he pulls his chair over to our table.

He's a university student in Marrakech, back home in Boumaine for the summer. His English is excellent so he speaks to me. The other man speaks French to Tamara.

"So what do you think of globalism?" my guy asks me.

"Ummm . . . I guess it's a good thing," I say, thinking its way too hot for an intellectual discussion.

"Why?"

"Because the world is becoming more and more connected and it makes sense that we're getting closer to creating a world economy."

He shakes his head. "I don't agree. For a developing country such as Morocco, it is not in our best interest to participate in a world economy."

"How come?"

"Because a global economy will only benefit nations that are *already* wealthy."

What I'd learned in university about economic development and world trade seem so distant now, as if my education has been sitting in a box for years, gathering dust. That my head feels like a fried egg isn't helping my ability to think.

He tilts his head slightly. "You haven't read Chomsky?"

"*Noam* Chomsky?"

"That's the only Chomsky I know of."

"I've read him," I say. "Although it's been awhile."

He smiles. "Then you know that Chomsky maintains that a global economy suits the needs of international corporations and finance, not the local people."

"I know."

"What about existentialism."

I take a sip of tea. "What about it?"

"Do you know what it is?"

I sigh. "I can't remember at the moment."

He leans back, folding his arms across his chest. "According to Sartre, it means that existence takes priority over essence."

"OK."

"Do you believe that?"

I wipe my forehead with the sleeve of my *jelabah*. "Do I believe what, sorry?"

"That a person's existence is more important than their essence – their fundamental nature – if there is such a thing?"

"I believe," I reply, after much mental strain, "that the essence of a person is of equal importance to their actual existence."

"Ah hah!" the philosopher cries, clapping his hands. "So there is a brain in there."

"I've been through a lot lately," I say snottily.

"So you think a person actually *has* a nature . . . an essence?"

"Absolutely."

I take a drink from my water bottle then pour water over my blue sarong, which I've taken to draping over my head and neck. Then I stick my straw hat back on top. In case Morocco isn't dazzled by my men's *jelabah*, this ensemble ought to do the trick. The Muslim watches all this with amusement.

"And does that essence exist before the person is born," he asks, "or is the person responsible for creating it himself?"

"I dunno."

"*I* think we're responsible for creating our own selves."

Then he asks me if I've ever walked through an oasis. I shake my head, hoping the experience involves water. The four of us leave the café and walk the ten minutes into the oasis on the edge of town. I can't help but notice that walking along, talking philosophy with these men in white robes, feels as if we've been transported back to biblical times . . . or ancient Greece.

"It doesn't rain much here, does it?" I ask my Muslim.

"The Sahara hasn't had rain in four and a half years."

I sigh, seriously starting to wilt. Then I dip my sarong in the running water and drape it over my head again.

"That won't cool your core body temperature," says the philosopher. "You're actually bringing heat to the surface."

"But the water feels cool on my skin."

"That is only temporary."

"Then I'll pour more water on."

"There might not always be water to waste."

I turn to him. "I'm usually pretty good about not wasting water."

My concern over water conservation used to drive Sam crazy. Last summer we'd been on a neighbourhood walk and had come across a sprinkler watering more of the sidewalk than the lawn, so I'd walked across the grass to the tap at the side of the house.

"What are you doing?" Sam had hollered after me.

"What does it look like I'm doing?"

"Trespassing! Use your head – there are better ways to get your point across."

Funny the things we'd fought over.

"I guess if you didn't care about anything but yourself," says the philosopher, "you probably wouldn't be traveling through Morocco, let alone Boumaine."

Though grateful for this stranger's faith in my ability to look beyond my own self, the truth is that although I've *thought* about bigger issues since Sam's death, my lack of action reflects the utter self-absorption that grief tends to demand.

"Perhaps you are not part of the bewildered herd after all," he says.

I stop walking. "Huh?"

"From Chomsky's book – *What Uncle Sam Really Wants* . . ."

Another long lost piece of knowledge clicks into place. "Right."

"Although I do think you live in Plato City."

"How so?"

"You live in the world of ideas, not reality. You are very idealistic."

It's true. I *am* living inside my ideas, dreams, hopes and fantasies because that's a hell of a happier place to reside than widowville.

"But at some point," he says, "you will be forced to return to reality."

I shrug. "When I'm ready."

"Sometimes the distance between ideas and reality is not so far."

I turn to him. "I think it's as far as we want it to be."

The philosopher looks as surprised at my comment as I am at making it.

Back in Tinerhir, Tamara and I buy corn on the cob and watermelon at the market and eat it in our hotel room. Then we lie on our beds, staring up at the mosaic tile ceiling.

"I think I had a chat with Sam today," I say. "The twenty-five year old version."

"How's he doing?"

"He's frustrated with me."

She sits up. "What did you guys talk about?"

"Noam Chomsky, globalism, existentialism, idealism and water conservation."

"Oh," she says and lies back down. "I finally figured something out."

"What's that?"

"I need to find an antelope with a sense of wonder . . . a guy who cares that a world exists beyond his own backyard."

I sit up. "An antelope?"

"Yeah. If we're gazelles then guys are antelopes," she says, as if this were the logical next step in renaming gender.

"What did *you* two talk about today?"

She smiles. "Love."

"Know what *I* want?"

"What?"

"To be a *pink* gazelle again. I want to be the apple of my antelope's eye . . . that's what I was to Sam and now I won't settle for anything less."

"I've never been a pink gazelle," Tamara says softly.

"You will."

"I'm almost forty, Adri."

"Your blue antelope just hasn't appeared yet."

We're both quiet for awhile, thinking our own thoughts, until I leap up. "I see a watering hole!"

"*What?*"

"A watering hole. And on one side, there's a row of white gazelles and on the other, a row of white antelopes. But there's one antelope that sticks out because he's blue – but he only appears that way to *you*, whereas to everyone else he'll be white. Same with you: your blue antelope will see you as a *pink* gazelle but all the other antelopes will see you as white."

"Gazelle," she says, "I think we're on to something here."

"Yeah – it's called the pink gazelle/blue antelope theory . . ."

A knock at the door interrupts our laughter. It's the desk clerk, telling us we have a visitor. So all three of us traipse downstairs to see our guide from the day before waiting in the lobby. He hands me a piece of paper.

"This is the name of the guide," he says, "who will take you into the Sahara tomorrow. He's expecting you."

We catch the morning bus to Erfoud, the city nearest the Sahara. On the outskirts of Erfoud, the bus stops and a man wearing a khaki vest gets on. He quickly scans the passengers and upon spotting our faces, breaks into a brown-toothed grin. Waving a piece of paper in my face, he says something in French that I don't understand.

I shrug. "*No merci.*"

Tamara takes the paper and reads aloud *our* names. So she asks him a few questions in French as I smile and wave at the staring passengers.

"Apparently," she says to me, "this is our Sahara guide."

"Just plucking us off the bus in the middle of nowhere?"

"He's expecting us, remember?"

Twelve

We climb off the bus and into a waiting Land Rover. Introductions are made, the price for a three-day camel trek negotiated and agreed upon, and then off we go in the non air-conditioned vehicle. An hour later, we pull up in front of a concrete compound. Tamara and I exchange glances. Our guide walks us to the building, where he stops briefly to kick awake a man sleeping on a mat, then leads us to the dining room.

"He said we can rest here for a while," Tamara translates to me, "because we won't be going into the desert until later."

"It's not even noon and it's already stifling in here."

She relays this to the guide.

He smiles at me with enormous teeth. "Come with me."

We follow him out of the dining room, past a swimming pool with no water in it, and into a room with no fan or air-con; just a small window through which the scorching wind blows straight off the desert.

"I'm going to shower to cool down," I tell Tamara once the guide has left.

But it only runs hot water and when I glance up, bright green algae drips from the showerhead. I return, soaking wet, to our room and lie on the bed, which is where I remain for the next six hours. At one point, I ask Tamara how hot it is.

"You don't want to know."

"Try me."

"I overheard them talking in the dining room."

"And?"

"It's fifty degrees Celsius."

I'd cry but I can't afford to lose the water.

Tamara sits on the end of my bed. "Why are we here, Adri?"

"Because Sam loves the heat."

"Sam's dead. He can't feel the heat – but *you* can."

Around dinnertime, we're relocated to the roof and soon hear the rumbling of a convoy of vehicles. I watch in amazement as half a dozen air-conditioned Land Rovers pull up beside the compound and tourists wearing khaki shorts and crisp white shirts climb out – and onto *our* waiting camels. We run downstairs and protest to our guide.

"He said they're going into the desert to watch the sunset," Tamara says to me.

"What the hell does he think *we've* sat around all day waiting for?"

Thus we, too, are boarded onto camels to accompany the cheating tourists – the smart ones who brought guidebooks – into the Sahara.

Back at the compound, Tamara whispers in my ear, "The guy leading my camel asked if we'd like two guides in the desert tonight."

I frown. "Why would we need two?"

She folds her arms across her chest.

"Uh oh," I say.

We watch the Land Rovers convoy back to Erfoud, where the occupants will be staying in air-conditioned hotels with pools with water in them. There is, however, one tourist – a guy in his fifties – left behind. He greets us cheerfully with an English accent. I ask him why he didn't go back with the others.

"Oh I've driven my own vehicle here – all the way from England."

I can't help but laugh. "Why?"

"A friend of mine knows the owner of this place but unfortunately he's not here."

Ah, the boss is away – *that* explains why we're being treated more like captives than customers.

"So what are you two ladies doing out here all on your own?" he asks.

"We kinda ended up here," I say sheepishly. "And we're going on a three-day camel trek."

Now it's his turn to laugh. "You can't be serious."

"We are," says Tamara.

"You're going out into the Sahara for three days in *June?*"

"It sounded like a good idea back home," I say.

"Would you like to join us?" Tamara asks.

He smiles. "Well, as intriguing as that sounds . . ."

Perhaps he notices the fear on our faces because he finishes his sentence with, "Oh why not?"

Although our guide does not appear at all pleased with this last minute change of plans, after a dinner of shish kebabs wrapped in sheep stomach lining, the four of us head out into the desert beneath the most magnificent night sky I've ever seen. For three hours, our camels plod up and down dunes until we come to a Berber tent. The guide asks if we'd like to sleep beneath the stars. We all nod and watch as he places a large carpet on the sand, then arranges bedding. I sit at one end of the carpet, the Englishman sits beside me, and Tamara beside him. The guide sits by my feet and leans back against my legs.

Shit.

When the guide goes into the tent a few minutes later, I hiss at the Englishman. "Quick! Trade places."

"Why?"

"Because he's putting the moves on me."

So we swap spots but when the guide comes back out and sees the Englishman in my place, he promptly sits beside me in my new location.

"I am responsible," he says.

"*Je suis uncomfortable.*"

He leans back on one elbow and stares at me. I suspect I'm a lovely shade of pink.

Tamara breaks the silence. "Check out those stars."

"Did you know that what we see as a star," says the Englishman, "is actually just light traveling towards us?"

"Most of the stars don't even exist anymore," Tamara adds. "They burnt out millions of years ago so it's just their light reaching us now. We're looking at the past."

The guide gets up and goes into the tent to sleep. Relieved, I stare up at the sky and find the Orien Belt. The three stars all in a row remind me of the three moles on Sam's forearm. What if my one and only blue antelope had been Sam? Will I spend the rest of my life staring at the past . . . living with the memory of a man who himself no longer exists?

A bright light streaks across the sky. "A shooting star!" I cry.

Tamara laughs. "That's just Sam saying hello."

In the morning, we get back on our camels and head further into the desert. By 9:00 a.m., the heat is excruciating. Watching the wind-rippled lines in the sand as our camels slowly bump along is mesmerizing and when I do lift my head, all I see is red dunes, the occasional clump of grass and bright blue sky. Around 11:00 a.m., we stop at a cluster of palm trees – the only shelter we've seen since breakfast – and we climb off our camels.

"Soon," says our guide, "too hot to move."

He's not kidding. For the next seven hours, we all fade in and out of consciousness. It's technically an oasis but since there hasn't been rain in nearly five years, it's a waterless one. Our only form of movement is to inch around the palm trees, following the scraps of shade as the sun passes overhead.

Around hour three, Tamara asks me what I'm thinking.

I've just poured a small amount of water onto my sarong and am draping it over my body for the two minutes of comfort. "That there must be a reason why the four of us are in the middle of the Sahara desert at an oasis with no water in it."

"And what do you think it is?"

"I haven't got that far yet," I reply groggily.

"Do let me know when you figure it out."

"Me too," mumbles the Englishman as the guide snores on.

Since we have limited water and my coping mechanisms clearly aren't working, I finally try the Boumaine philosopher's suggestion to not cool my skin with water.

"Gazelle?" I say, an agonizing hour later.

Tamara slowly turns her head. "Uh?"

"I think water is connected to the soul."

"Of course it is," she says, eyes still closed. "We *are* seventy percent water."

"So's the earth," adds the Englishman.

I look over at the poor guy sprawled out on his back, starfish-style.

"Are ya glad you came?" I ask.

He gives me a very slow thumbs-up.

By hour seven, I'm actually getting used to the heat. Around 6:00 p.m., we board our camels and the guide leads us back to the Berber tent. He prepares beef tagine for dinner while we visit a nomadic Berber woman and her children living a couple of dunes over. That we've been away from any form of refrigeration for more than twenty-four hours does not bode well with the reality that we're eating beef for dinner. Thus I spend much of the night squatting in the sand. By morning, my stomach is a gurgling balloon.

"*Tu es tres malade*," the guide says, taking my hand and rubbing the skin between my thumb and index finger.

I nod forlornly, disgusted by his touch yet also partially comforted.

"When we get back," he whispers, "I'll give you a special Berber massage."

So over the dunes I go . . . a lamb headed for slaughter and too sick to care.

At the compound, the Englishman returns to his room and Tamara leaves ours to wash her feet. This means I'm alone when the guide arrives. It's a special massage all right – more conducive to increasing the Berber population than healing a stomach ailment. When his hand brushes my bra, I realize he's expecting participation from me. When his fingers touch my panties, I suspect dehydration will soon be the least of my worries. Yet I don't say anything because being intimately touched by a man again – even one that repulses and frightens me – seems better than no touch at all.

Besides, this is a *medicinal* massage. I close my eyes and hear him panting.

"Just one kiss?" His hand slips inside my bra.

Shaking my head, I swat his paw away. And besides, Sam wouldn't let this man hurt me. But the hand comes back and begins moving slowly down my stomach.

I open my eyes. "No," I hear myself say and watch as my finger points to the door. "Get the fuck out."

The guide shrugs and leaves the room. I pull my shirt back down. If I ever want another blue antelope to perceive me as a pink gazelle, then I'm going to have to learn how to see *myself* that way first.

"Gazelle?" Tamara says from the doorway. "Are you OK?"

"Not particularly. We better get back to Spain – I'm gonna need a hospital."

Thirteen

Two days and ten packages of re-hydration salts later, Tamara and I are back on the ferry to Algeciras, swapping travel tales with a Swiss backpacker. I mention the Ourzazate military man who spoke of Northrop Frye and earth, wind, fire and water.

"Archetypes, you mean?" the Swiss girl clarifies.
I search my dusty mental filing cabinet but come up empty.

"Supposedly," she says, "archetypes are part of our collective consciousness. Carl Jung wrote about them. The sacred elements of earth, wind, fire and water are an ancient way people perceived the world around them."

Another piece of dormant education flickers to life.

"And with the environmental crisis today," she continues, "it totally makes sense that these elements are resurfacing from our subconscious into our *conscience*."

Tamara looks at me. "What were you saying in the desert about water?"

"That it's connected to the soul."

I'm hit with another stomach cramp and race to the toilet. When I get back, the Swiss girl is telling Tamara about a recently intercepted e-mail between the CEO's of two large American corporations. "It caused quite a fuss because it mentioned that the race for control of the world's water supply is already well underway. Contrary to popular belief, we *can* live without oil – but not without water."

"Are you all right?" Tamara asks me.

I rest my head against the window. "I think *I'm* outta water."

"She lost her soul mate eight months ago," Tamara says to the woman.

The backpacker looks at me. "I don't think anything real is ever lost."

Tamara laughs. "Oh, we've figured out that much. He pops up all over the place."

In Ronda, Spain, Tamara sleeps in the hospital waiting room while I spend the night in emergency, hooked up to an IV recovering from severe dehydration.

In the morning, I call my mom and fill her in. She freaks.

Then I call Sam's parents and chat to his dad. Having a great time, I say.

Next on the clipboard of fun is Seville, where we're inside a Roman Catholic Church when Tamara, staring at a large metal sculpture on the wall, suddenly bursts into tears. I lead her outside and we sit together on the church steps.

"What was that about?" I ask.

"I have no idea. I was just looking at that sculpture and then it . . . transformed into this huge twisted mass of metal. And there was all this smoke and people were screaming and I – well, it was like I could feel *their* pain."

"Wow," I say. "That's kinda weird."

"I just can't believe how much it *hurt*."

We end our journey in Lagos, Portugal. Now Tamara is the one drinking while I frantically try to complete the first draft of the manuscript by the nine-month anniversary. It's not quality material I'm cranking out but at least I'm keeping my promise to myself.

Tamara places a glass of wine on the patio table for me. "Look at you go."

I put down my pen and take a sip of wine. "I'm trying to describe the mixture Sam's mom prepared for his forty-day anniversary."

"What's significant about forty days?"

"The Greeks believe that on the fortieth day after a person dies, Michael the Archangel takes their soul to God and they're told what work they'll do in heaven."

"So what's in the mixture?"

"Wheat seeds, which represent the soul that goes on to eternal life after the death of the body. But there were also these red pomegranate seeds in there and now I can't remember what *they* symbolized."

She thinks about this. "Remember the red light I saw above the door in Nerja?"

"Yeah."

"That was about the size of a pomegranate seed."

On the morning of June 29th, I complete the first draft of the manuscript. It's an ugly baby but it's out. In celebration, Tamara and I are spending the afternoon sipping fruity cocktails beneath our beach umbrella when a man wearing a big, floppy hat and carrying a canvas bag comes up to us. Carved animals for sale, he says.

I smile. "Do you have a gazelle?"

He frowns. "A gazella?"

"Yeah."

"No. But I have giraffes, elephants and many beautiful necklaces."

I buy a necklace for my mom.

But just as he's about to leave, he roots around in his canvas bag again, pulls out a wooden gazelle and hands it to me. "I guess I have one after all."

Tamara laughs. "When we get back to Canada, I'll make her a tiny pink *jelabah*." .

After a dinner of sea bass and beer, we're walking back to our *pension* when we pass a building with graffiti on the side that reads: *Without truth you are the loser.*

I'm wearing funky new tie-dyed pants, a fitted t-shirt and my favourite jean jacket. On the outside, at least, I'm looking better. I hand Tamara my camera then stand beneath the statement.

She leans back and snaps my photo. "Got it."

Fourteen

Life back home in Canada, however, is no quiet beach in Portugal. Within twenty-four hours, I'm completely overwhelmed again by phone-calls, drop-ins, answering machine messages, unopened mail, unread e-mails, and social functions to attend. However, it's a minor oversight by the police service that sends me over the edge.

"THERE WERE NO GODDAMN TRUMPETS PLAY-ING," I scream at the unfortunate person in Human Resources on the other end of the line, "BECAUSE NOBODY WAS IN-VITED TO ATTEND THE CEREMONY!"

In the police administration building downtown, there's a glass display cabinet that holds plaques in memory of officers who have passed away in the line of duty. While I was away, Sam's plaque had been placed in the cabinet without his family being informed. Instead, Angela had read in the newspaper: "There were no teary eyed crowds or soulful trumpets playing to commemorate the officer . . ."

"We made a mistake," the police chief tells me when word reaches him. "We're very sorry."

No, I say to the water fountain after hanging up. Sorry isn't good enough. In fact, no to a lot of things. No to Sam going to work and never coming home again. No to him giving his life searching for a non-existent intruder. No to him choosing his stupid job over me. No to the doctor who told me he was brain-dead but could I spare a coupla organs? No to the dozens of people who paraded through his ICU room, constantly interrupting our last fucking day on earth together. No to the prayer service where I stood in a receiving line in front of his dead body, shaking hands with five hundred people. No to the public funeral with cameramen on the roof taking my picture. No to the company that couldn't give a shit about safety. No to the multiple false alarms that night. No to the . . . wait: how did they *know* those other two alarms were false?

The phone rings.

"Fuck off!" I scream at the handset. "Leave me alone!"

No to the bloody phone that won't stop ringing. And no to having to sit under a palm tree in the middle of the goddamn Sahara to be able to finally get some peace.

Did it take the heat of the desert to finally thaw the rage frozen inside nine and a half months of grief? Regardless, I know I need to be left alone for the flood. I vow to say no to every demand placed upon my time, including the wretched baby showers popping up at an alarming rate. I resolve to not answer the phone or door and instead, focus my efforts on accomplishing the one thing I do have control over: creating a *publishable* manuscript.

So I begin typing into the computer what I'd handwritten while traveling. Unfortunately, I have enough piss and vinegar flowing through me to poison an elephant; not a state of mind conducive to effective storytelling. For not a wheel must grind, said Virginia Woolf. Yet on I forge, making one hell of a racket, until one morning in mid-July when I come screeching to a halt. I have no new deadline to aim for. I glance up at the bookshelf and John Irving's *A Widow For One Year* again catches my eye. Done. A year it is for the manuscript and me. The Latin meaning for the word widow is 'empty.' But I am NOT going through the rest of my life defined as a hollow vessel . . . something left behind. I was signed up for a contract position and I'm not renewing it once the year is up.

And look what's beside my John Irving book: Sam's copy of Noam Chomsky's *What Uncle Sam Really Wants*. So I spend the rest of the day reading shocking facts about U.S. foreign policy and the propaganda behind it. In the late afternoon, I come to Chomsky's reference to Walter Lippmann's "bewildered herd."

Comprising 80% of the American population, the herd is supposed to follow orders and keep out of the way of the important people. The herd is the target of the real mass media – and must be kept diverted by reinforcing the values of passivity, submissiveness to authority, the overriding virtue of greed and personal gain, lack of concern for others, and fear of real or imagined enemies. The bewildered herd *must* remain bewildered because if they trouble themselves with the reality of what's really going on in the world, they may set themselves to change it. And the other 20% cannot allow that.

Thus, into my manuscript thunders the bewildered herd, followed by findings from the other homework assigned to me in Morocco. I track down Northrop Frye's *Anatomy of Criticism* and also discover his *Spiritus Mundi*. Between the two books, Frye articulates much of what I've been thinking and experiencing since Sam's death in regards to religious beliefs. Frye warns of the danger in taking stories from the Bible, or any religious document, as literal truth. Analogies and metaphors are tools to understand valuable human lessons – not truths in themselves. *This* is what bothered me so much about Christianity's resurrection belief.

On January 10th, I'd finally faced the truth that it was physically impossible for a human being – Jesus or otherwise – to come back from the dead. Reading Northrop Frye clarifies the message behind the tale: when a person dies, the best of him or her rises up and continues on in our own hearts and lives. Jesus doesn't need to come back and save us; he already gave us the tools to save ourselves.

Then I read up on Carl Jung. Sure enough, earth, wind, fire and water were ancient archetypes that have, over the course of our evolution, resurfaced from our collective consciousness with different twists, depending on the culture and point in history.

I finish reading *The Sacred Balance* by David Suzuki and Jane Goodall's *A Reason for Hope* and start in on Al Gore's book, *Earth in the Balance; Ecology and the Human Spirit.* The message in all three is clear: our environmental crisis is dire; we cannot sustain the path we are on; and we're going to have to change the way we relate to the natural world. Simply put: we need a new worldview.

What, am I busy?

Not particularly. So I get to work creating one. I look at the archetypes of earth, wind, fire, water and add a fifth – life itself. Then I think about what love means to me and wonder if it, too, is experienced on five levels: body, mind, heart, soul and spirit.

I reflect on some of the strange occurrences – possible 'signs' from Sam – that have happened over the past year: Sam having a seizure when I kissed him in the hospital, *after* he'd been declared brain-dead; the pee in the toilet in the Toronto hotel room during the howling snowstorm; the gold heart pendant floating in the melted wax of the mysteriously re-ignited candle around Valentine's Day; and the wolf pendant given me by the girl on the plane while thinking about a symbol to represent what Sam stood for.

I connect the dots and come up with my own little way of viewing the world: the earth represents the body; wind represents the mind; fire represents the heart; life represents the spirit; and water . . . well, I suspect it represents the soul but I haven't yet received a clear sign from Sam.

So I pour my 80% complete worldview into the manuscript stew, then return my attention to Voltaire and Emilie du Chatelet in the *E=mc²* book. I read again how Emilie's work, two hundred and fifty years earlier, had led to Einstein squaring the speed of light in his famous equation.

Light.

What about the red light? I haven't incorporated *that* into my worldview – but surely it must be significant, especially since I'm pretty damn sure it is somehow Sam. But *how* can that be?

I start scribbling down thoughts. $E=mc^2$ means that the amount of energy 'hidden' inside matter is determined by multiplying it's mass by the speed of light squared. I first saw the red light right after Sam's heart had been removed. Love is the energy of the soul. Energy can neither be created nor destroyed, it just changes form. The spirit is the life-force of the soul.

Is the spirit *light*? What is light but packets of photons, which are . . . energy.

I resume reading and come to the part where Emilie had been writing madly to finish her work before the baby arrived. Surrounded by books and piles of papers, she'd been sorting out ideas by candlelight. I look to my own desk, covered in books and papers as I try to sort out ideas, and ponder again the possibility of reincarnation. Or am I just resonating with Emilie's story because there's a significant life lesson in there for me? For as much as I love working at this level of intensity, I can't help but wonder if I'm rushing to get my book done because I *do* want to have a child?

My phone rings and a man from the Human Resources department of the police service starts to leave a message on the machine. I'm surprised they're still speaking to me after the trumpet incident.

I pick up the phone mid-message. "Hi."

The officer – I think it's the same guy who drew stick figures for me to explain Sam's funeral procession – asks me if he's interrupting anything.

"Oh no, no," I say, waving at the bookshelf.

Then he tells me the police service would like to send me to Ottawa at the end of September for the national memorial weekend for fallen peace officers.

"I didn't realize there was such a thing."

"There is." He clears his throat. "And it actually falls on the one year anniversary of Sam's death."

"I see."

"We'll also be sending a police representative along with you and Sam's family."

"Who?" I ask, even though my stomach tells me I already know the answer.

Fifteen

For navigational assistance through this latest tidal wave of guilt, I call Amanda and she joins Sasha, Sven and I at the dog-park. I tell her that Tom and I will be in Ottawa together for the national memorial service.

She throws the ball and Sasha races after it. "The future must seem pretty daunting on your own," she says finally.

"I'm OK."

Amanda smiles. "Oh I know you are. But I just wonder if deep down, you're worried about your future – and the *idea* of one with Tom makes you feel better. And if so, there's nothing wrong with that."

I let out a snort. "Except that it's not real."

"It is to you. I mean, it's where you're at right now."

"Did you know the memorial service for fallen officers coincides with the one year anniversary of Sam's death?"

"No," she says. "But that makes sense because September 29th is St Michael's Day and since he's the patron saint of police officers, that's probably why they hold the national memorial service then."

"And Sam just happening to die *on* St Michael's Day is . . . what?"

"Very odd."

I throw up my hands. "Then why am I the only person who questions this stuff?"

"You're not." She tosses the ball again and Sasha chases it. Sven charges her on her way back and the two of them tussle in the long grass. "I told my sister-in-law about Sam's dream – the one where you cheated on him."

I turn to her. "I thought we came to the conclusion that Sam was worried I would betray my own *self* by having a baby before I got my book published?"

"There might be more than one meaning," she replies, "because apparently when you dream you're being cheated on, that means the person cheating on you is going to be honouring you in the near future."

"That's not what *Sam* got out of the dream."

Amanda smiles. "I asked about that too. My sister-in-law said that was probably Sam's *ego* responding to the dream, not his real self."

I stop walking. "His real self? As in his soul?"

"I guess. Do you remember when we went for lunch last November and you told me how it felt like you had two selves?"

"Yeah."

"But that you only show people the person *you* want them to see."

"Uh huh."

"So maybe that's what the ego is – the fake self we show others. Maybe we think that outer shell, that . . ."

"Crust?"

Amanda nods. "Yeah – that's a good word for it. Maybe we think that crust will somehow make us less vulnerable."

"On the day Sam died, when the social worker walked me down the hallway towards the ER, I had the sense there were two of me. I mean, I was walking but I could also *see* myself walking. Then when I went into the emergency room and saw Sam on the gurney, it happened again: it was like I was in two places at once. I was looking at Sam *and* watching myself looking at Sam."

"Really?"

"Yeah. And one of your teammates was in the room and he later told me how incredibly vulnerable I looked in that moment. So I wonder if somehow my ego, you know . . . fell down for just a sec so that what your teammate saw was the *real* me – my soul – and not the widow crust I was already creating."

"Which you had to," she says, "to survive."

"I know." I throw the ball. "But do ya think it's possible that I was actually *in* your teammate? I mean, how else could I have seen myself?"

"Shit, you think a lot."

"Well, if departed souls can move from one person to the next, why couldn't the souls of the living?" I let out a squeal. "Or maybe it was SAM who was in your teammate, watching me! *That* would make more sense . . . he could probably do tricks like that since he was already so close to death."

Amanda looks at me. "But how could *you* experience that?"

"Oh, that's easy. Sam and I are soul mates so we're pretty much interchangeable."

When I get home, I call Jodie and tell her about the memorial service in Ottawa. "And since I'm going to be down East anyway, I think I'll go to New York. Sam and I always wanted to go, so here's my chance."

Pause. "Are you sure you want to go there without him, Adri?"

"Do I have a choice?"

"What I mean," she says, "is that you don't have to go yet."

"But I want to – and I was wondering if you'd like to come with me?"

"I'll have to get back to you on that. And by the way, we're selling our SUV. I think at one point, you were interested in buying it."

"I'll take it for a test drive," I say. "See how it feels . . ."

The next morning, I drop Sasha and Sven off at the puppy parlour and am pulling up alongside my house when I notice how brown the grass is. I fiddle with the soaker hose for a few minutes but can't get it to work properly, so I decide to use the brass spray nozzle that Sam preferred to hand water the lawn with. I'm standing in front of the tap and have just seen the spray nozzle resting on the ledge of the hose holder – but when I go to reach for it, it's not there. I blink. It's gone. I look around the yard and find it on the fence, right beside the gate I've just walked in and out of three times.

I close my eyes to ponder this impossibility – and Water-world at Universal Studios comes to mind. I recall Sam's laughter watching the reactions of the people being squirted with the hose by the undercover actor.

Did I just receive the fifth and final sign from Sam to complete my worldview?

Inside the house, I turn my attention to more practical matters and write a letter to the police chief. The police association's lawyer was right: not being 'allowed' to remarry is bullshit. Even if *I* never manage to lassoo another antelope, what about the next person in my shoes, God forbid there is one? It's been four months since I'd learned of the remarriage clause and although I know the lawyer is looking into the issue, I dare say it's time to expedite the process. I cc the chief's letter to the president of the police association and the lawyer, then pop all three envelopes into the mailbox.

After lunch, I retrieve Sasha and Sven from the puppy parlour then take them to my mom's apartment. I make it as far as the foyer when a crotchety senior snaps: "You can't bring those dogs in here!"

I turn to her. "Oh yes I can."

She wags a finger at me. "No you can't!"

"Oh, but I can," I say, in a very Sam-like manner, "and I will. There's no rule that says I can't bring dogs to visit."

"How dare you speak to me that way!" she hisses.

"How dare you speak to *me* that way?" is my reply.

Then all three of us march – heads and tails held high – past her and on to my mom's apartment.

Over tea, my mom asks me if I'd like to join her for a festival of plays next weekend. Since I'm finding meaning in every conversation, book, magazine article, newspaper headline, movie, TV sitcom, current event and misplaced household item, attending an entire weekend of theatre will surely be a buffet for the mind.

Indeed, at the festival, every play *was* written for me.

"It is the search for truth and beauty," says one actor, "that shall set you free."

OH YES! I want to cry out from the audience.

But as I'm leaving the theatre, I wonder just how free I am in my supposed search for truth because finding potential meaning everywhere I look is starting to feel increasingly more like self-imprisonment. Perceiving life to be a mere unfolding of some pre-determined plan, in which my role is merely to pick up the pieces of the puzzle and snap them into place, is not a particularly empowering way to live.

Over dinner, I find myself asking my mom why she had four kids.

"We didn't have the choices you do today, Adri."

"Given the choice, would you still have us?"

"Yes."

"Even though you know the world is such a shitty place?"

She winces. "It's also a very beautiful place. And new life needs to go on."

"But don't you think we should be solving our problems instead of just bringing more people onto the planet?"

"And what are *you* doing to solve our problems?"

"I'm trying," I say, "to write a book."

"I know. And I realize you've been through an awful lot but at some point you're going to have to actually *do* something instead of just complaining about what's wrong."

Ah the two by four of truth.

Sixteen

Monday morning is my first appointment with the personal injury lawyer and on the way there, I stop in to have a chat with Sam. I'm walking from my car to his grave when I see there is a huge *hole* in the ground. I break into a run.

Sure enough, right in front of his headstone is a hole about three feet long by two feet deep. I drop to my knees and look down but thankfully, I can't see his casket – just dirt and a candy wrapper that blew in. I reach in to retrieve the garbage and I think to myself that if I were in a horror movie, a hand would reach up right about now and pull me in. But instead of being terrified, it occurs to me that, given the opportunity, I'd go anywhere to be with Sam again. I let out a sigh of relief, *finally* feeling how I figure a normal widow ought to.

I lift my head to look at his shiny black headstone – but it's a beautiful woman in capri pants and a white shirt kneeling at her husband's grave I see. As difficult as it was to hear at the time, maybe Ed *had* been right when he said that Sam lives on in me.

"Do I sue or not?" I ask Sam's photo, recently set into the stone.

I'd given in to his parents' repeated request for a photo – but I chose which one.

"I'm not even sure I have a legal case yet," I continue. "But if I do, is there any point in me spending all that time and energy in the courts?"

A bird chirps.

"Besides, what am I really after here? Money? Trying to force a corporation to take responsibility? Creating awareness about the issue?"

Silence.

"What exactly *is* the issue?"

I hear an aircraft, possibly a helicopter, in the distance.

"Because of an unsafe workplace, you never made it home."

It *is* a helicopter.

"But is suing the company going to change that fact?"

It flies overhead.

"No. Not unless the money is directed to dealing with workplace safety."

On my way out of the cemetery, I stop in at the office and tell the staff about the hole. They assure me it's likely just the ground shifting as the result of an air pocket.

"We've done a preliminary review of Sam's case," the personal injury lawyer tells me half an hour later, "and to be honest, the circumstances are quite unusual."

"That seems to be the general consensus."

"And I don't have a clear-cut answer for you at this point."

I lean forward. "As in?"

"As in whether or not to advise you to proceed with litigation against the company where Sam fell. And because it was a Worker's Compensation Board claim, you might not even be entitled to pursue legal action anyway."

"Oh?"

"I'm looking into that right now. However, what *is* clear is that according to Alberta legislation, a safety railing should have been in place. But I'm concerned this could be a long drawn out process and frankly, the evidence thus far doesn't suggest this is necessarily the wisest road to take. I think you need to ask yourself what it is you hope to gain from pursuing legal action."

"Awareness," I reply. "Sam's fund is going to produce a public service announcement about workplace safety, so any money I receive from litigation will go towards this."

"Then there's the possibility of approaching the company *outside* the legal system and explaining what the memorial fund is planning to do."

"And?"

"And hopefully, they'll do the right thing."

I lean back in my chair. "Well, whatever we do, it's pretty safe to say that Sam would . . ." I stop speaking and my hand flies up to my mouth.

"What?"

"I was just going to say that Sam would roll over in his grave if I spent the next five years of my life dealing with this in the courts – but that's an odd choice of words considering I just came from Sam's grave and there *was* a big hole in the ground!"

The lawyer's face goes pale.

I give him the wave. "Oh don't worry, I'm sure it was the ground shifting. It's just the timing that's weird – but this kind of thing happens quite a bit."

Back home, there are two messages on my machine. The first is
from Jodie; she'll be joining me in New York. I immediately go
on-line and purchase outrageously expensive tickets for us to see
La Boheme at The Met.

Then I deal with the second message. It's from the police
association lawyer and he does not sound pleased.

"What the HELL were you thinking?" he snarls when I
muster up the courage to call him back.

"About?"

"Those letters you sent about the remarriage clause! Adri,
you wrote the chief of police *and* the president of the police
union."

"Yeah . . . so?"

"*So*? So in the middle of contract negotiations, you com-
municated about a major flaw in the contract with the top dog
in management AND the head of the union. THEY ARE ON
OPPOSITE SIDES OF THE FENCE."

"But they needed to hear my perspective," I say rather quietly.

"That's *my* job."

"Sorry."

He sighs. "Well, I guess you didn't know any better."

"So what happens now?"

"Your guess is as good as mine."

By early September, the long days on the computer are taking
their toll on my body. My wrists and forearms ache from ten-
donitis so I book a massage. The masseuse, not one I've met
before, asks me to remove my necklace and upon seeing the
wolf pendant given me by the girl on the plane, asks if that's my
power animal.

"My what?"

"Power animal. It's a native belief that each person has an
animal to which they turn for strength and guidance. Sometimes it also symbolizes the type of person you are."

I shake my head. "Actually, the wolf symbolizes the spirit of
my husband. He passed away a year ago."

"Were you soul mates?"

"Yes."

"Then you probably have more wolf-like attributes than you realize."

"Maybe . . . but I think the animal that best symbolizes me, at least at this point, is the butterfly."

"That tends to represent transformation and change."

"That's me all right . . . I just hope I'm through the damn caterpillar stage – eating everything in sight."

She laughs.

"Or maybe I'm more like a dragonfly," I muse. "They're bigger, tougher and louder, plus they're always trying to mate."

"I'm shooting a documentary about that right now."

I lift my head to get a better look at this person. "You're a filmmaker?"

"Yup. I'm just on call here to help finance my films."

I lie flat again. "And you're making a documentary about *mating*?"

"Pretty much . . . it's called *The End of Evolution*, which is where the human race is headed if we don't start changing the way we think and live."

When I get home, there's another message from the police association lawyer.

"It's gone," he says when I call him back.

"Pardon me?"

"The remarriage clause has been removed from the contract. I won't pretend to guess what happened – but clearly, your letter had an impact."

Smiling, I hang up the phone. "Well, whaddya think of them apples?" I ask my little wooden gazelle all the way from Portugal, now sporting a tiny pink *jelabah*.

Tonight I dream that I'm in my basement office writing when I hear someone come in the back door. Expecting Sam, I race upstairs to say hi but it's Tom standing in my kitchen. I'm the same age I am now but he's about thirty years older, has white hair and is very thin. We hug tightly and are about to kiss but I quickly pull away. "No!" I say. "We can't do this yet."

In real life, Tom and I meet later in the day for ice cream and I tell him my dream.

"You do realize I am in love with my girlfriend?" is his response.

I dip my spoon into the sundae we're sharing. "I thought you guys weren't gonna make it?"

"We're still trying."

I eat a spoonful of ice cream. "Did I ever tell you that both your and Sam's regimental numbers add up to eleven?"

"No."

"They do. So I had an actuarial friend calculate the odds of that happening."

"And?"

"It's less than .01 percent."

Tom folds his arms across his chest. "And what do you make of that?"

"I think eleven is the number of my soul mate."

He sighs and sticks his feet into the aisle, crossing one leg over the other.

I glance down. "Are those traffic boots?"

"Yeah."

"Why are *you* wearing them?"

"I'm back in the traffic unit. I got transferred last week."

"Oh." I scrape out the walnuts and chocolate sauce.

"You need to move on, Adri."

"I'm taking a dance class."

His face brightens. "That's a start. What kind?"

"Hip hop. I start tomorrow."

"And the book?"

"It's in rough shape . . . maybe I'm not cracked up to be a novelist."

Tom frowns. "How so?"

"What if I just needed to write this book to make sense of Sam's death – and my life without him in it?"

"But he's still in it! You have a stronger relationship with your dead spouse than most people do with a living one."

"True," I say. "So maybe I just needed to write this book to help me grieve – but that doesn't mean I have to publish it."

"But if writing it helped you, then reading it will help others."

I shake my head. "Not the way it reads now."

Tom folds his arms across his chest. "What would Sam say if he knew you were thinking of not publishing this book?"

"He'd throttle me," I say, reaching for my purse. "I finally saw *Gladiator*."

"And?"

I look Tom in the eye. "And I know perfectly well I can't be with Sam."

"But you still want to be," he says softly. "And that makes all the difference."

Seventeen

The next morning I pick up Jodie's SUV and drive it downtown for my first hip hop class. Inside the studio, I find a spot in the last row of students, furthest from the mirror that takes up the entire front wall.

"The only rule in my class," the teacher tells us, "is to fake it till you make it."

This sums up my past year quite nicely.

On the drive home, I ask the rearview mirror how it feels driving a $32,000 SUV home from dance class on a Monday afternoon.

Like I'm a spoiled princess considering using blood money to purchase a luxury vehicle to cart muddy dogs to and from the off-leash park.

I give the mirror a wave. "Don't be ridiculous."

At home, I call my financial advisor and request that he sell some stocks so I can purchase the SUV.

There is a definite pause before he replies. "Have you researched this purchase?"

"I need a new vehicle," I say, "and I'm sure this is as good as any."

"OK. I'll get that money out of the market for you."

I'm having coffee the next morning when I hear my mother sobbing on the answering machine, telling me to turn on the TV *now*. I do so and along with a few billion others, watch a replay of the south tower of the World Trade Centre collapsing.

I phone Jodie. "If one were biblically inclined, this might appear to be the beginning of the end."

"Adri?"

"On a personal note, however, I certainly have some idea of the hell that lies ahead for a few thousand people."

"Are you . . ."

"But the worst part is that everybody else will move on. Oh sure, people will be shocked for a little while but unless *they've* lost the person they love the most in the world, they'll just roll over and go back to sleep, carrying on with their busy little lives while the broken-hearted get left behind, staring at the last towel her husband touched and then one day, she'll go to take her birth control pill but soon realize how silly *that* is because someone else has made that decision rather fucking final FOR her. And then, she'll start to hear how it's best to accept her husband's death as part of God's plan but not to worry her pretty little head about actually trying to figure *out* said plan."

"Ummm . . ."

"And then she'll start to see her dead husband everywhere because he can't *really* be gone, see, because he loved her more than she loved herself and that kind of love DOES NOT DIE."

"Oh boy."

"And I won't be buying your SUV," I finish, "because what's probably behind these attacks is an absolute hatred of this very attitude."

"What attitude?"

"The selfish, ignorant, irresponsible materialism of people such as myself. The World Trade Centre of the world's superpower is now a pile of burning rubble. I'd say that's a rather direct attack on globalism and capitalism."

"They're saying terrorists are responsible."

"Obviously. But terrorism is only a symptom of a far deeper problem."

"Which is?"

"The inequitable distribution of wealth on the planet – speaking of which, thanks to you, I just managed to get thirty-two grand out of the market before it tanks."

Silence.

"That's the truth," I say.

"I just don't understand what kind of monsters would do this . . ."

"The same kind who probably *hired* the terrorists in the first place."

"Huh?"

I ask her who would be the *least* likely to attack the World Trade Centre.

"The U.S. government, I guess."

"Uh huh. And who's behind Uncle Sam?"

"Whaddya mean?"

"Who's behind the scenes . . . pulling the strings in the political puppet show?"

"I dunno."

"The wealthy!" I cry. "Big business. Multinationals."

"I can't believe we're having this conversation."

"And yet we are."

"But why would the U.S. government destroy their own symbol of power, never mind killing all the *business* people inside?"

"Because it's completely unbelievable, that's why. I betcha if anyone ever has the balls to do a study on who didn't go into work today, they'll discover the *really* important people were conveniently otherwise engaged."

"I don't believe it."

"Nor will the American public, which is exactly why the plan is gonna work."

"But *why* kill all those innocent people?"

"Because," I say, "the best way to get the masses to support a government's agenda is to give them an enemy – real or imagined – to fear. It's the oldest trick in the book. Keep the bewildered herd bewildered and provide them with a bad guy to hate, so you can do whatever the fuck you want behind the scenes."

"Adri, where's all this coming from?"

"Read your history! What makes you think a government wouldn't kill a couple thousand of their own if the agenda justified doing so? Or maybe the tower wasn't supposed to *collapse*. Or maybe it's a case of willful blindness where the powers that be knew of a likely attack but chose to ignore the warnings because it would give them a perfect excuse. At any rate, just wait and see what the Republicans do in response to this – that'll tell ya what they're really after . . . probably oil."

"But . . ."

"Now if *Al Gore* was President," I cut in, "which he *would* be if it wasn't for the Florida recount fiasco which was, gee, not at all suspicious, I betcha the future would unfold very differently."

"How so?"

"Ya think issues like global warming, species loss, rainforest clear-cutting, water conservation, poverty, AIDS, hunger, overpopulation, healthcare and education are gonna get *any* attention now?"

"I don't know."

"Well I do – and trust me, the Fundamentalist Christians running this popsicle stand don't give a flying fuck about the average person, let alone the environment. The U.S. is being run by a buncha right-wing traditionalists who are just *using* religion to hide their backwardass ultra-conservative beliefs. They don't believe in God or Jesus. They believe in money and power. But guess what?"

"What?"

I take a deep breath. "I think Jesus *did* come back but then he left again because he was so goddamn disgusted by what he saw here."

Pause. "What are you talking about?"

"Ya remember last fall when I thought I was the Second Coming of Christ?"

"Of course."

"Well, it wasn't me."

"I thought we already determined that."

"You haven't figured it out yet, have you?"

"Figured what out?"

"It was *Sam*," I say as the north tower collapses. "Sam was Jesus."

Eighteen

"Did you just say what I think you did?" asks Jodie.

"Hang on, my other line's going. I gotta go."

"No! Don't —"

"I'll call ya later."

I hang up and push call-waiting. It's Tamara.

"That's what I saw," she whispers.

"Huh?"

"In that church in Seville! The twisted metal and smoke . . . it was the World Trade Centre collapsing."

"But how could you have seen that *before* it happened?"

"You tell me," she snaps.

"I'll go talk to Sam."

I load Sasha and Sven into the car, roar up to the cemetery and stomp over to Sam's grave. The hole is filled in.

"What the hell is going on?" I demand, hands on my hips.

But Sam just keeps on smiling, holding tight to the brass pole of his white horse.

"Are you still working?" I ask, shakily lighting a Colt's. "Because this strikes me as rather high on the priority fucking crimes list."

If you're working, I'm working.

"Oh for God's sakes," I snap, then turn and stride back to the car.

I drive the dogs to the off-leash park, where I ask a woman walking her poodle what she thinks of the attacks.

"This," she replies proudly, "will sure change air travel."

I give birdbrain the goldfish. Air travel? *That's* what you're taking from the fact that thousands of people went to work this morning and simply vanished? What about asking a few questions? Like why the attacks took place? How can so much hatred exist in the world? What state of mind must one be in to fly a plane into a building? Will tightened airport security be yet another band-aid solution placed on top of a gushing stab wound?

Home again, I call Jodie back. "I guess we better finish our conversation."

"I'll say."

"I know you think I'm crazy but here's the scoop: I suspect Sam was the Second Coming – but he wasn't sent back to save humanity, he came to save *me*."

"Why you?"

"Because I'm the poor sap who's gonna have to coordinate the clean-up of the goddamn mess we've made. Why do you think I'm getting paid his salary?"

"Because he died on the job, Adri."

"I don't blame you for not believing me – but how many other thirty-three year olds do you know who receive their dead husband's paycheque?"

"That doesn't mean you're supposed to save humanity."

"And I have no intention of doing so. I'm just a writer. My job is to wake up the bewildered herd and get the Stampede started. The masses can save their own damn asses, should they so choose: that's what *I* had to do. Sam gave me everything he could in life and what he couldn't, he gave me in death. Then Tom stepped in and gave me hope for falling in love again, which came in rather handy when the suicide scene rolled around. *Those* are the kinds of things soul mates do for each other."

"Are you saying that both Sam and Tom are your soul mates?"

"Yup."

"How do you know?"

"Eleven is the number of my soul mate – both their regimentals add up to that."

"Today's the eleventh."

"Yes," I say. "I realize that. But the catch, see, is that soul mate or not, in the end, no one could save me but me. Likewise with the planet, no one can save us but us – and we're dangerously close to the suicide scene. And yet we *insist* on holding on to archaic belief systems that only serve to ensure we continue acting like children of a very shitty father simply because we don't want to grow up and take responsibility for our own actions."

"Geez," she says. "When you say it like that, it kinda makes sense."

"You're a mother. Would *you* raise your kids to remain dependent on you?"

"Of course not."

"And would you tell them to kill each other when they don't get along?"

"No!"

"How about telling them they can do whatever they want to the place while you're away, as long as they promise to love *you*, you'll fix whatever mess they make when you come back?"

"Don't be ridiculous."

"Well, that's Christianity in a nutshell for ya – and whether you're a believer or not, the underlying assumption that Jesus is coming back to save us is so deeply ingrained in our Western psyche, we don't even see it anymore. It's the Saviour syndrome . . . believe me, I know all about it."

Jodie doesn't say anything.

"But it's our war on the *environment* that's the real apocalypse," I continue. "We're destroying the planet and yet we refuse to accept this, let alone address it. What we need to do is stop exploiting the natural world and learn again how to work *with* it, which is exactly what people like Al Gore, David Suzuki, Jane Goodall and many others are doing. But I bet you today's events will send us in the complete opposite direction."

"Maybe not."

I let out a snort. "I wish I had your faith. Remember how I mentioned last fall that a more female-oriented perspective was needed in the world?"

"Yeah."

"Well, I came up with my own little worldview this summer."

I tell Jodie the details, ending with the hose nozzle incident that confirmed the soul/water connection. When I finish, there isn't a peep on the other end of the line.

"And in light of what's happened today," I add, "I guess all that must sound childish and silly. But I just thought it might be a useful tool for us to help understand that much of what is going on around us is also going on *in* us."

"Are you saying that when there's a . . . hurricane, for example, that could be an indication that our *thoughts* are out of control?"

"Yeah."

"Or when a tsunami hits, that's an indication that our souls are in trouble?"

"It's *possible* . . ."

"I kinda like it," she says.

"You're kidding."

"Except that it's pretty fragmented."

"But maybe that's a necessary step before we can become whole again . . . kinda like the way the medical staff perceived Sam's body after his brain-death. Because of his organ donation, he was viewed as a collection of body parts instead of a human whole – which is understandable since he was on his way out anyway. But we're treating the earth the same way: as a collection of natural resources to be exploited versus an interconnected whole."

"You're right."

"You know," I say, "it actually makes sense to me now why Sam was taken out of the game. He accomplished what he was here to do and now it's my turn."

"Are you saying Sam really was Jesus but now that he's gone, *you're* taking on that role?"

I laugh. "Don't tell me you believe any of this?"

"I don't know what I believe anymore . . . except that the U.S. government couldn't be behind today's attacks."

"Why not?"

"Because they wouldn't treat their own people like that."

"Why is that possibility so hard for you to accept?"

"Because if I did, then I'd have to lose faith in democracy itself."

"Sometimes losing one's faith is the best thing that can happen. I mean, nothing real is ever lost, right?"

No response.

"Look," I say, "Let's just see what the next few years bring – that'll show us what the Republican boys *really* think of the average American. Whoops! Sorry, gotta go . . . there's my other line."

I hang up and push call-waiting. It's Katrina.

Nineteen

Three days before the one-year anniversary of Sam's death, I print off a fatter version of my ugly baby and take the meandering mess of a manuscript with me to the ceremony at Sam's church where I meet up with Jodie.

"I know it's wretched," I say, handing it to her, "but I also know you're the one person on the planet who will still encourage me."

"Ya gotta start somewhere. I'm sorry I can't go to New York with you now."

On September 30th, Sam's family, Ed and I have front row seats at the national memorial service for fallen officers at the Parliament Buildings in Ottawa. I've tried to mentally prepare myself for today. Tom will be carrying a police hat, representing Sam, on a pillow. There will be thousands of officers from across North America. The media will be filming family members of officers who have passed away in the line of duty during the past year. There will be speeches. There always are.

What I've forgotten to factor in, however, is that although I've survived a year of widowhood, I am nowhere near healed. Thus it isn't pride, respect and honour I feel as the pipe band marches by; it's anger. *Boom, boom, boom* goes the drum and I'm back at Sam's funeral watching the pallbearers climb the church steps, struggling beneath the weight of his casket. Who *did* take more than a fucking date square from his funeral? Has any positive change come from his death? Are workplaces any safer?

Or is it me who is now carrying Sam's casket?

Boom. I open my eyes and see Tom, holding the pillow and hat, fighting back tears. I am so ashamed for wanting a relationship with him but God knows I've tried to love a soul, or a spirit or a memory or whatever it is, instead of a husband.

Boom. I am in the future. Who will be sitting in my seat next year?

The speeches reflect the usual rhetoric: God's plan, greener pastures, fallen heroes and societal gratitude. Cause and effect, anyone?

Then the bagpipes play Amazing Grace. I hang my head and cry; can a wretch like me be saved?

After the ceremony, Ed and I go to the cemetery where our grandma – our mom's mom – is buried.

"I wouldn't want to be you," Ed says as I place pink carnations on her headstone.

"Thanks a lot."

"It's just that I know how much you loved Sam," he explains, "so I can't fathom what this last year has been like for you."

"It's been the shits. And not a goddamn thing has changed either."

"What did you expect to change?"

I shrug. "I dunno."

"Ghandi said you must be the change you wish to see in the world."

"And what about everyone else?"

"Most people won't change unless they absolutely have to," he says, "and that's usually not until the eleventh hour."

I sit down on the grass. "Ed, do you believe in fate?"

He smiles. "I believe destiny is waiting for you at the corner store – but if you don't leave your house to go buy that carton of milk, you won't meet it."

"I guess that answers my question about going to New York tomorrow."

"Why wouldn't you go?"

"Because I'm scared shitless."

"At this point, Manhattan is probably the safest place on earth."

"But it sucks having to go alone."

"It also takes courage," he says, nodding towards my grandma's headstone. "Luckily, you come from a long line of strong women."

At the age of 32, my grandmother left England for Canada with plans to marry a Saskatchewan farmer. But on the boat over, she fell in love with my grandfather, an engineer and army major from Ottawa. They married within the week and their daughter, my mother the lioness, arrived shortly thereafter with a birth weight of 3 pounds, 6 ounces. In 1925, it was a miracle she survived but a testament to her inner strength.

"What if I don't have a baby?" I blurt. "Will that line end with me?"

Ed frowns. "Do you even *want* a child?"

"I dunno."

"Then you better do some serious soul-searching to find out."

"I think I'm in love with Tom."

He smiles. "That's certainly plausible."

"He's not in love with me, though."

"Tom *can't* be, Adri. For lots of reasons."

I pick a dandelion, nodding.

"And besides, he already has kids, doesn't he?"

"Yeah," I reply. "So?"

"So as much as you don't want to be alone, I strongly suggest you make wise use of this time. You need to figure out what you *really* want out of life and then slowly start working towards that. There are no short-cuts."

"That's not the answer I wanted to hear," I say.

"Then you shouldn't have asked the question."

I throw the dandelion at his head.

With a laugh, he catches it. "Better than a cookie."

We walk together back to his car. He opens the rear door on the driver's side, pulls out my knapsack and hands it to me. "You forgot this at the memorial service."

"You're going to the war-torn streets of Manhattan," the U.S. customs officer says to me the next day, "for a *holiday?*"

"Yeah. I planned this trip before the World Trade Centre, er . . . fell."

"That was only three weeks ago."

"I realize that."

After scrutinizing my passport, he hands it back. "Well, have a good trip."

First stop is Yankee Stadium where dozens of police officers stand guard outside the building. Inside, I buy my Yankees ball cap, a hotdog and a beer then walk up the ramp to watch a ball game in a near-empty stadium.

After a mammoth American breakfast the next morning, I walk from my hotel on Broadway all the way to the financial district. Past the jazz bars of Greenwich Village I stroll but there are no crowds of cheerful patrons singing. Nor do I see steam rising from manhole covers. The remains at Ground Zero, however, are still smoldering.

I stop in front of a flower-laden shrine to fallen police officers and firefighters and bow my head. I say a prayer for the dead as well as a fanciful wish for the loved ones left behind: may their year ahead be less horrific than the past one has been for me.

Walking towards Battery Park, I see a group of Marines armed with machine guns, standing at a checkpoint. One of them stares out across the water. I turn my head to follow his gaze and there, through the barbed-wire fence, I see the real Statue of Liberty for the first time.

"There she is," I whisper.

I close my eyes and I'm on the bridge again with Sam in the Venice of Vegas. I see the gondolier, in his cheerful red scarf, gently paddling his gondola through the canal as beautiful Italian music fills the air. I smell Sam's cologne, now mixed with the scent of smoke and flowers, and feel the soft weight of his hand on my shoulder as we stand together, looking out over the . . .

"Ma'am?"

I open my eyes and turn around. The Marine who had been staring at the Statue of Liberty is now standing behind me. The Empire State Building looms in the background. His hand drops to his side. "Are you all right?"

"Uh huh."

"Then I'm going to have to ask you to head back the way you came," he says, "because this is a restricted area."

So I begin the long walk back to my hotel, past the thousands of missing-persons' photographs flapping on telephone poles.

The following afternoon, I'm sitting on a park bench in Central Park, watching the ducks in the lagoon, when a teenager sits down beside me and asks how I'm doing.

"Not bad, thanks."

"That was quite something, huh? About those towers?"

I nod. "No kidding. I . . ."

"A group of us have come from Texas to see if we could help." He shifts so he's facing me. "Have you let Jesus into your heart?"

I stare at the ducks. "That's an interesting question."

"We're here to spread the word of God," he says, patting his bible.

I turn to him. "I see. And what is *that*, exactly?"

He holds up the bible. "This is the word of God."

"No," I say, "that's a book. What's the *word* of God?"

"Ma'am, are you a Christian?"

I throw back my head and laugh. "I'd have to go with no."

He pats his bible again. "This is the truth. This is the word of God."

"You still haven't told me *what* that word is."

The teen turns and stares at the ducks for a few minutes. "Love," he says finally.

I smile. "Bingo."

Clearly unimpressed with me, he wanders off. So I head

over to the Bronx Zoo and am standing in front of the bear enclosure, watching an old timer snoozing in the sun, when an older woman comes up to me.

"He's not too worried about world events," she says.

"No kidding."

The woman, a zoo volunteer, proceeds to enthusiastically tell me about the bear's history, personality and daily habits. I'm inspired by her commitment. This is her tiny corner of the world and despite all that's happened she still takes her job seriously.

Then I go to the New York Public Library bookstore and buy *The Metaphysical Club* by Louis Menand. I sit on the front steps and am flipping through the book when a quote catches my eye: "Organisms don't struggle because they must evolve; they evolve because they must struggle." Clunk. Because of my struggles this past year, *I* am evolving. I can feel a faint stirring inside, as if that part of my self that fell alongside Sam is finally trying to get back up again.

I head over to the Metropolitan Museum of Art, where I find myself almost running from one exhibit to the next . . . from Greece to China, Mesopotamia to Peru. Then I hit the Natural History Museum and look for Lucy – the three and a half million year-old hominid I'd read about in university. When I find the exhibit, I wave at her through the glass. Science blooms again in the garden of my mind – alongside a few persistent religious weeds.

At the space exhibit at the other end of the museum, where I'd heard complimentary snacks were being offered, I down a glass of wine and a few meatballs then catch the Imax show, narrated by Tom Hanks. Inside the empty theatre, I gaze up at the replica night sky.

"We are in the universe," says Tom, "and the universe is in us."

I scan the sky for the Orion Belt and when I spot the three stars in a row, I smile.

In the gift store on the way out of the museum, I buy a pink dragonfly necklace and matching earrings to symbolize the year of transformation I've made it through.

My final evening in New York is spent at a sold-out performance of *La Boheme* at the Met.

"It's beautiful, isn't it?"

I turn to my right and see a guy about my age sitting where Jodie – or Sam in an ideal world or Tom in a next-to-ideal one – should be.

I smile. "Yeah it is."

Twenty

Eleven days later, home in Canada, I'm driving home from the dog-park and come across a dead squirrel in the middle of the road. I stop the car, get out and am bending over to pick up its little body to put in a plastic bag, when the police helicopter flies overhead.

I place the squirrel in the garbage can in my back alley then head inside the house. The phone rings. Another young police officer in our city has died in the line of duty – the eleventh one in the history of our city – this one in a training incident. I sit down in my big blue chair and cry.

But this is not about me. I will not go off the deep end again. Yet, for the next few days, *my* phone rings relentlessly. The parallels to Sam's death are uncanny: the same time of year, the result of an unbelievable sequence of events, a childless widow the same age as me left behind. The media interview me. How do I feel? What do I think? How is it similar to losing Sam? What advice can I offer the new widow? How have I coped over the past year?

"WHY THE FUCK DIDN'T YOU CALL ME?" I scream at Tom over the phone, after two days pass with no word from him.

Silence.

"What's your problem?" I ask.

"I didn't call you," he says, "because I didn't want to give you the wrong idea."

"I thought we were friends," I snap and hang up the phone.

The next morning, he asks me for coffee at our usual place.

"You were very upset yesterday," he begins.

"Yeah, well . . ."

He leans across the table. "Adri, I don't want to hurt you but you need to understand that nothing is EVER going to happen between us."

"But I feel something between us."

"You feel what you want to feel," he says, "not what's really there."

I fold my arms across my chest. "Why don't I believe you?"

"Maybe because you're not ready to."

Neither of us says anything for a few minutes. Then he points to the necklace I bought in New York. "I'm surprised to see you wearing a cross."

"It's not. It's a dragonfly."

Tom squints. "So it is."

I am about to stand up when he says, "By the way, I was thinking about your number eleven."

"And?"

"Well, that's a logical number to represent the concept of soul mates because the number eleven is two ones side by side – and one plus one equals two. And I bet the key to a healthy relationship is that both individuals need to be happy on their own first."

In the afternoon, the police chief phones me, figuring I might have some sort of sage advice for the new widow.

What am I supposed to tell her? The truth?

Dear Widow,

   Hello and welcome to hell. I've just finished my one-year contract and now it's your turn to give it a go. Regardless of the path you choose, you've just entered what will undoubtedly be the shittiest journey of your life. But for what it's worth, here are a few pointers on how NOT to grieve:

Don't underestimate the immense power of love and its unexplainable mysteries. Yet do not lie to yourself about the fact of death, choosing instead to become consumed by the psychological reaction to it – what we call grief. Do not deny yourself the experience of *feeling* the pain. Don't pretend you're OK, when it feels as if your heart has been ripped from your body but you're not lucky enough to die along with it.

Don't be angry with the idiots who whisper in your ear to 'be strong' and not worry because 'you're young.' Or that it's a GOOD THING you didn't have children together – or that your loss couldn't *possibly* be as bad as losing a child. And try not to dwell on the fact that you're 33 and might not *get* the chance to have a child now.

Don't take it too personally when those around you move forward with their own lives while you're left sitting at home, staring at the walls, kissing photos of your dead husband and wondering what the hell just happened. And do not fool yourself into thinking that it's your job, and your job only, to ensure your husband's memory is honoured.

Do not twist a religious belief to fit your desires. If and when the suicidal thoughts come, do not give in to the self-pity monster. Be careful about fantasizing about another guy because doing so makes you temporarily feel better about the great one you've just lost. Yet if a new relationship feels right with all your heart, don't let guilt stop you from being happy again.

And don't let anyone tell you how long it will take for you to heal – but be aware that time is passing, whether you're healing or not. Don't search for meaning in every greeting card and graffiti message. Don't look to external belief systems to give you the answers

– because the only truth that matters is within you
and the relationship you shared with your husband.

Love from a former widow

P.S. Don't eat too many cookies
P.P.S. When you're ready, you *can* legally remarry and
still receive compensation
P.P.P.S. The national memorial service for fallen officers, which you'll be attending next year in Ottawa,
is about as much fun as poking a knitting needle in
your eye

Of course I don't give her the letter. When I do meet her, I
simply say, "I'm sorry," then shut up and listen. For I know the
only right way to grieve will be her way.

On the day of her husband's funeral, there's an unexpected
October snowstorm to complete the parallels to Sam's funeral.
When Louie B. Armstrong's *It's a Wonderful World* is played during the service, I can't stop crying, thinking it's not one whatsoever.

In the procession afterwards, I walk along in my brown
swing coat – worn again at a police funeral instead of lunch with
a New York publisher – past the hundreds of saluting emergency
services personnel from across North America. When I hear the
familiar chopping sound, I look up and watch the police helicopter doing the fly-over.

I feel a hand on my shoulder. "Hey."

I turn to see Mark beside me.

Nodding towards the helicopter, I say, "Sometimes I wonder if the big guy's up there, watching us."

"And if he is, what would he be saying?"

"Are you learning *anything* down there?" The sun's coming
out again so I put on my Jackie O sunglasses. "We've got so much
work ahead of us . . . with the workplace safety stuff, I mean."

"It'll get done," Charlie says, joining me on the other side.

Then the three of us break away from the dwindling procession to take a short cut back to the church, where there will inevitably be an array of baked goods at the reception. As we walk through the parking lot, Mark asks me how my book is coming.

"It's in pretty rough shape," I reply. "I reckon it'll be awhile yet."

He smiles. Funny . . . I've never noticed before how nice his teeth are.

"I'm sure it'll be worth the wait," he says, opening the church door for me.

Plan M.

Epilogue

July 2002
A farmhouse in central Alberta

I dare say I found your road.
That you did.
It wasn't in the middle of an Iowa cornfield.
I told ya it wouldn't matter where it was.
Well, you were right about the feeling free part.
I know.
Now can you see what's beyond the field . . . the bigger picture?
I can see more of it than you can, put it that way.
And am I on the right track?
Are you happy?
I'm getting there.
Then you're on your way. You've certainly got quite the imagination.
You're one to talk! You don't get much cornier than Pucdeuos.
If you'd left me alone once in awhile, I coulda come up with something better.
You can go now, I say with a giggle.

We tell ourselves stories in order to live.
—Joan Didion

Acknowledgements

A sincere thank you to my mom and dad, family, friends and colleagues, John's family, friends and colleagues as well as the Calgary Police Service and Greek community for all the support given to me in the days after John's death and in the years to follow.

Thank you to my editors who have helped me transform a broken heart into a coherent story: Jennifer Barclay, Jill Roberts, Alex Pope, Shannon Lyons and Judy Millar.

Special thanks to the officers who started the John Petropoulos Memorial Fund – Cliff O'Brien, Joel Matthews and Glenn Laird – and continue, along with Ian Wilson, to fulfill the Fund's purpose of educating the public that workplace safety for emergency services personnel is a shared responsibility.

And thank you to John, for believing in my dream of becoming a writer.

Bibliography

Albom, Mitch. *Tuesday's with Morrie*. Doubleday, 1997.

Ban Breathnach, Sarah. *Simple Abundance; A Daybook of Comfort and Joy*. New York: Warner Books, Inc, 1995.

Bodanis, David. *E=mc² A Biography of the World's Most Famous Equation*. Doubleday Canada, 2000.

Bodson, Gerard. *Cracking the Apocalypse Code*. USA: Element Books, Inc, 2000.

Chomsky, Noam. *What Uncle Sam Really Wants*. California: Odonian Press, 1992.

Dickinson, Emily. *Collected Poems*. New York: Barnes & Noble, Inc, 1993.

Frye, Northrop. *Anatomy of Criticism*. UK: Princeton University Press, 1957.

Frye, Northrop. *Spiritus Mundi; Essays on Literature, Myth, and Society*. Canada: Fitzhenry & Whiteside, 1991.

Goodall, Jane. With Phillip Berman. *Reason for Hope; A Spiritual Journey*. New York: Warner Books, Inc, 1999.

Gore, Al. *Earth in the Balance; Ecology and the Human Spirit*. New York: Penguin Group, 1992.

Irving, John. *A Widow for One Year*. Toronto: Alfred A. Knopf Canada, 1998.

King, Stephen. *On Writing: A Memoir of the Craft*. New York: Pocket Books, a division of Simon & Schuster, Inc. 2000.

Menand, Louis. *The Metaphysical Club: A Story of Ideas in America*. New York: Farrar, Straus and Giroux, 2001.

Suzuki, David. With Amanda McConnell. *The Sacred Balance; Rediscovering our Place in Nature*. Vancouver: Douglas & McIntyre, 1997.

Tolle, Eckhart. *The Power of Now: A Guide to Spiritual Enlightenment*. Vancouver: Namaste Publishing, 1999.

Woolf, Virginia. *A Room of One's Own*. Great Britain: Hogarth Press, 1929. London: HarperCollins Publishers, 1994.

Zukav, Gary. *The Seat of the Soul*. New York: Simon & Schuster Inc, 1990.

Related Projects

John Petropoulos Memorial Fund
www.jpmf.ca

Keep Your Workplace Safe for Everyone; 30 second Public Service Announcement, 2004

This PSA uses Cst John Petropoulos' on-duty death – the result of a preventable fall at unsafe workplace – as an example of why workplace safety for everyone is a priority.

SLOW DOWN: It's no Picnic Out Here; 30 second Public Service Announcement, 2005

This PSA educates motorists about the importance of slowing down when passing emergency services personnel working on the road.

Put Yourself in Our Boots; 7 minute safety video, being produced fall 2008

This video will educate building owners, managers, safety coordinators, etc. about why and how to make their workplaces safe for everyone, including emergency services personnel who may have to attend the premises after hours and in unfamiliar conditions.

Pink Gazelle Productions Inc
www.pinkgazelle.com

Whatever Floats Your Boat . . . Perspectives on Motherhood;
53 minute documentary and educational resource kit

To be or not to be…a mom? is the question of the weekend as a group of women set sail on a houseboat. With beautiful British Columbia as Mother Nature's backdrop, the mother of all topics is brought to the surface with courage and candour. Produced in partnership with the National Film Board of Canada.

The Widow's; one act dramatic comedy play script

While backpacking through India, two widows take a morning off from the rigors of travel in their hotel room. Tucked beneath the safety of mosquito nets, they have a discussion to remember as public service announcements, uncircumcised penises and a pink flip-flop battle it out against men, motherhood and malaria. Received the Dorothy White award in the 2005 Ottawa Little Theatre One-Act Playwriting Competition.

Saviour; full length dramatic play script

Virginia Woolf meets Jesus in this theatrical exploration of an emotional, psychological and spiritual journey through grief. Received Honourable Mention in the 2006 Alberta Playwriting Competition and the 2005 Julia Young Memorial Playwriting Prize.

Face the Future; environmental awareness campaign

www.facethefuture.ca

This will be a series of 30 second Public Service Announcements that will educate viewers about environmental statistics should society continue with business as usual. By demonstrating the *cumulative* effect of seemingly harmless individual actions, such as vehicle idling, the PSAs, corresponding products and community campaigns will be a call to consumers to face the future by thinking globally and acting locally.

Various short stories including:

Girl with the Pink Purse	*The Shoeshine Boy*
Logan and the Girdle	*Squirrel at the Birdbell*
The Moroccan Carpet Salesman	*The Turtleneck*
Nakoda	*Venice of Vegas*
Pray for Us	*Zookeeper*

Photo by Ada Casello

About the Author

Maryanne Pope is the Chair of the John Petropoulos Memorial Fund and the Founder and CEO of Pink Gazelle Productions Inc. Maryanne writes short stories, play scripts and screenplays and lives in Calgary, Alberta with her dad and two dogs.

The John Petropoulos Memorial Fund (JPMF) is a non-profit society in Alberta, Canada. The JPMF educates the public that workplace safety for emergency services personnel is a shared responsibility. When communities work together, risks can be minimized. Please visit www.jpmf.ca for more information on the Fund's safety initiatives.

Pink Gazelle Productions Inc (PGP) creates works that inspire readers and viewers to affect positive change in themselves and the world around them. PGP produces books, short stories, children's stories, play scripts, screenplays, documentaries, feature films and public service announcements. Please visit www.pinkgazelle.com.